92

104

116

CARRIER STRIKE

COVER ART:
Carrier Strike by Neil Roberts

AUTHOR
Donald Nijboer

PRODUCTION EDITOR
Dan Sharp

PAGE DESIGN
Sean Phillips, ATG-media.com

COVER DESIGN
Mike Baumber

PUBLISHER
Steve O'Hara

PUBLISHING DIRECTOR
Dan Savage

MARKETING MANAGER
Charlotte Park

COMMERCIAL DIRECTOR
Nigel Hole

PUBLISHED BY
Mortons Media Group Ltd.
Media Centre
Morton Way
Horncastle
Lincolnshire
LN9 6JR
Tel. 01507 529529

PRINTED BY
William Gibbons and Sons,
Wolverhampton
ISBN: 978-1-911276-99-9
© 2019 Mortons Media Group Ltd.
All rights reserved. No part of this publication may be reproduced or transmitted in any form or by any means, electronic or mechanical, including photocopying, recording or any information storage retrieval system without prior permission in writing from the publisher.

CHAPTER 1

PLANTING THE SEEDS OF VICTORY

Development of US Naval Carrier
Air Power 1922-1941

"The Navy will resemble a vast and efficient organism, all the parts leagued together by a common understanding and common purpose."

Bradley A. Fiske, 1916

ABOVE: American battleships during fleet manoeuvres, September 1940. A mixed formation of monoplane and biplane carrier aircraft pass over the fleet. US NAVAL HISTORICAL CENTER

THE BIG PICTURE

BELOW: Aircraft from *Essex* (CV-9) attack two Japanese aircraft carriers at Kure March 19, 1945. An SB2C Helldiver on the upper right is pulling out of its dive. The carrier at the bottom is either *Amagi* or *Katsuragi*. The smaller carrier is *Kaiyo*.
US NAVAL HISTORICAL CENTER

CONTENTS

06 — **Chapter 1: PLANTING THE SEEDS OF VICTORY**
Development of US naval carrier air power 1922-1941

16 — **Chapter 2: YEAR OF ATTRITION**
Carrier raids and battles of 1942

34 — **Chapter 3: TOOLS OF THE TRADE**
New weapons and equipment

50 — **Chapter 4: CARRIER STRIKES 1943**
'Hit hard, hit fast, hit often'

60 — **Chapter 5: OPERATION HAILSTONE**
The Truk Lagoon raid and how it revolutionised naval air warfare 1944

72 — **Chapter 6: THE END OF THE JAPANESE FLEET**
The Great Marianas Turkey Shoot and the Battle of Leyte Gulf

92 — **Chapter 7: STEEL RAIN**
The kamikaze war, October 1944-August 1945

104 — **Chapter 8: THE FORGOTTEN FLEET**
British carrier strikes in the Pacific 1944-45

116 — **Chapter 9: TOKYO BOUND**
Japan carrier strikes 1945

06

16

34

50

60

72

On August 31, 1943, just 308 days since the last carrier battle of 1942, the US Navy returned to the offensive. Centred on the brand-new fleet carriers USS *Essex* (CV-9), USS *Yorktown* (CV-10) and the new light carrier USS *Independence* (CVL-22) America's new Fast Carrier Task Force (Task Force 15) launched its first strike of the Pacific war.

The target was the Japanese occupied island of Marcus, just 700 miles from Tokyo. Escorted by one battleship, two cruisers and attending destroyers the three flattops had on board 84 new Grumman F6F-3 Hellcat fighters, 45 Douglas Dauntless SBD-3 dive-bombers and 27 Grumman TBF-1 Avenger torpedo bombers. For the majority of the navy fliers this would be their first taste of combat.

At 0415 hours the first Hellcats began taking off. After radio checks were made, throttles and RPM set the Hellcat pilots formed up, climbed for altitude and pointed their noses toward Marcus.

As the sun rose over the Atoll the young Hellcat pilots saw their target for the first time. Straps were tightened, gunsights switched on and guns armed. As they scanned the sky ahead they were surprised by to find the airspace above Marcus void of enemy aircraft. Now was their chance. Shoving their sticks forward they dove into the attack. Roaring over the airfield the Hellcats announced their presence with a hail of machine fire.

The Japanese were caught completely by surprise and as they ran to their fighters they were cut down by the strafing Hellcats. Not a single Japanese fighter rose to the defence. Next in were the SBD dive-bombers and Avengers dropping their deadly loads of 500 and 1,000lb bombs. With each explosion jagged shrapnel and concussive blast waves shattered nearby aircraft and buildings. Within minutes Marcus Island became a shooting gallery. Ground targets were limited but all of the Japanese aircraft caught on the ground were destroyed and for the young fighter and bomber pilots it was a first. They fired at the enemy and enemy shot back. The smell of cordite, sweat and fear filled their cockpits as they made their bombing and strafing runs. And once they landed back on their carriers the unique exhilaration of having survived their first combat mission would be remembered for the rest of their lives.

After four air strikes the atoll was left a smoking wreck with approximately 80% of the facilities destroyed.

In sharp contrast the US Navy's first carrier raid on Marcus Island, which occurred on March 4, 1942, consisted of one carrier with just 36 SBD-3 dive-bombers and six F4F-3 Wildcats. The damage from the first raid was minor.

The second raid announced the return of the US Navy carrier force. One that was growing in strength and bristled with incredible offensive and defensive capability centred on the new Grumman F6F Hellcat and Essex class carrier. It was also the first time the US Navy had grouped three carriers into one task force.

Previous US naval doctrine called for each fleet carrier to operate independently (the Marcus raid March 1942), but by 1943 Admiral Chester W. Nimitz, Commander in Chief, US Pacific Fleet (CINPAC) adopted the Japanese method of concentrating his carriers into a single task force. With the new Essex and Independence

ABOVE: Aviator Eugene B. Ely stands by his Curtiss pusher biplane, just before taking off from USS *Pennsylvania* to return to land, January 18, 1911. Earlier in the day he landed on the ship's deck, the first time an airplane had alighted on a warship. US NAVAL HISTORICAL CENTER

ABOVE: Eugene Ely's plane taking off from the cruiser USS *Pennsylvania* in 1911. US NAVAL HISTORICAL CENTER

class carriers, the Hellcat, the vast improvement in fighter interception and control and improved anti-aircraft defences, the US Navy now had the ability to mount offensive operations and protect the fleet task force at the same time – something it was unable to do during the carrier battles of 1942. A year after the carrier battle of Santa Cruz the 'new' US Navy had been transformed and was ready to take the war directly to Japan.

Many historians have credited the Essex class of carriers and the Hellcat for winning the great battles in the Pacific and destroying the Japanese Navy. But it was more than just technology. The seeds of victory in the Pacific had been planted long before the first Essex carrier took to the sea. In the end it would be a mix of technology, leadership, sound doctrine, training, logistics and most importantly, the ability to adapt and learn that would lead the US Navy to the greatest naval victory in history.

On the eve of December 7, 1941, the US Pacific fleet lay shattered. The Japanese surprise attack on Pearl Harbor left five battleships sunk, the core of the US Navy's Pacific Fleet. In one devastating attack the Imperial Japanese Navy (IJN) had clearly demonstrated the striking power and range of a combined carrier strike force. For the next seven months the Japanese First Air Fleet (which consisted of six fleet carriers) bulled its way across the Pacific and Indian Ocean, seizing positions from the Aleutians to Singapore. The result of this massed carrier air power and the excellence of its long-range aircraft and combat experienced aircrew overwhelmed even the best Allied resistance. While the defeats had been crushing and humiliating, just a year later, Admiral Chester W. Nimitz reclaimed the initiative from the Japanese in the Guadalcanal campaign and began advancing in the South Pacific. It was a remarkable recovery. The US Navy's quick recovery after Pearl Harbor can be traced to the Navy's change in culture nearly 50 years before.

In the early years of the 20th century the US Navy changed from a traditional institution into a modern, professional organisation based on education and innovation. The Navy's introduction of a new learning system allowed for new approaches to officer education. Competitive war games and problems at the Naval War College exposed students to the challenge of making quick decisions in a chaotic environment. Individual creativity was emphasised and

ABOVE: USS *Langley* (CV-1) under reconstruction from the collier USS *Jupiter* at Norfolk Navy Yard, Portsmouth, Virginia, late 1921. US NAVAL HISTORICAL CENTER

ABOVE: A Douglas DT-2 taking off, circa 1925. The DT-2 had a maximum speed of 100mph and was capable carrying a 1,800lb torpedo. US NAVAL HISTORICAL CENTER

ABOVE: USS *Lexington* (CV-2) seen here with a full complement of 78 aircraft shortly after entering service in 1928. US NAVAL HISTORICAL CENTER

ABOVE: USS *Langley* (CV-1), 1922. *Langley* was capable of carrying 34 aircraft. Early carrier aircraft lacked the range and payload capacity to be truly effective. US NAVAL HISTORICAL CENTER

that there was no 'staff solution' to a rapidly changing situation. The Navy also reformed its promotional system. In the late 19th century promotion was based on seniority and not ability. As the navy grew, commanding larger formations of ships required new levels of skill – abilities that could only be learned through experience. The improved system placed skill and initiative over seniority, greatly improving the quality of the young officers on the rise.

When the Atlantic Fleet was established in 1907 the Navy began to employ similar learning methods at sea. Officers explored the most effective and efficient ways of coordinating men and ships in combat. It was also a top down exercise where fleet commanders like Rear Admirals Charles J. Badger and Frank Friday Fletcher and junior officers developed and incorporated the lessons learned from operational exercises and tactical drills. The exercises also exploited the creativity of every officer to produce 'common doctrines'.

Frequent conferences and simulated combat situations helped develop problem solving techniques that created a shared sense of how to act in battle – tactical doctrine. During the interwar period these two levels of learning combined to create a planning process that integrated the development of war plans, fleet exercises and the work of the Naval War College. This transformation led to the 'Fleet Problem' – large operational exercises that involved both major and minor vessels in various scenarios.

Beginning in the early 1920s the first exercise, known as Fleet Problem I, led to a series of annual exercises that continued right up to the eve of war. This sophisticated learning system combined with the numerous Fleet Problems created an extremely effective tactical doctrine that centred on the ability to exploit lessons learned from combat and quickly turn them into new tactics, plans and force structures. With the system in place the US Navy was able to overcome initial Japanese advantages during the first year of war and generate a faster rate of learning. Just as they failed to match America's industrial might, the Japanese were unable to keep pace and by late 1943 the Navy's fast carrier strike force with its sophisticated tactics and refined doctrine largely assured victory in the Pacific.

FIRST FLIGHTS

Despite the success and popularity of the Wright brothers and other aviation pioneers, it wasn't until 1908 did the US Navy took any interest. It was understandable – early aircraft were flimsy, had unreliable engines and little to no range. Despite its reluctance the US Navy became the first to launch an aircraft from a ship. In late 1910 Eugene Ely, flying a Curtiss floatplane, took off from a wooden platform built on the cruiser USS *Birmingham*. Just two months later, on January 18, 1911, Ely made the first landing on a warship by setting his Curtiss pusher biplane onto the deck of the USS *Pennsylvania* shortly after he took off – completing the first takeoff and landing of an aircraft from a warship. This demonstration piqued the Navy's interest and by March it had allocated $25,000 (over $600,000 in today's money) to the acquisition of naval aircraft. Instead of pursuing their initial lead in carrier technology however, the Navy pursued catapult launched seaplanes, but none were in service when the First World War broke out.

America entered the war in April 1917, spurring on the expansion of naval aviation. But not a single carrier or ship dedicated to operating aircraft was commissioned. Training and procurement did expand though, with more than 37,000 officers and men trained as pilots or technicians during the war.

The first detachment of naval planes and pilots arrived in France in June 1917. Their combat debut was delayed due to the desire to train more pilots and determine the right role for their

ABOVE: USS *Saratoga* (CV-3) at sea on February 7, 1932. The forward deck park is crowded, indicating aircraft recovery is in operation. US NAVAL HISTORICAL CENTER

aircraft over the battlefield and sea. It wasn't until the last few months of the war that these aviation units, primarily Marine, saw service. A few land targets were attacked along with 25 attacks made against enemy submarines by patrol aircraft.

By the end of the war the Royal Navy had the clear lead in naval aviation with several carriers in service (one Argus and three Glorious class carriers). The fear of falling behind led to the construction of the US Navy's first carrier, the USS *Langley*. Converted from the slow collier USS *Jupiter*, *Langley* was a compromise. In order to begin experiments with aircraft from ships and unable to procure funding for a modern aircraft carrier, the Navy settled on a conversion. Completed in March 1922 the USS *Langley* was given the designation CV-1 (CV representing a fleet carrier and 1 being the first ship of this designation). In reality *Langley* was a technology demonstrator and not a dedicated carrier.

Langley was small, just 542ft long. While it could carry up to 42 aircraft (she started her service with just eight to ten aircraft) its top speed was only 14 knots, far too slow when operating with the rest of the fleet. After three years of flight operations and fleet maneuvers the *Langley's* contribution was disappointing. The small number of aircraft and the time it took to land its air group (30 minutes) hampered its effectiveness. By 1927 under the guidance of Joseph Reeves, Commander, Aircraft Squadrons Battle Fleet, landing times had been drastically reduced. Instead of lifting each recovered aircraft down to the lower deck, the aircraft were simply moved to a section of the deck not needed for take-off or landings. This 'deck park'

ABOVE: USS *Yorktown* (CV-5) tied up at Naval Operating Base, Norfolk, Virginia, in October 1937. The retractable navigation light mast on the flight deck can be clearly seen. US NAVAL HISTORICAL CENTER

method increased aircraft handling dramatically and was *Langley's* greatest contribution to carrier warfare. It also increased the sortie rate per aircraft, increasing its effectiveness.

Langley's service in the fleet gave the US Navy a greater appreciation for carrier launched aviation. Even though it was small, *Langley* was capable of carrying a large number of aircraft for its size, a practice continued with every other prewar carrier. During the numerous fleet exercises in the 1920s *Langley* developed scouting, air combat, battleship artillery spotting and dive bombing tactics. It also demonstrated the offensive capability of a carrier by launching large numbers of bombers.

Langley was taken out of service as an aircraft carrier in 1936 and converted into a seaplane tender. When the US entered the war, it was used at an aircraft transport. While ferrying 32 P-40Es to the south coast of Java it was attacked ▶

BELOW: *Ranger*, *Lexington* and *Saratoga* anchored off Honolulu during fleet exercises, 1938. During the 1930s, the US Navy rarely grouped its carriers into a single task force during training exercises, instead single carriers were pitted against each other for limited results. NARA

SPECIFICATION

★ **USS LEXINGTON (CV-2)** ★

Displacement: 36,000 tons
Dimensions: Length 888ft; beam 105ft; draught 32ft
Maximum speed: 34kts
Aircraft capacity: 90
Radius of action: 6,960nm
Crew: 2,122 (prewar)

ABOVE: *Lexington* launching Martin T4M-1 torpedo planes, 1929. The T4M entered service in 1938. Powered by a Pratt & Whitney 525hp R-1690 Hornet 9 radial engine, it had a top speed of 114mph. US NAVAL HISTORICAL CENTER

ABOVE: USS *Enterprise* carried an avgas stock of 178,000 gallons which allowed for about 10 sorties per aircraft before replenishment was needed. US NAVAL HISTORICAL CENTER

by nine Mitsubishi G4M1 bombers and hit by several bombs. Shortly after it was abandoned and torpedoed by destroyer USS *Whipple*.

Langley's sacrifice was not in vain. Its contribution to the evolution of carrier aviation was instrumental in demonstrating the clear potential of carrier borne aircraft. The tactics and technologies tested on *Langley* helped pave the way for the creation of the US Navy's fast carrier task force.

ENTER THE LEXINGTONS

The two Lexington class carriers were not built by design but by circumstance. By 1921 the US Navy realized that Japan would be the future enemy of the United States in the Pacific. The Navy planners focused their gaze on the possible control of the former German-held northern island and atolls in the Marianas, Marshalls and Carolinas by the Japanese. Once in Japanese hands, they would threaten the lines of communication to US possessions at Guam, Wake and the Philippines. If these were cut off, and in the absence of land-based airfields within range, retaking or neutralising those island bases would require seaborne air power.

In 1922 the Washington Naval Treaty was signed by the US, Britain, France, Italy and Japan. The treaty strictly limited both the tonnage and construction of capitol ships and aircraft carriers. With its 5:3 (United States to Japan) ratio in capitol ship tonnage, the US was forced to cancel all of its battle cruisers already under construction. New carrier construction was also limited to 23,000 tons, but an exemption was granted for conversions up to 33,000 tons from existing hulls.

Conversion of *Lexington* (CV-2) and *Saratoga* (CV-3) from existing cruiser hulls began in 1922. When commissioned in 1927 they were the largest carriers in service and would remain so until the completion of the Japanese *Shinano* in 1944. They were also the fastest American carriers with a top speed of 34 knots. Their steel flight decks were not armoured but covered with wood planking. Although the protection was minimal against dive-bombing attacks, the construction allowed for rapid repair and the quick return to air operations.

When first completed, the Lexingtons were armed for both surface and anti-aircraft action. Eight 8in guns, housed in four twin turrets provided the firepower to deal with any cruisers. Anti-aircraft protection against dive-bombers was provided by 12 single 5in/38 gun mounts positioned on the corners of the flight deck.

To counter the growing threat of dive-bombing attack, both ships increased their AA defences with the addition of a large battery of .50cal water cooled machine guns. Lexington, the more modern of the sisters, also installed a CXAM air search radar in 1940. The .50cal machine guns, while reliable and accurate, didn't have the range or hitting power to deal effectively with dive-bombers or torpedo bombers. In 1940 five 1.1in (28mm) quadruple machine cannons were installed, reducing the number of machine guns to 28.

By their sheer size and number of aircraft carried, the Lexingtons helped create the 'fleet carrier' concept to US Navy. Entering service in 1928, both *Lexington* and *Saratoga* were assigned to the Pacific Fleet. Both would quickly show their value and combat potential. During Fleet Problems in 1929, both ships were able to demonstrate their ability to launch large single deck-load air strikes in all weathers. After a series of Fleet Problems in the 1930s, the Lexingtons developed a number of tactics that became standard practice during the war: the creation of the separate carrier task groups with escorting cruisers and destroyers, long-range strikes by carrier aircraft and most importantly, the independent offensive use of carriers.

There were, however, problems that remained unresolved. As the threat of aerial attack grew, battleship commanders realised their ships were now vulnerable. After one of the Navy's annual Fleet Problems, the main complaint of the battleship officers was that the carriers had basically fought amongst themselves, depriving the battle line of vital air cover. Providing adequate fighter cover for both carriers and battleships would remain a major weakness during the first year of the war.

USS RANGER (CV-4)

Ranger was the first US carrier designed from the keel up. In contrast to the Lexingtons, the *Ranger* was directly influenced by the experiences gained by *Langley* during tactical simulations the mid-1920s. The Naval College concluded that the ability to find the enemy first and launch the largest number of strike aircraft in the shortest amount of time would determine the success of an operation. There was also the fear that concentrating the

RIGHT: USS *Enterprise* (CV-6) docked at Ford Island, Pearl Harbor, March 1942. This view of the aft end of the island clearly shows the heavy deck crane, two 1.1in guns mounts, and the Mk.33 director at the top of the crane. US NAVAL HISTORICAL CENTER

SPECIFICATION

★ USS RANGER (CV-4) ★

Displacement: 14,500 tons
Dimensions: Length 769ft; beam 80ft; draught 20ft
Maximum speed: 29.5kts
Aircraft capacity: 90
Radius of action: 9,960nm
Crew: 2,245 (including air group) and 216 officers

ABOVE: Grumman F3F-3 Fighters from Fighting Squadron Five (VF-5), USS *Yorktown* (CV-5) in a three-plane formation over the southern California coast. The F3F was the last biplane fighter to serve with the US Navy. When introduced it had a top speed of 264mph at 15,250ft. US NAVAL HISTORICAL CENTER

ABOVE: USS *Ranger* (CV-4). The aft elevator is partially lowered. *Ranger* was easily distinguished by its six parallel stacks on either side of the flight deck. During flight operations these stacks were hinged and rotated to a position parallel with the hangar deck. US NAVAL HISTORICAL CENTER

SPECIFICATION
★ USS YORKTOWN (CV-5) ★
Displacement: 19,576 tons
Dimensions: Length 810ft (*Hornet* 825ft); beam 80ft (114ft); draught 25ft
Maximum speed: 33kts
Aircraft capacity: 81 (*Hornet* 85)
Radius of action: 11,200nm at 15kts
Crew: (1941): 227 officers, 1,990 enlisted personnel (including air group)

fleet's entire air strength in one or two large carriers, rather than four, was a major weakness. Having nearly half of the 135,000 tons allowed for the US Navy under the Washington Treaty taken up by the two Lexingtons meant that other carriers would have to be smaller and more efficient.

The eventual size selected for *Ranger* was 13,800 tons and this was seen as adequate for building a carrier with a sufficient number of aircraft and good handling facilities. Commissioned in 1934, *Ranger* featured several attributes that would become standard in future US prewar carrier designs: an open hangar, a gallery deck around the flight deck, and provision for cross deck catapults mounted on the hangar deck.

Ranger was designed for 76 aircraft – the maximum number possible. These comprised 36 fighters, 36 scout/dive bombers and four utility aircraft. Armament consisted of 8 5in/38 guns and 40 .50cal machine guns. Of the seven prewar carriers, *Ranger* was the only one never to see action in the Pacific.

YORKTOWN CLASS
Designed with the benefit of fleet experience, the Yorktown class were the first modern US carriers to be built. The basic design was so successful it provided the template for the next generation of carriers, the Essex class. The design parameters for the new Yorktowns came directly from the failed Ranger class. The three ships of the new class, *Yorktown* (CV-5), *Enterprise* (CV-6) and *Hornet* (CV-8) provided the nucleus of the US Pacific Fleet. While the Lexingtons were larger, these were without a doubt the best of the Washington Naval Treaty-designed carriers.

One of the primary design features of the Yorktowns was their protection against torpedo attack. A 4in side armour belt was fitted over the machinery spaces, gasoline storage tanks and magazines. In addition, 1.5in of amour was added for vertical protection over the machinery spaces. A further 4in of armour was fitted to the machinery spaces bulkheads. Torpedo protection was also enhanced by a side protective system of three tanks: an inner tank that was void and two outer tanks filled with liquid. These were designed to absorb the shock of any torpedo. Like the Lexingtons, the flight deck was unarmoured and built of light steel. The use of large roller curtains allowed the hangar deck to be opened, providing aircraft to the chance to warm prior to launch, and closed for weather.

Yorktown and *Enterprise* were commissioned in and 1937 and 1938 respectively. The third ship, USS *Hornet* entered service in 1941. The Yorktowns were impressive designs and capable of operating 90 aircraft, but during combat operations fewer were carried. All three ships had two deck catapults and three elevators. A deck hangar catapult was fitted to permit the launching of scout aircraft when the flight deck was occupied by a full deck of strike aircraft.

In terms of anti-aircraft protection, the Yorktowns were well equipped with eight new 5in/38 dual-purpose guns, controlled by a pair of Mark 33 Directors mounted on the island. For medium range defence and close in protection, four 1.1in quadruple mounts were positioned fore and aft of the island and 24 .50cal water cooled machine guns for dive-bombing defence were fitted on the gallery deck.

All three Yorktowns were fitted with radar in 1940 with the *Yorktown* being fitted with one of six prototype CXAM radars, the *Enterprise* received the improved CXAM-1 unit and the *Hornet* was equipped with the smaller SC radar.

The *Yorktown* class was arguably the most successful carrier design by any navy prior to World War II. Their ability to sustain heavy damage and remain afloat was remarkable. As larger aircraft (F6F Hellcat, F4U Corsair, SB2C Helldiver) were introduced the Yorktowns proved remarkably adaptive, capable of operating large air groups.

ABOVE: USS *Hornet* (CV-8) late 1941, soon after completion. The light construction of US flight decks meant that bombs penetrated easily. One or two bombs would be sufficient to render a flight deck inoperable. US NAVAL HISTORICAL CENTER

ABOVE: This obsolete Navy floatplane was subject to .50cal and 1.1in fire to determine the amount of damage caused by each shell. US NAVAL HISTORICAL CENTER

ABOVE: A pair of Vought O2U-2 Corsairs of Marine Corps Scouting Squadron VS-14 in the circuit prior to landing about USS *Saratoga*, 1930. US NAVAL HISTORICAL CENTER

THE WASP (CV-7)

The USS *Wasp*'s unique design was tied directly to the US Navy's treaty carrier allocation. With just 14,500 tons left to be used it would be impossible to build another Yorktown class, but the designers did their best to incorporate all the best features of the larger ship into the *Wasp*. The results were disappointing with *Wasp* being a slightly improved version of *Ranger*. Shorter than *Ranger* by 40ft, her top speed was a mediocre 29.5 knots. Armour was provided with the hangar deck receiving 1.25in and the 3.5in armoured bulkheads protected the aft magazine and steering compartment.

Anti-aircraft protection was provided by eight 5in/38 guns arranged in pairs on the port and starboard bow and quarter. Four 1.1in quad guns were fitted forward and aft of the island and for close in protection 24 water-cooled .50cal machine guns were fitted.

Wasp, like *Ranger*, was not originally intended to carry torpedo bombers. The new carrier war changed that and by 1942 *Wasp*'s air group consisted of 32 fighters, 28 dive bombers and ten torpedo aircraft.

Wasp's carrier war in the Pacific was brief and it did not participate in any of the carrier battles of 1942. After providing air cover for the landings on Guadalcanal in August 1942 it would be lost on September 15, when the Japanese submarine I-19 put three torpedoes into its side. At the time *Wasp* was refuelling aircraft. Fires quickly spread and a series of gasoline explosions quickly overwhelmed the ship. After just 35 minutes the vessel was abandoned for the loss of 193 men. While *Wasp* never struck the Japanese directly, its destruction actually played a useful role in the design of the new Essex class. As the second US carrier to be lost due to gasoline induced fires and explosions, extensive changes were made to the gasoline storage system of the new *Essex* design. The resulting changes meant that no fleet carriers would be lost to this cause during the war.

ANTI-AIRCRAFT GUN DEFENCE

American planners paid more attention to anti-aircraft gun defences then did their Japanese counterparts. Against torpedo attack the carriers would rely on their 5in/38 guns and more importantly evasive manoeuvres at sea. By 1929 the introduction of the dive-bomber posed a new threat. Many senior officers became increasingly concerned with this new form of attack. Rear Admiral Luke McNamee, director of fleet training was one of the first to voice his concern: "Even if the defensive fire begins at the earliest possible instant, only about 30 seconds of actual firing times are available to get on the attacking planes and damage them sufficiently to prevent the attack from being completed." None of the anti-aircraft guns then in service – 50cal machine guns, the 3in anti-aircraft gun, and the 5in/25 dual purpose gun – was designed for the purpose.

The Bureau of Ordnance (BuOrd) recognised the urgent need for a new weapon to counter the new dive-bomber. Opinion within the bureau varied as to which caliber of ammunition would be the most effective. To find out, the bureau began testing using .30cal, .50cal and the new 1.1in projectile against statically mounted obsolete fabric covered aircraft. Test results showed that while the .30cal bullets were capable of penetrating the engine block (at close range), they would be ineffective at preventing a dive-bombing attack once the bombers were in their dive. The .50cal shell performed very well, being capable of penetrating the engine block and reaching the

SPECIFICATION
★ USS WASP ★
Displacement: 14,700 tons
Dimensions: Length 749ft; beam 81ft; draught 20ft
Maximum speed: 29.5kts
Aircraft capacity: 70
Radius of action: 12,000nm at 15kts
Crew: 201 officers, 2,046 enlisted personnel (including air group)

BELOW: By 1937 American carriers fielded a potent strike package consisting of Grumman F3F fighters, Curtiss SBC-4 dive-bombers, and the first monoplane torpedo bomber, the Douglas TBD-1 Devastator. US NAVAL HISTORICAL CENTER

pilot's position. The impact, however, wasn't enough to render the plane uncontrollable unless the pilot was injured or killed. It must be remembered that the first job of the anti-aircraft gun was to cause the bomber to miss its target. That meant making a torpedo/dive bomber drop its ordnance before the optimum height, range and speed. Hotter accurate metal sent up meant less cold accurate steel coming down.

Many still believed that to be effective AA fire had to cause a total loss of control of the diving aircraft by either killing the pilot or causing enough damage to the engine or flight controls to render the dive bomber inoperable. The results of the 1.1in shell were the most promising and favoured by the bureau. Firing explosive projectiles, the 1.1in had the ability to cause the loss of control with a single shell in the right spot (engine, cockpit, wing, tail plane). The 1.1in gun's rate of fire was considerably less than the .50cal's however, resulting in a quadruple mount being necessary. The BuOrd concluded that because of the small size of a dive-bomber, "a weapon of greater destructiveness than [could] be delivered by a solid [.50cal] projectile was essential." This led to the development and acquisition of the 1.1in/.75cal quadruple machine cannon.

Test firing of the gun began in 1937 but proved disappointing. Excessive vibration and smoke adversely affected its aim. In service the gun was difficult to maintain and prone to failure after firing just a few rounds. Regardless of these problems, when the gun was well maintained it was a welcome addition a carrier's anti-aircraft defences and would play an important role in the first two carrier battles of the war.

The US Navy's constant focus on AA gun defences would lead directly to the adoption of the Swedish 40mm Bofors gun, the best AA gun of the war and the Oerlikon 20mm cannon. Both these weapons replaced the 1.1in and .50cal machine guns. In comparison, Japanese gun development stagnated and remained unchanged throughout the war.

At the beginning of the war US carrier AA defences were considered poor, but much better than the Japanese carriers and escorts. Neither side had enough barrels or guns of adequate range to effectively engage dive-bombers and the American 5in/25 was only marginally effective against torpedo bombers. Early American AA defences, however, proved more effective at shooting down and damaging Japanese aircraft after they had released their ordnance.

CARRIER AIR GROUP

Prior to the outbreak of hostilities, US Navy carriers generally carried more aircraft than Japanese flattops. US aircraft were just as a capable as their Japanese counterparts and in some cases were superior. The US Navy practice of keeping a large number of aircraft parked on the deck meant US Navy air groups were larger, with 60-70 fighters and bombers available for action. A typical air group consisted of one fighter squadron (VF) of 18 F4F Wildcats, one squadron (VT) of 12-18 TBD Devastator torpedo bombers, and two squadrons of SBD Dauntless dive-bombers (16-21 aircraft each). One squadron of SBDs was designated as a 'bombing' squadron (VB) and the other as a 'scouting' squadron (VS). In practice there was little difference between the two with the VB squadrons sometimes carrying 1,000lb bombs (with shorter range) and the VS would carry a 500lb bomb for longer-range scouting missions. But both could do the job equally well.

US NAVY CARRIER AIRCRAFT 1942

GRUMMAN F4F-4 WILDCAT

The F4F Wildcat has often been described as outclassed and no match for the Japanese Zero-sen carrier-based fighter. While each fighter had its strengths and weaknesses (the Zero was faster and more manoeuvrable) the Wildcat held some distinct advantages. Lieutenant Colonel Joe Bauer of the famous Cactus Air Force said this about the Zero: "A Zero can go faster than you can, it climbs faster than you can, and it can outmanoeuvre you. Aside from those things, you've got a better fighter plane."

First flown in 1937 the Wildcat was designed for carrier use from the outset. To help pilots cope with the difficult task of taking off and landing on a small flight deck, the Grumman designers put a large wing far forward of the fuselage. This large wing area gave it high lift, giving pilots the ability to take-off quickly and land at slow speeds.

The F4F-4 joined the Pacific Fleet in April 1942, replacing the earlier F4F-3. The new version featured folding wings, six .50cal machine guns, factory installed armour, self-sealing fuel tanks, air-to-air and air-to-carrier radios, all powered by a Pratt and Whitney R-1830-36 Twin Wasp radial engine with a two-speed, two-stage supercharger. It was one of the first production fighters anywhere to be equipped with a mechanical supercharger of that type. The Wildcat's best speed occurred around 21,000ft – about 2,000ft higher than the Zero's. When well flown the F4F proved to be the Zero's equal.

SPECIFICATION

Crew: One
Armament: Six wing-mounted M2 Browning .50cal machine guns with 240 rounds per gun, or 1,440 total (18 seconds firing time).
Maximum Speed: 318mph at 19,400ft
Range: 720 miles (effective combat radius 175 miles)

ABOVE: USS *Lexington* (CV-2) test firing in its 5in/.25cal anti-aircraft guns, 1928.
US NAVAL HISTORICAL CENTER

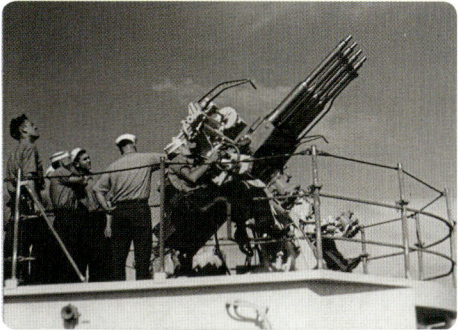

ABOVE: The 1.1in AA quad gun first appeared in 1931 with limited production starting in 1934. It did not enter service until 1936 and was not available in quantity until 1940. NARA

BELOW: Grumman XF4F-2 Wildcat prototype. The aircraft was progressively modified from its first flight in September 1937 until it appeared as the F3F-3 production variant in late 1939. At the time of Pearl Harbor the Navy counted 131 Wildcats in operational squadrons – 103 in the Atlantic Fleet and 29 with the Pacific. NARA

DOCTRINE

After over a decade of fleet exercises and the introduction of modern monoplane fighters and bombers, US carrier doctrine centred on the premise of 'first strike'. Knowing carriers could not withstand significant damage, it became imperative that the primary task of the carrier was the destruction of any opposing carriers as soon as possible. It was certainly doctrine in 1938, for the carrier air doctrine manual of that year stated the following: "It is highly improbable that control of the air can be gained by employing aircraft to shoot down enemy aircraft. The surest and quickest means of gaining control of the air is destruction of enemy carriers... by bombing attacks.

In order to improve the survivability of carriers, US doctrine called for the separation of the carriers from the main battle fleet in order to escape early detection and destruction by enemy aircraft. It also called for the launch of entire air groups at one time. In order for this to happen the entire 'deck load' strike had to be on the flight deck and launched as quickly as possible.

STATE OF THE FLEET

In December 1941 the US Pacific carrier fleet was well equipped with aircraft, men and ships. The three operational carriers of the fleet: *Lexington*, *Saratoga* and *Enterprise* were joined by *Yorktown* in January 1942 and *Hornet* in April. The Lexingtons were large well-designed carriers with the Yorktowns being arguably the best designs in the world. The Yorktowns' overall design provided the template for the even more successful Essex class. US carriers had sufficient speed (30 knots plus) for fleet operations and were big enough to carry a large four squadron (18 aircraft each with several reserves) air group. The carriers had adequate underwater protection against torpedo attack

ABOVE: The third production Brewster F2A-1 Buffalo, the US Navy's first monoplane fighter. Powered by the Wright R-1820 34 engine rated at 950hp, the F2A-1 had a top speed of 311mph at 18,000ft. NARA

DOUGLAS TBD-1 DEVASTATOR

The Douglas TBD-1 Devastator was a significant aircraft in the history of US Navy carrier aviation. It was the first monoplane torpedo bomber to enter service with modern design features including hydraulically-operated landing gear, flaps, folding wings and fully enclosed cockpit. In combat the Devastator proved a better weapon than conventional history has given credit. If it wasn't for the faulty and unreliable Mk XIII torpedo, the Devastator may very well have earned its name.

In 1937 the US Navy received its first Devastator. After extensive testing, "the TBD was found to be superior in performance to any horizontal bomber or torpedo plane in use by the Navy, has excellent flying characteristics, and is considered to be entirely suitable for operation from aircraft carriers or from flying field".

By 1942 the Devastator's shortcomings were evident. Its slow speed and short combat radius in combination with the Mk XIII torpedo made it obsolete. The Mk XIII torpedo, which could not be dropped above 100mph or above 120ft, made the TBD-1 extremely vulnerable to AA fire and fighters. A total of 130 TBD-1s were built, with 76 being assigned to the Pacific Fleet. Of those aircraft, 59 would be lost in combat or operational causes. In December 1941, 99 TBD-1s were available to form seven fleet squadrons.

SPECIFICATION
Crew: Three
Armament: One 2,216lb Mk XIII torpedo or 1,000lb of bombs; one .30cal or one .50cal nose mounted machine gun and one flexible rear mounted .30cal machine gun.
Maximum speed: 206mph at 8,000ft
Range: 700 miles (effective combat radius with ordnance was just 150 miles)

BELOW: A Douglas TBD-1 Devastator torpedo plane drops a Mark XIII torpedo during exercises in the Pacific, October 20, 1941. The low level and low speed required to drop the Mk XIII torpedo made the TBD-1 extremely vulnerable to AA fire and fighters. US NAVAL HISTORICAL CENTER

GRUMMAN TBF-1 AVENGER

Entering service in June 1942 the Grumman Avenger would become the most widely-produced naval strike aircraft in history. It's rugged construction, speed, range and payload made it the most effective carrier torpedo/bomber aircraft of the Pacific War.

A quantum leap forward the new Avenger featured power folding wings, hydraulically operated landing gear, electrically powered turret and internal bomb bay all powered by a Wright R-2600-8 radial air-cooled engine, rated at 1,700 horsepower.

Designed as a replacement for the Devastator, the first XTBF-1 prototype flew on August 7, 1941. Incredibly, one year later Avenger units provided carrier-based air support for the marine offensive at Guadalcanal. At the time of the Battle of Midway Grumman was producing 60 TBFs per month and by the end of 1942 646 aircraft were built.

Like its predecessor the TBF relied on the ineffective Mk XIII torpedo, limiting its ability to mount successful airborne attacks.

SPECIFICATION
Crew: Three
Armament: 2,000lb of bombs or one torpedo; one forward firing .30cal machine gun, one .30cal ventral machine gun, and one .50cal machine gun in the dorsal turret aft of the cockpit.
Maximum speed: 271mph at 12,000ft
Range: 1,215 miles (effective combat radius 260 miles)

ABOVE: A SBD-2 Dauntless dive-bomber. The SBD's dive flaps can be clearly seen. The tennis ball sized holes allowed the slipstream to pass through the flaps without losing air flow over the tail surfaces which were required for recovery from a dive. NARA

gave top priority to the area of damage control and all crew members were well trained in this regard. This stood in sharp contrast to their Japanese counterparts who received very little or no training in this critical area. US flyers also had the advantage of superior radios, for both air-to-air and air-to-ship communication. This allowed for more effective intercepts, but also improved survivability during an attack.

For all its advantages, the US Pacific carrier fleet was lacking in two crucial areas. First was combat experience. While its aircrews were well trained, motivated and led, none of them had fired their guns in anger. They would also enter the war with a defective torpedo that was horribly unreliable. In contrast the Japanese had an abundance of combat experience and their Type 91 aerial torpedo would prove deadly accurate. ∎

BELOW: Vought SB2U Vindicators of VS-41 and VS-42 and a Grumman F4F-3 Wildcat of VF-41 getting ready for a patrol flight aboard USS *Ranger*, November 1941. US Naval Historical Center. US NAVAL HISTORICAL CENTER

VOUGHT SB2U VINDICATOR

The Vought SB2U Vindicator was the second modern monoplane aircraft to enter US Navy service. The first, accepted in July 1937, incorporated the most advanced technologies of the day. Hydraulics controlled the landing gear and flaps and drooped the ailerons up to twelve degrees for additional lift on takeoffs and landings. The SB2U had manually folded wings and much of the aircraft was skinned with aluminium sheet, with fabric covering portions of the wing, tail and fuselage.

The SB2U was designed as a long-range scout bomber capable of carrying either a 500lb or 1,000lb bomb under the fuselage or two 100lb bombs under the wings. The lack of adequate dive brakes limited the Vindicator's dive angle to just 30 to 45 degrees.

In 1941, as America prepared for war on two fronts, the Navy moved its Vindicators to the Atlantic. The Marines went in the opposite direction, moving their SB2Us to Hawaii and Midway island.

Like the Devastator, the Vindicator's combat career was short. The Vindicator was never launched in anger from a US carrier, but it did see its first and last combat operation during the Battle of Midway flying from Midway Island on June 4, 1941.

SPECIFICATION

Crew: Two
Armament: One 1,000lb, one 500lb or two 100lb bombs. Two wing mounted .50cal machine guns and one flexible .30cal rear gun.
Maximum speed: 242mph at 9,500ft
Range: 2,640 miles with a 50 gallon center line drop tank (effective combat radius with a 1,000lb bomb was 560 miles)

CHAPTER 2

YEAR OF ATTRITION

★

Carrier raids and battles of 1942

ABOVE: Yokosuka B4Y1 Type 96 carrier attack bomber. This type was used during the first stages of the Sino-Japanese War. The B4Y1 was capable of carrying a 1,764lb torpedo or 1,102lb of bombs. NARA

"I think our principal teacher in respect to the necessity of emphasising aircraft carriers was the American Navy. We had no teachers to speak of besides the United States in respect to the aircraft themselves and to the method of their employment. We were doing our utmost all the time to catch up with the United States."

Admiral Osmai Nagano, IJN, 1945

By 1937 the three carrier navies of the world (Britain, Japan and United States) had in service both large and small carriers. At the time each had come to the same conclusion as to how carrier air power would be used in the future. Each navy still believed in the supremacy of the big gun battleship as the final arbiter of naval combat, but they also knew that any future clash between capitol ships would be affected by carrier air power.

Up to that point the evolution of carrier naval aviation depended upon studies, fleet exercises, and research internal to each navy. This was supplemented by intelligence reports and information that shone some light on the technological developments on the other side. For the Americans and Japanese, assessing the viability of specific aircraft, carriers, weapons and tactics was still largely guess work. All this would change, however, with the world's first combined carrier strikes. These strikes revealed the versatility of the aircraft carrier and its dual role capability – attacking surface vessels and striking ground targets.

The outbreak of Japan's war in China in the summer of 1937 caught the Japanese navy off guard. This major continental war seriously interrupted its plans for an orderly expansion of carrier naval aviation. Construction of additional aircraft carriers and seaplane tenders would be delayed and all of the navy's operational frontline aircraft – the Nakajima A1N (Type 90) and Nakajima A4N (Type 95) fighters, the Aichi D1A (Type 94) dive-bomber and the Mitsubishi B2M (Type 89) and Yokosuka B3Y (Type 92) torpedo planes – were fabric covered biplanes with limited range and payload.

Adequate when first introduced, these types were obsolete in terms of speed and combat durability by the time war broke out in China. Initially the navy's two land-based long-range (G3M twin engine medium bombers) groups and the carriers of the 1st and 2nd Carrier Divisions – *Hosho, Ryugo* and *Kaga* – provided the air power needed to destroy Chinese air units and their bases along with supporting the army's ground operations.

Just 24 hours after hostilities began, Japanese carrier planes began striking targets along the Chinese coast. Even though the Chinese were unable to launch air attacks against the fast-moving carriers, their fighters did take a steady

ABOVE: The Aichi D1A Type 96 dive-bomber. Based on the German Heinkel He 50, the D1A was capable of carrying a single 551lb bomb and two 66lb bombs. NARA

toll of attacking bombers. In the first two weeks of the war Japanese Navy bomber losses, both carrier- and land-based totalled 33. The slow Mitsubishi B2M2 carrier attack bomber proved easy prey for the more nimble Curtiss Hawk fighters flown by the Chinese. Fighter escort was needed, but the short range of the Type 90 and Type 95 fighters made that all but impossible.

These losses were unsustainable and to the Japanese naval leaders the clear solution lay with an improved fighter design with a longer range. After air battles of August 1937 the Second Combined Air Group submitted a report calling for a new escort fighter. The report clearly spelled out the specifications required which included: a monocoque construction, heavier calibre weapons and greater operational range. These specifications led directly to the development of the famed Mitsubishi A6M1 Zero-sen. Work on the new fighter began in October 1937 and it would be three years before the Zero-sen entered service.

In the meantime, the Japanese introduced the Mitsubishi A5M2 Type 96 'Claude' – the world's first monoplane carrier fighter. With its greater speed and rate of climb, the all metal 'Claude' had a distinct advantage over the assortment of Chinese biplane fighters. It was also one of the first monoplane fighters to use a drop tank to extend its range. In late September 1937 the first A5M2s began carrier operations providing escort for both carrier- and land-based bombers. As more came into action the Japanese navy established air superiority.

In early October the 1st and 2nd Carrier Divisions with their new A5M2s were assigned to provide tactical support for Japanese army units and their drive towards the Chinese capitol. With no training Japanese carrier pilots engaged in close support bombing missions and strafing attacks using the A5M2 with good results.

The Japanese experience in China showed clearly the tremendous offensive potential of carrier-based air power and that massive air strikes with good fighter escort were needed to deal with well defended land targets. Before the advent of the 'Claude' and 'Zero', fighter aircraft were used in the purely defensive role; now they were seen as offensive weapons for both the air superiority role and ground attack. The navy also began to experiment with the use of fighters to strafe surface vessels, particularly the bridges of enemy ships while carrier dive and torpedo bombers made their runs.

For the Japanese the modest number of aircraft (80) assembled from the carriers *Kaga, Ryujo* and *Hosho* clearly showed what the concentration of carrier air power could accomplish and just four and half years later that concept led directly to the formation of the semi-independent fast carrier task group and the attack on Pearl Harbor.

JAPANESE CARRIER V1941

In December 1941 the Imperial Japanese Navy (IJN) had nine carriers ready for action: *Akagi* (66 planes), *Kaga* (75 planes), *Hiryu* (54 planes), *Soryu* (54 planes), *Shokaku* (72 planes), *Zuikaku* (72 planes), *Zuiho* (27 planes), *Ryujo* (34 planes) and *Hosho* (19 planes).

Japanese carrier design centred on speed and aircraft capacity and generally mirrored that of US Navy designs. Following the experimental carrier *Hosho*, the first fleet carriers *Akagi* and *Kaga* entered the fleet. Both the *Akagi* and *Kaga* were

ABOVE: Three Mitsubishi A5M4 'Claudes'. At the time of its introduction in 1937 the A5M4 was the fastest carrier fighter in the world. Maximum speed was 270mph with a range of 750 miles. NARA

CARRIER STRIKE 17

SMALL VIEW SHOWS JETTISONABLE FUEL TANK

T.O NAVY FIGHTER (JAPAN)

conversions based on capitol ship hulls. These were followed by the first true carrier design the *Soryu* class. These ships, *Soryu* and *Hiryu*, featured minimal protection but had a large strike capability. The best Japanese carriers was the *Shokaku* class. Designed without reference to the Washington Treaty limitations the *Shokaku* and *Zuikaku* possessed a good balance of speed, aircraft capacity, defensive armament and protection and were considered by many to be the finest carriers in the world in 1942.

Where aircraft capacity was concerned, American doctrine called for most of a carrier's aircraft to be parked on the flight deck, with the hangar deck assigned to maintenance and storage. Japanese aircraft capacity was determined solely by the size of the hangar. All fueling, arming and maintenance was done in the hangar deck.

The flight deck and hangars on Japanese carriers were unarmoured.

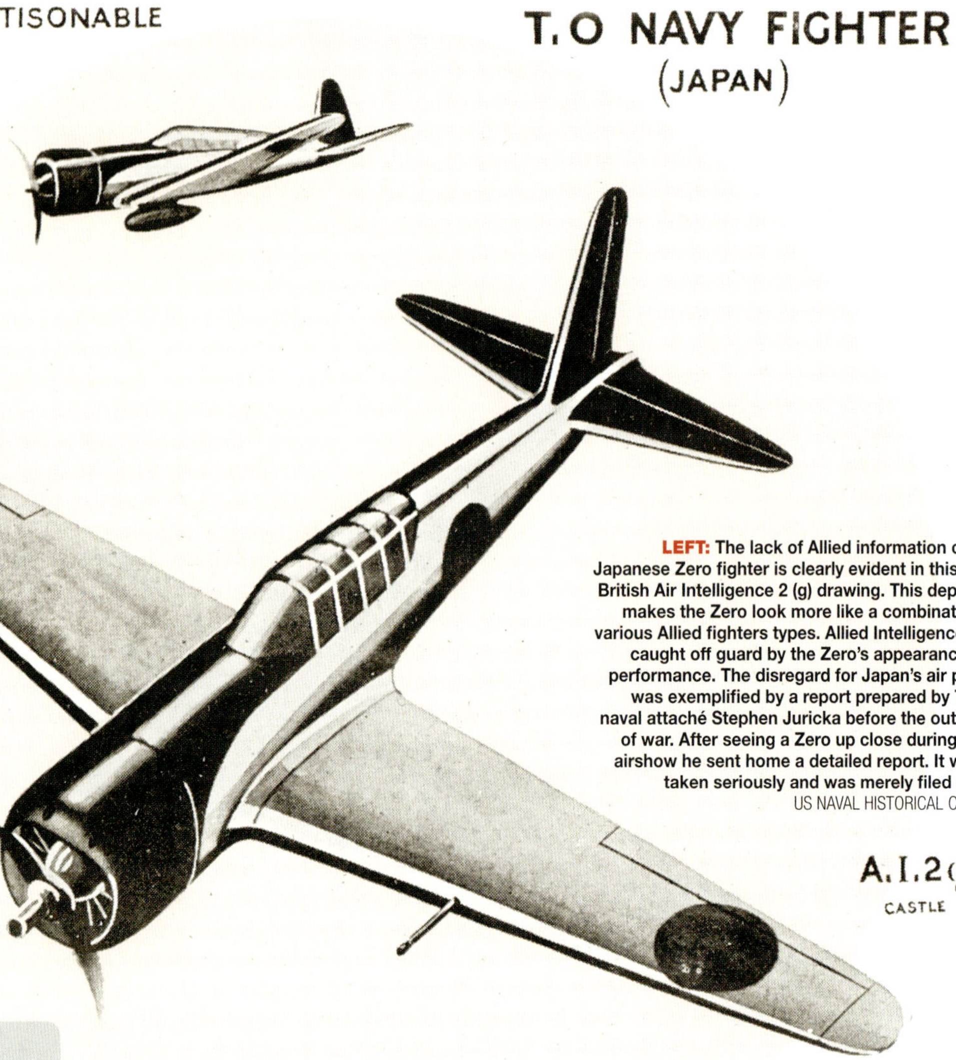

LEFT: The lack of Allied information on the Japanese Zero fighter is clearly evident in this early British Air Intelligence 2 (g) drawing. This depiction makes the Zero look more like a combination of various Allied fighters types. Allied Intelligence was caught off guard by the Zero's appearance and performance. The disregard for Japan's air power was exemplified by a report prepared by Tokyo naval attaché Stephen Juricka before the outbreak of war. After seeing a Zero up close during at an airshow he sent home a detailed report. It wasn't taken seriously and was merely filed away.
US NAVAL HISTORICAL CENTER

A.I.2(g) CASTLE

MITSUBISHI A6M2 TYPE 00 MODEL 21

Designed from specifications first issued in 1937, the first Mitsubishi A6M1 fighter took to the air in April 1939. Code named 'Zeke' by the Allies the A6M possessed exceptional performance and because of its exceptional range was the world's first escort fighter. Powered by a 950 horsepower Sakae radial engine, the A6M2 Model 21 entered service in 1941 with more than 400 delivered prior to the outbreak of war. An inspired design, the Zero possessed exceptional manoeuvrability, speed, great climb and acceleration, cannon armament and the greatest range of any single seat fighter, but these qualities came at a price. The Zero's low engine power (by 1941 Allied engines were developing well over 1,000 horse power) and demanding specifications forced Zero designer Jiro Horikoshi to make his aircraft as light as possible. That meant no armour or self-sealing fuel tanks making the Zero extremely vulnerable to damage even from small calibre weapons.

SPECIFICATION
Crew: One
Armament: Two 7.7mm machine guns with 500 rounds each and two 20mm cannon with 66 rounds each
Maximum speed: 336mph at 19,685ft
Range: 1,160 miles

To help negate the effects of a bomb hit, the hangars were designed to vent the force of an exploding bomb outward instead of upward. In combat the opposite frequently occurred – resulting in a ruptured flight deck. Japanese design also incorporated the fuel tanks as part of the structure of the ship. Resulting shocks from bomb hits would be absorbed by the tanks, creating leaks and explosive fumes. An inability to vent these fumes from the hangar and the poor training of damage repair crews when it came to addressing battle damage meant Japanese carriers were extremely vulnerable.

By the early 1930s carrier aviation and carrier design had reached a turning point. Carriers were now seen as viable striking platforms in their own

ABOVE: Japanese carrier *Akagi* with three Mitsubishi A6M2 Zero fighters at sea during the summer of 1941.
US NAVAL HISTORICAL CENTER

ABOVE: The Japanese carrier *Kaga* at sea following her 1934-36 modernisation. Kaga was capable of operating 75 aircraft. The *Kaga* stored 154,000 of avgas compared to the USS *Lexington*'s 132,000 gallons.
US NAVAL HISTORICAL CENTER

NAKAJIMA B5N2 TYPE 97 MODEL 12

Torpedoes were greatest ship killers of the Second World War and at the beginning of the Pacific war the Japanese possessed the best carrier torpedo bomber and aerial torpedo. The Nakajima B5N2 Type 97 carrier attack aircraft, codenamed 'Kate' by the Allies entered service in 1939. Compared to the American Devastator, the Type 97 was far superior in the key areas of speed, rate of climb and range. It was also equipped with the reliable and deadly Type 91 aerial torpedo. This allowed for higher dropping altitudes and higher attack speeds, limiting exposure to anti-aircraft fire.

SPECIFICATION
Crew: Two
Armament: One 551lb centreline bomb; two 132lb bombs under the wings; two forward firing 7.7mm machine guns, and one rear firing 7.7mm machine gun
Maximum speed: 240mph at 9,845ft
Range: 840 miles with bombload

ABOVE: Often cited as a B5N2 Type 97 'Kate' torpedo bomber taking off for the Pearl Harbor attack, this is in fact a still image taken from a film depicting a B5N1 model taking off from the carrier *Akagi* during a training mission in March-April 1942. Another clue is the dented torpedo and lack of air box aerodynamic fins at the tail.
US NAVAL HISTORICAL CENTER

right, capable of over the horizon strikes with bombs and torpedoes. The Japanese like the Americans focused on enemy aircraft carriers as the main threat and their quick destruction was the key to victory. Both knew their carriers were highly vulnerable to attack and for the Japanese that meant the essential precondition for carrier combat was to find the enemy first and strike first with overwhelming force.

The Japanese also recognized the need to mass their carrier power by using two or more carriers in a single formation. This important advantage would give them greater striking power and tactical initiative. In April 1941, the Japanese organised all their fleet carriers into a single formation, the First Air Fleet.

The operational component of the First Air Fleet was the *Kido Butai* meaning literally 'mobile force' or 'striking force'. The *Kido Butai* was made up of three carrier divisions: The 1st with the *Akagi* and *Kaga*, the 2nd with the *Soryu* and *Hiryu* and the 5th with the *Shokaku* and *Zuikaku*. The *Kido Butai* conducted operations as a multicarrier formation. The two carriers in a division fought together and during a strike each carrier would launch a combined force of dive and torpedo bombers, escorted by six or nine Zeros from each carrier. Each carrier retained a strike squadron as a reserve or second wave. In comparison to US Navy doctrine, the IJN was able to integrate operations from different carriers with greater efficiency and achieved a higher level of coordination and destructive power.

Japanese fleet carriers had their own air group made up of dive bombers, torpedo bombers and fighters. Each squadron had 18 aircraft with three in reserve. These aircraft, along with well-trained and experienced aircrews and deck crews, made the IJN's carriers formidable and versatile striking platforms.

As war approached both the IJN and US Navy shared a similar doctrine, but each had its share of combat strengths and weaknesses. Where the Japanese aircraft dominated in terms of well-trained aircrew, aircraft with exceptional range and performance and reliable torpedoes and bombs, the American answered with better intelligence, leadership, rugged aircraft, radar, better damage control and robust AA defences. At the beginning of the war nine Japanese carriers (six fleet carriers), opposed five American fleet carriers. In terms of striking power, the Japanese embarked 533 aircraft compared to the 427 aircraft of the US Navy.

AICHI D3A1 TYPE 99 MODEL 11

Of the three carrier aircraft in service at the outbreak of the war the Aichi D3A1 'Val' dive bomber was the weakest, but remained effective through 1942. Unable to carry the same maximum bombload of the SBD Dauntless, it was not as rugged and wasn't equipped with self-sealing fuel tanks. Ordered into production in December 1939 it saw limited combat operations in China from land bases and carriers.

SPECIFICATION
Crew: Two
Armament: One 551lb centreline bomb; two 132lb bombs under the wings; two forward firing 7.7mm machine guns, and one rear firing 7.7mm machine gun
Maximum speed: 240mph at 9,845ft
Range: 840 miles with bombload

BELOW: An A6M2 Type 21 is seen lashed to the flight deck of the IJN carrier *Akagi* in Hitokappu Bay, the Kurie Islands in late November 1941. The Japanese fleet gathered here prior to heading south to attack Pearl Harbor. AUTHOR'S COLLECTION

OPENING MOVES

In 1940 the US Navy transferred the Pacific Fleet from San Diego to Pearl Harbor. For Japanese military strategists this was seen as a direct threat and a major obstacle to their planned expansion into Indochina, the Philippines and numerous islands and atolls in the Pacific. The Japanese plan was to establish a defence perimeter in depth far into the Indian and Pacific oceans as practicable. This was to be achieved by intricately coordinated multiple surprise attacks. The Japanese would then reinforce their new territories with impunity, providing the US Fleet could be neutralised. This strategy centred on the strength and speed of the *Kido Butai*.

An attack on Pearl Harbor was seen as equally likely by both the United States and Japan. The Americans knew an attack by the Japanese somewhere in the Pacific was coming, they just didn't know where. While the Pearl Harbor attack was a surprise, it was not entirely unexpected.

The Japanese Carrier Striking Task Force of six fleet carriers was truly formidable. As it

> ### "The moment has arrived. The rise or fall of our empire is at stake..."
> #### Admiral Yamamoto

ABOVE: This chart of Pearl Harbor was recovered from a Japanese midget submarine captured after the attack on December 7, 1941. The chart shows ship locations but is clearly inaccurate and out of date. US NAVAL HISTORICAL CENTER

ABOVE: This cine still from a Japanese newsreel shows a B5N2 'Kate' taking off from *Shokaku* on December 7, 1941 heading for Pearl Harbor. US NAVAL HISTORICAL CENTER

ABOVE: An Aichi D3A1 Type 99 'Val' dive-bomber over Pearl Harbor. Equipped with a generous wing area, the 'Val' was very manoeuvrable, but like all Japanese carrier aircraft, it was lightly built with no armour or self-sealing fuel tanks. US NAVAL HISTORICAL CENTER

headed for the Hawaiian islands it was escorted by two fast battleships, two heavy cruisers, six destroyers and three submarines. From a position of 200 miles north of Oahu, the carriers turned into the wind and began to launch their aircraft. At 0751 hours on December 7, 1941, 183 aircraft (49 level bombers, 51 dive-bombers, 43 fighters and 40 torpedo bombers) of the first wave began their attacks. Surprise was total and the effect devastating.

This was followed by a second wave at 0900 hours of 40 fighters, 54 level bombers, and 80 dive-bombers. The primary targets of the attack were the three carriers of the Pacific Fleet. The Japanese would be disappointed however. *Enterprise* was not in harbour – instead it was steaming back from Wake Island. *Lexington* was cruising close to Midway Island and *Saratoga* was in San Diego. While the carriers had been saved the damage to the Pacific Fleet was severe.

Twenty-one ships were sunk or damaged: five battleships, one mine layer, three destroyers, two service craft, and auxiliary sunk; one cruiser and one auxiliary severely damaged; three battleships, two cruisers, one destroyer moderately damaged. One hundred and eighty-eight aircraft were destroyed and 159 damaged. Japanese losses were just 29 aircraft shot down, with 111 damaged – mostly by AA fire. As the Japanese retired, the *Kido Butai* had clearly established the supremacy of carrier airpower, making it the most formidable striking force in the Pacific.

In a single stroke the US Navy carrier air doctrine for the defence of the battle line had been altered forever. With the bulk of the battleship force lying on the bottom of Pearl Harbor and with the carriers unscathed, the naval aviators now had a chance to implement what they had been arguing for, for so long: task force strike operations built around the fast carrier.

Japan's carrier force achieved a great but limited victory. Its leaders went to war knowing their immediate objectives but were in many ways willfully ignorant and naïve about what would follow.

For the first six months of 1942 success followed the *Kido Butai* wherever it went. By using

ABOVE: Japanese Aichi D3A1 'Vals' of the second Pearl Harbor attack wave prepare to take off with the carrier *Soryu* in the background. US NAVAL HISTORICAL CENTER

carriers en masse and in combination with high-quality aircraft, tested tactics and experienced aircrews the Japanese were able to focus massive amounts of airpower on a single target or multiple ships. Shortly after Pearl Harbor, *Soryu* and *Hiryu* provided air support for the invasion of Wake Island. The first Japanese attempt to capture Wake Island began simultaneously with the attack on Pearl Harbor. Air attacks by land based bombers started on December 8 and on the 11th the first landing attempt was repelled by the defenders. This forced the Japanese to dispatch the *Soryu* and *Hiryu* to provide air support for a second, successful, landing on December 23.

After a brief respite in Japanese waters to refuel and replenish, the *Kido Butai* moved south in support of the invasion of the Dutch East Indies. In order to protect their operations from Allied interference the Japanese decided to conduct a major raid on the Australian city of Darwin. This would be the second significant attack mounted by the *Kido Butai* on a major Allied harbour and supporting airfields. On February 19 the Japanese launched 188 strike aircraft from the carriers *Akagi, Kaga, Shokaku* and *Zuikaku*. Two hours later 54 land-based Navy G3M 'Nell' and G4M 'Betty' bombers finished off the attack. The effectiveness of the *Kido Butai* resulted in another successful surprise aerial attack on a naval target and came as a great shock to the Australians.

In April, minus the carrier *Kaga*, the *Kido Butai* with five carriers sortied into the Indian Ocean to attack British naval bases and shipping. The British now had the carriers *Formidable, Indomitable* and *Hermes* in the Indian Ocean. On April 5, the Japanese struck the port of Colombo (128 aircraft) on the island of Ceylon (present day Sri Lanka). The British carriers were not in port, but two days later the *Kido Butai* found the British heavy cruisers, *Cornwall* and

Dorsetshire. Fifty-three D3A1 'Val' dive-bombers made short work of these vessels, sinking both in just 19 minutes with an incredible hit rate of close to 80%. More strikes against shore targets continued and on April 9 the Japanese sighted *Hermes*. Eighty-five 'Val' dive-bombers fell on the carrier. With no hope of survival against such a force, HMS *Hermes* became the first aircraft carrier to be sunk by aircraft from another carrier. From December 1941 to April 1942 British losses to Japanese carrier and land based torpedo bombers were shocking: one battleship, one battlecruiser, one aircraft carrier, two heavy cruisers and several destroyers.

Flush with victory, the Japanese carriers returned to Japan on April 22 unscathed. Aircraft losses had been relatively light, but maintenance had to be done, new aircrews integrated and for those who had seen constant action a period to rest. It was short lived, however, when the 5th Carrier Division was ordered south to cover the invasion of Port Moresby on New Guinea.

In the first five months of the war, the power of the *Kido Butai* was nothing short of astonishing. No ships had been lost and almost every objective in the early stages of the war had be achieved. The doctrine of massed air strikes, equipped with excellent aircraft and well-trained aircrew simply overwhelmed Allied forces. But while the victories had been impressive, the Japanese had yet to face a force that could match its own capabilities and training. Like the early German victories in Europe in 1940, the Japanese became infected with an overconfidence they would later identify as 'victory disease'. It was an advantage the US Navy was quick to exploit.

The Japanese rampage across the Pacific in early 1942 did not go unanswered. Not waiting for reinforcements, the three operational carriers – *Lexington, Saratoga* and *Enterprise* began a series of carrier raids against the newly captured Japanese held islands. The raids were designed to keep the Japanese off balance and let them know US carriers were ready and able to fight back.

Just eight weeks after the Pearl Harbor attack the first US carrier strike of the war was conducted on February 1. *Enterprise* launched a full-deck strike of 67 aircraft (SBD-3s, TBD-1s and F4F-3s) against Japanese targets on Kwajalein in the Marshall Islands. At the same time *Yorktown* attacked targets in the Marshall and Gilbert Islands with 42 SBD Dauntless and TBD Devastators. The results were negligible, but the IJN did react by sending two carriers in search of the Americans. They quickly abandoned the pursuit. American aircraft losses were light, but the experience gained by the Navy flyers proved invaluable in the coming battles.

Shortly afterwards, on February 20, *Lexington* sortied to attack the newly captured Japanese base at Rabaul in the South Pacific. Before its aircraft could be launched, *Enterprise* was attacked by 17 long-range Mitsubishi G4M1 'Betty' bombers equipped with bombs instead of torpedoes. *Lexington's* F4Fs, SBDs and anti-aircraft gunners destroyed 15 of 17 attacking bombers. More raids followed, with *Enterprise* striking Wake Island on February 24 and Marcus Island on March 3.

On March 10 the US Navy launch its first multi carrier raid of the war. *Lexington* and *Yorktown* each launched 52 aircraft, striking Japanese naval forces at Lae and Salamaua, New Guinea. Surprise was complete and Japanese fighter and AA defences were negligible. However, despite the high number of American dive-bombers and torpedo aircraft launched, just three Japanese transports were sunk. It was a poor performance but the overall series of attacks demonstrated that the easy period of Japanese expansion and free movement in the Pacific was nearing an end.

In April, that point was driven home in one of the most audacious carrier attacks of the war. On April 18 *Hornet*, with *Enterprise* providing air cover, launched 16 Army Air Force B-25B Mitchell twin engine bombers. Each B-25 carried a single 500lb bomb and incendiary cluster. The raid caught the Japanese napping and although the physical damage was slight, the psychological effect was far worse. The fact that two American carriers had sailed undetected to within striking distance of the homeland came as a complete shock and would alter Japanese planning in the weeks and months ahead. This raid, more than any other before, forced the Japanese to react to a US offensive operation and not the other way around.

BELOW: SBD-3 Dauntlesses from VS-6 and VB-6 warming prior to take-off for the strike on Wake Island on February 24, 1942. The forward SBDs at the front of the formation carry a single centre-line bomb, while the SBDs behind, with more deck space to take-off, are armed with additional 100lb bombs beneath the wings. NARA

ABOVE: After finishing its bomb run a Douglas TBD-1 from USS *Enterprise* flies over Wake during the February 24 raid. Note fires burning in the lower centre. US NAVAL HISTORICAL CENTER

RIGHT: Some of the B-25B 'Doolittle Raiders' secured to the flight deck of USS *Hornet*, while en route to Japan and their takeoff point. US NAVAL HISTORICAL CENTER

'EGGSHELLS WITH HAMMERS'

At the beginning of the war the Americans held a distinct advantage. Prior to the attack on Pearl Harbor US Navy code breakers were able to crack the IJN's secondary code system – known as JN-25. This allowed for key insights into the movements of Japanese carriers. On April 8, Navy intelligence predicted the Japanese were heading for Port Moresby in Papa New Guinea. Initially they thought five carriers would be involved but by early May the number had been confirmed as three.

At the beginning of May the US Navy had five carriers in the Pacific. Repairs on *Saratoga* were almost complete; *Yorktown* and *Enterprise* were returning from the Doolittle raid, leaving *Lexington* and *Yorktown* for operations. After Pearl Harbor both *Yorktown* and *Lexington* improved their AA defences by replacing their .50cal machine guns with Oerlikon 20mm cannons and 1.1in quadruple gun mounts. When they entered battle both carriers were well equipped with long-range, intermediate, and close in AA weapons. *Lexington* had twelve 5in/25 guns, twelve 1.1in mounts, 22 Oerlikons and roughly 24 .50cal machine guns. *Yorktown* carried eight 5in/38 guns, four quad mounts, 24 20mm guns and 24 .50cal machine guns.

Japanese intentions in the Coral Sea were two-fold: capture Port Moresby and in the process strengthen their outer defensive position in the South Pacific. Covering the troop and supporting ships was the small carrier *Shoho* with just 18 aircraft (12 Zeros and eight Kates). Long range cover against US fleet ships was provided by the fleet carriers *Shokaku* and *Zuikaku* with 121 aircraft. To meet the threat the US had 134 aircraft on *Lexington* and *Yorktown* designated Task Force 17 (TF-17).

On May 4, Japanese forces landed on Tulagi island in the Solomons. In response *Yorktown* launched 40 strike aircraft sinking a destroyer and three minesweepers. The presence of American

CARRIER STRIKE 23

carriers was now clear. On May 5 *Lexington* joined *Yorktown*. On the morning of the 6th, a Japanese reconnaissance aircraft spotted the carriers, but they were out of range.

On the morning of May 7, both sides were ready for action. First off the mark were the Japanese with *Shokaku* launching a reconnaissance aircraft at 0722 hours. A carrier was reported sighted just 150 miles south of the Japanese carriers. Rear Admiral Chuichi Hara ordered a strike group of 78 aircraft (36 Vals, 24 Kates and 18 Zeros) launched from both carriers.

As the strike force arrived, what they found was not the American carriers but a fleet oiler and a destroyer. Prior to the attack at 0820 a floatplane from the cruiser *Furutaka* found the American carriers and this was later confirmed but it was too late to alter the first strike. After searching for the American carriers, the dive-bombers were finally ordered into action, sinking the oiler *Neosho* and destroyer *Sims*. The Japanese lost a single bomber shot down and four others lost to operational causes.

Just as the Japanese had trouble finding their quarry, the Americans were also having problems with sightings and target identification. At 0815 hours *Yorktown's* scouts reported two carriers and four heavy cruisers and this was quickly interpreted as the Japanese main force. In accordance with doctrine Rear Admiral Frank Fletcher ordered a two deck load strike of 50 aircraft from *Yorktown* and 43 from *Lexington* (53 SBDs, 22 TBDs and 18 F4Fs). When the scout returned, Fletcher learned the report had been miscoded and should have read, 'two cruisers and two destroyers'.

LEFT: The Japanese carrier *Shoho* is torpedoed, during attacks by US Navy carrier aircraft in the late morning of May 7, 1942. The TDB-1 Devastators from *Yorktown* and *Lexington* claimed 19 hits from the 22 torpedoes dropped, but the accepted figure is seven torpedoes finding their mark. US NAVAL HISTORICAL CENTER

BELOW: Douglas SBD-3 Dauntless scout bombers of VS-5 preparing to take off from *Yorktown*, during operations in the Coral Sea, April 18, 1942. NARA

BELOW: Three SBD-3 returning to Hornet in October 1942. Two of the rear gunners remain vigilant while the third has secured his guns. Both Navy and Marine SBD squadrons racked up an impressive score during 1942 sinking, in whole or in part, six aircraft carriers, one battleship, three cruisers and four destroyers.

Fletcher's first strike was now heading for a low-priority target. Recalling the strike would be too risky with a Japanese attack expected at any moment. At 1013, Fletcher received a report from a US army bomber that the light carrier *Shoho* and her escorts had been spotted. Breaking radio silence, Fletcher redirected his strike package to the *Shoho*. At 1040 the first bombs began to fall. The Japanese launched a mix of A5M 'Claudes' and A6M2 Zeros – resulting in the first combat between Zeros and Navy F4Fs.

The Wildcat pilots claimed two A5Ms and one A6M2 for no losses. After 13 bomb hits and seven torpedo strikes (19 hits were claimed, but most of the torpedoes missed) the *Shoho* was sunk. Deprived of its air cover, the Japanese invasion fleet turned for home – giving the Americans their first victory.

That same afternoon the Japanese received information on American carriers located 330-360 miles to the west. Hara launched a dusk raid with a 27-aircraft strike force (12 dive-bombers and 15 torpedo bombers) crewed by his most experienced pilots. To meet the raid were 30 F4Fs. Aided by ship-based radar, the F4Fs descended on the Japanese and shot down nine, damaging two more. It was a fiasco for the Japanese and triumph for the carrier's CAP (combat air patrol).

As May 8 dawned the Japanese had on strength 109 aircraft of which 95 were operational (37 A6M2 fighters, 33 D3A1 dive-bombers, and 25 B5N2 torpedo planes). US aircraft strength numbered 128 aircraft, of which 117 were serviceable (31 F4F fighters, 65 SBD dive-bombers, and 21 TBD torpedo planes). Shortly after 0800 hours scouts from both sides reported sightings approximately 210 miles from each other. At 0847 hours the Americans got going first – launching 75 aircraft from their two carriers. At 0915 hours the Japanese carriers launched 33 dive-bombers, 18 torpedo bombers and 18 fighters.

At 1057 hours, after waiting for the slower TBD-1 Devastators to start their attack, the *Yorktown's* SBDs rolled in on *Shokaku*. That gave *Zuikaku* enough time to find cover in a rain squall and escape attack. As the dive-bombers began their runs on the *Shokaku* the F4F escort engaged the Japanese air combat patrol of 13 Zeros. The F4Fs didn't make any claims, but the SBDs scored two hits with 1,000lb bombs (AN-M64 GP with 530lb explosive weight) for the loss of two dive-bombers to AA fire. The Devastator torpedo bombers were less successful with no hits recorded.

Next came *Lexington's* attack group (15 dive-bombers, 12 torpedo bombers, and nine fighters) at 1130 hours. Poor weather prevented the SBD dive bombers of VB-2 from finding their target, but the rest found *Shokaku* and scored just one bomb hit. All torpedoes missed.

At 1055 hours, *Lexington's* CXAM radar detected the first of 69 Japanese strike aircraft at 68 miles out (18 B5N2 torpedo planes, 33 D3A1 dive bombers and 18 A6M2 fighters). Flying CAP were 17 F4Fs and an additional 18 SBDs, posted at 800 to 900ft to intercept the low flying B5N2 torpedo bombers. Before reaching the carriers, the CAP managed to shoot down four torpedo bombers and six dive-bombers, but they lost five SBDs and three F4Fs to the escorting Zeros.

The attack began at 1113 hours and was well coordinated. The first to attack were 14 B5N2s. Ten against the *Lexington* with four attacking *Yorktown*. Breaking through the AA fire and intercepting fighters all four torpedoes launched at *Yorktown* missed. Against the *Lexington* the remaining ten B5N2s split to set up a classic anvil attack. With aircraft attacking from both bows the *Lexington* had no room to evade. Flying through the AA fire and fighters, nine Kates attacked the *Lexington* while two others turned their sights on an escorting cruiser. The first five torpedoes missed. The remaining four were dropped at just 700 yards scoring two hits. One of the torpedoes struck near the port forward gun gallery, cracking the port aviation fuel storage tanks and eventually sealing the ship's fate. Four Kates were shot down by AA fire.

With the *Lexington* hit, but not sinking, the Japanese D3A1 dive-bombers began their attacks on *Lexington* and *Yorktown*. Diving to 1,500ft before releasing their bombs, 19 'Vals' went after *Lexington* – smothering the ship in what seemed like a devastating attack. Only two bombs hit causing minor damage. Fourteen dive-bombers from *Zuikaku* went after *Yorktown*. The Japanese claimed eight hits, but only one bomb, a single 551lb Type 99 No.25 Mk 1 semi-amour piercing round found its mark. After penetrating through four decks it exploded causing considerable damage. Even with this damage, *Yorktown* remained operational.

Between 1250 hours and 1430 hours, both sides recovered their respective strikes. All Japanese aircraft were ordered to land on *Zuikaku*. While the Japanese attack had damaged the US carriers, both were operational and neither seemed in danger of sinking. During the attack on the Japanese carriers American losses amounted to three F4Fs and nine SBDs to enemy fighters and AA fire. The Japanese suffered similar losses. American CAP shot down five dive-bombers, eight torpedo planes and one escorting Zero. The number of damaged aircraft was far higher. Seven ditched on the way back to their carriers and 12 were so severely damaged after landing that they were thrown overboard. That left the Japanese with just 39 operational aircraft – 24 fighters, nine dive-bombers and six torpedo planes. Low on fuel and no longer capable of mounting another strike, Hara was forced to retire.

Early damage control efforts on *Lexington* kept the vessel operational, but the build-up of dangerous aviation fuel vapours spread throughout the ship. At 1247 hours the first of several explosions rocked the great carrier. With the fires out of control, more explosions followed. Finally, at 1707 hours the order was given to abandon ship. At 1952 hours torpedoes from the destroyer USS *Phelps* sent *Lexington* to the bottom. The majority of *Lexington's* aircraft were transferred to *Yorktown* giving it 72 aircraft of which 50 were operational. With offensive operations over, the damaged carrier was sent to Pearl Harbor for immediate repair.

ANALYSIS
This was the first true carrier battle of the war fought entirely by aircraft. While a tactical victory for the Japanese it was huge strategic victory for the US Navy. For the first time in the war the Japanese had been forced to retreat and abandon their plans, preventing the seaborne invasion of Port Moresby.

Both sides had committed many errors and a major operational weakness was revealed. Both sides had too few fighters for both escort and CAP over the carriers. While the Americans had the advantage of radar, their fighter direction sent many fighters to the wrong altitude and in the confusion of combat radio discipline broke down, overloading the network. But it was still much better than the Japanese system.

Japanese CAP was rudimentary at best. Even

BELOW: *Shokaku* under attack during the Battle of the Coral Sea. SBDs from *Yorktown* and *Lexington* scored four hits on the 20,000 ton carrier causing heavy damage. US NAVAL HISTORICAL CENTER

BELOW: *Lexington* burning and sinking after her crew abandoned ship during the Battle of Coral Sea, May 8, 1942. Note planes parked aft, where fires have not yet reached. US NAVAL HISTORICAL CENTER

with the superior A6M2 Zero, the lack of radar or any type of fighter control made the job of the CAP all but impossible. The Japanese relied on lookouts on escorting ships and gunfire to alert the CAP. Each fleet carrier maintained nine Zeros for air defence: one three-fighter Shotai airborne, a second Shotai readied for launch and a third in a lesser state of readiness.

Without effective radio direction, the pilots in each Shotai had to vector themselves. During the attack on *Shokaku* and *Zuikaku* the CAP consisted of just 15 to 18 Zeros, the standard number of a two-carrier division. The Americans made a coordinated dive-bomber and torpedo attack and in the confusion the US aircraft managed to deal with the Japanese CAP. Just four SBDs and three escorting F4Fs were shot down and while the torpedo attack failed, the Devastator rear gunners managed to shoot down three Zeros for no losses.

The introduction of the Grumman F4F-4 with folding wings allowed the Americans to increase their carrier fighter complement to 27. The Japanese continued with the standard 18 fighters for each fleet carrier.

The combination of CXAM radar and the Combat Information Centre (CIC) gave the American carriers a greater chance of survival over their Japanese counterparts. Radar eliminated the chance of surprise and gave them more time to launch and direct fighters. It also enhanced the AA defences. AA crews were no longer caught flat footed. Carriers and their escorts had time to prepare, knowing the approximate direction from which to expect the attack and the time it was likely to occur. For Japanese aircrew US carrier AA fire was intense and unexpected. Lieutenant Commander Shimazaki Shigekezu from *Zuikaku* was one of the first torpedo attackers to experience American AA fire.

He said: "When we attacked the enemy carriers we ran into a virtual wall of anti-aircraft fire; the carriers and their supporting ships blackened the sky with exploding shells and tracers. It seemed impossible that we could survive our bombing and torpedo runs through such an incredible defence."

In the weeks and months ahead these AA defences would only increase in both the number of barrels and sheer weight of fire with the replacement of the 1.1in machine cannon with the superb Bofors 40mm AA gun.

BATTLE OF MIDWAY, JUNE 1942

By the late spring of 1942, both the IJN and Imperial Japanese Army (IJA) had reached their intended territorial goals and begun to strengthen their outer perimeter defences. The only major stumbling block that remained was the continued presence of the American carriers.

The Japanese needed to bring the American carriers into battle and defeat them in one decisive action. The island of Midway was chosen as the bait. The planned operation to engage the remaining strength of the US Pacific Fleet would be the largest mounted by the IJN in the first year of the war. All eight of its operational carriers were committed, along with 11 battleships, 14 of its 18 heavy cruisers and the bulk its light cruiser and destroyer force.

For the attack on Midway, Admiral Yamamoto Isoroku employed the carriers *Akagi, Kaga, Soryu* and *Hiryu* of the *1st Kido Butai* with a total of 247

ABOVE: A Japanese cruiser, circa 1937 mounting the 5in/40 type twin mount AA gun. This gun equipped the carriers *Kaga, Soryu* and *Hiryu* and had an effective range of 8,750 yards. US NAVAL HISTORICAL CENTER

aircraft. The Battle of the Coral Sea had caused severe losses on both sides. The light carrier *Shoho* had been sunk, *Shokaku* was hit by three bombs and under repair and *Zuikaku's* air group was so battered it would take weeks to rebuild. This left Yamamoto with just four fleet carriers instead of the desired six but this force was still deemed more than adequate for the upcoming battle.

After the Battle of the Coral Sea *Yorktown* was quickly repaired at Pearl Harbor. Its air group was re-formed using squadrons from the damaged *Saratoga* air group and made ready for action. Fletcher remained in overall command, exercising direct control direct control of Task Force 17 (TF-17) centred on *Yorktown* with 75 aircraft (25 F4F-4s, 37 SBD-3s and 13 TBD-1s). Rear Admiral Raymond Spruance commanded Task Force 16 (TF-16) with *Enterprise* and *Hornet*. Each carried 79 aircraft with 27 F4Fs, 38 SBD-2/3s, and 14 TBD-1s on *Enterprise* and 27 F4F-4s, 27 SDB-2/3s and 15 TDB-1s on *Hornet*. The three American carriers embarked 234 aircraft.

The island of Midway, the 'unsinkable carrier', gave the Americans a distinct advantage. It also highlighted the good cooperation between the three services, Navy, Army Air Force and Marine. Commanded by Captain Simard, Midway's defensive and offensive assets included 20 operational F2A-3 Buffalo fighters, seven F4F-3 Wildcats, 18 SBD-2 Dauntless, 14 SB2U-3 Vindicators, six TBF-1 Avengers, four B-26 Marauder medium bombers, 14 B-17E and one B-17D heavy bomber, plus 29 PBY-5s.

And the Americans knew the Japanese were coming. The steady progress of cracking the Japanese Navy code gave the Americans some key insights into the Japanese plan. This allowed the American carrier groups to be placed north of Midway in a perfect ambush position.

The Battle of Midway has often been framed as an incredible victory against all odds but in truth the Japanese task force entered the battle as the weaker side. Losses in the early months of the war had been light, but the aircraft strength of the *Kido Butai* had declined nevertheless. Japanese aircraft factories were unable to keep pace and as a result the four carriers at Midway had 16% fewer aircraft than they did at Pearl Harbor. On the plus side the *Kido Butai's* aircrew were the most experienced in the Pacific.

The *Kido Butai's* four carriers embarked an air group with three squadrons. *Akagi* carried 54 aircraft (18 A6M2s, 18 D3A1s, 18 B5N2s). *Kaga* embarked 63 (18 A6M2s, 18 D3A1s and 27 B5N2s). *Hiryu* carried 54 (18 A6M2s, 18 D3A1s, 18 B5N2s) and *Soryu* carried 53-54 (18 A6M2s, 16 D3A1s, 18 B5N2s and 1-2 D4Y1s). All four carriers carried the 21 A6M2 Zeros from the 6th Air Group earmarked for Midway protection once the island was captured.

At 0345 hours on June 3, Midway's PBYs spotted the Japanese minesweeper group. Less than an hour later, the troop transport group was spotted 700 miles west of Midway. The Japanese hope for strategic surprise had been lost and ironically the first attack of the battle was delivered by US Army Air Force B-17s from the 431st BG at 1200 hours. The strike on the transport group was not a success, but at 0130 hours four radar-equipped PBYs armed with two Mk.XIII torpedoes made a night attack, scoring one hit on the tanker *Akebono Maru*. This was the only successful air-launched torpedo attack by US aircraft during the entire battle.

At 0430 hours on June 4, the Japanese joined the battle with the launch of 108 aircraft for a strike on Midway. Escorted by 36 Zeros were 36 D3A1 dive-bombers and 36 B5N2 level-bombers armed with high explosive bombs. To meet the attack, six Wildcats and 18 F2A Buffalos were scrambled. Tearing through the defenders, the Japanese shot down 15 of them. No American aircraft were caught on the ground however and the AA defences was extremely heavy. When the smoked cleared the Japanese had lost 11 shot down or ditched, 14 heavily damaged and rendered non-operational and a further 29 damaged.

The moment Captain Simard received the Japanese carrier contact report he launched all available strike aircraft. 51 US Navy, Marine Corps and Army Air Corps took off without escort. Just after 0700 hours they began their attack. The first in were six TBF Avengers torpedo planes and four Air Corps B-26 Marauder medium bombers armed with torpedoes. To meet them were 29 Zero fighters flying CAP. Lacking escort they were easy prey for the experienced Zero pilots. Just two TBFs were able to launch torpedoes towards *Hiryu* and a single B-26 dropped its fish towards *Akagi*, all missed. Just one Avenger and two B-26s survived.

At 0800 hours, the 16 SBD-2s of VSMB-241 joined the fray. *Hiryu* was spotted as their target, but 19 Zeros on CAP quickly decimated the formation. No hits were recorded and eight SBDs were shot down. Next over the carriers were 14 B-17s which delivered an attack from over 20,000ft. No hits scored.

Midway's final strike consisted of 11 obsolete SB2U-3 dive-bombers. Seeing too many Japanese fighters, a glide bomb attack was delivered with no hits and three aircraft lost.

At 0530 hours Midway reconnaissance aircraft reported the position of the Japanese carriers. According to plan, at 0700 hours Fletcher launched TF-16's strike group of 116 aircraft (67 dive-bombers, 29 torpedo planes and 20 fighters). At 0800 hours, *Yorktown* launched 17 dive-bombers, 12 torpedo bombers and six fighters.

At 0740 hours, an Aichi E13A 'Jake' floatplane from the cruiser *Tone* sighted the American ships, but no report of carriers was made. This was followed by another message at 0830 hours: "The enemy is accompanied by what appears to be a carrier."

As the Midway strike aircraft returned, Nagumo still had a large strike force of 43 torpedo bombers with a few re-armed with bombs and 34 dive-bombers. But Nagumo hesitated and instead of launching the strike aircraft available he opted to recover his Midway strike and then head northeast towards the Americans. At 0918 the recovery was complete, but it was too late. At 0753 hours, the battleship *Kirishima* reported American aircraft approaching.

Up until this point the *1st Kido Butai's* fighter CAP had turned away all attackers. The Midway strike had been an uncoordinated, makeshift operation. At 0915 18 Zeros were flying CAP when the first 15 Devastators from *Hornet* began their runs. Eleven more Zeros were launched. Flying as low as possible to avoid destruction, the slow Devastators were hacked from the sky. Between 0920 and 0937 hours all 15 Devastators were shot down, with just one torpedo launched towards *Soryu*. Next to appear were the 14 Devastators of VT-6 from Enterprise. Japanese lookouts spotted the approaching aircraft and the CAP was now up to 27 Zeros with another seven launched by *Akagi* and *Soryu*. Under heavy fire, the Devastators began their attack. Five torpedoes were launched. No hits were recorded and just five aircraft returned to *Enterprise*.

At 1003 hours *Yorktown's* three squadrons spotted the Japanese carriers. At the time 41 Zero fighters were aloft to meet the threat. First to attack were the 12 Devastators of VT-3. This time the torpedo bombers had an escort of six Wildcats. Up to 20 Zeros attacked and in the process drew the remaining fighters to low level. The Wildcats shot down three Zeros, but 10 Devastators were lost for no torpedo hits.

With the Japanese fixated on *Yorktown's* approaching torpedo bombers, no one spotted the arrival of the American dive-bombers. This was the key turning point of the battle. With Japanese CAP at low level and with no way to communicate the presence of the new threat, the dive-bombers went in unmolested. The 32 dive-bombers from VB-6 and VS-6 targeted the carriers *Kaga* and *Akagi*. Most dove on the *Kaga*, scoring four 1,000lb bomb hits. *Akagi*, initially overlooked, was attacked by three dive-bombers who scored a single hit between them.

The 17 dive-bombers of VB-3 selected *Soryu*, the hangar decks of which were jammed with fully fueled and armed aircraft. Three 1,000lb bombs ripped through the decks igniting an inferno the Japanese had no hope of extinguishing.

Between 1035 and 1040 hours eight bombs hit three carriers. The *Kaga* was the first to sink, scuttled at 1925 hours. *Soryu* followed at 1930 with *Akagi* scuttled the next morning. Only the *Hiryu* remained unscathed. At 1058 *Hiryu's* first strike of 18 'Val' dive-bombers and six Zeros was launched. At 32 miles out American radar detected the strike. To meet the attack were 18 Wildcats flying CAP. Their head-on defence resulted in 11 dive-bombers and three Zeros shot down. Seven 'Vals' survived long enough to dive on *Yorktow*n. Three 551lb SAP bombs found their mark with two damaging near misses. It was a remarkable achievement but the *Hiryu's* dive-bombing unit had been shattered; 13 'Vals' and three Zero fighters had been shot down by fighters and AA fire.

The damage to *Yorktown* seemed severe, but by 1400 hours the fires were under control and the vessel proved capable of steaming at 24kts. *Hiryu's* second strike lacked numbers. By 1245 hours a makeshift force of 16 aircraft was available: nine of *Hiryu's* torpedo bombers plus one from *Akagi*, escorted by six Zeros. At 1430hrs the *Yorktown* was spotted and just six Wildcats were flying CAP. Flying through repeated fighter attacks and heavy AA fire, seven aircraft survived long enough to drop their torpedoes, scoring two hits. Staggered by the hits, *Yorktown* was soon dead in the water, listing by 17 degrees. Incredibly, superior American damage control parties almost saved *Yorktown*. By 1455 hours,

BELOW: Torpedo Squadron 6 prepares for take-off on *Enterprise's* flight deck on the morning of June 4. Only four of these aircraft would survive their part in the Battle of Midway and return to *Enterprise*. US NAVAL HISTORICAL CENTER

ABOVE: F4F-3 Wildcats from VF-6 prepare to take-off from *Enterprise*, May 12, 1942. The F4F-3 was armed with four .50cal machine guns and had a maximum speed of 335mph.
AUTHOR'S COLLECTION.

however, the order to abandon ship was made. On June 5, the Japanese returned. In a well executed attack, two torpedoes from the Japanese submarine I-168 found their mark and the next morning *Yorktown* finally sank.

At 1445 hours *Hiryu* was spotted and by 1530 hours 25 Dauntlesses were launched from *Enterprise*. Thirty-minutes later *Hornet* dispatched 16 dive-bombers. As the *Hiryu's* second strike returned to its ship, the American strike was on its way. At 1705 hours the American dive-bombers pushed over into their dives and once again caught the Japanese by surprise. With just 13 Zeros flying CAP the defenders were quickly overwhelmed. Four bombs found their mark forward of the island, creating large fires. *Hornet's* strike arrived 15 minutes later and seeing *Hiryu* heavily damaged attacked her escorts for no results. Three Dauntlesses were shot down by fighters.

After two attempts to scuttle the carrier, the *Hiryu* finally sank at 0912 hours.

ANALYSIS

The Battle of Midway was a major defeat for the IJN. Belief in the 'decisive battle' concept had resulted in the loss of four fleet carriers, 247 aircraft, one heavy cruiser and one heavily damaged. 110 aircrew were lost along with 721 highly trained aircraft technicians, vital for carrier operations. The total number of Japanese dead was 3,057 personnel.

For the Americans the battle was an incredible victory. Despite the loss of one fleet carrier, 144 aircraft, one destroyer, 362 sailors, marines and airmen, the Americans were able to check Japanese expansion in the Pacific and render the IJN carrier force incapable of further strategic offensive operations. The Japanese defeat at Midway had allowed the Americans to grab the initiative. In August, US forces launched their first strategic offensive of the war by invading the Japanese held islands of Tulagi and Guadalcanal.

Operationally, many flaws in tactics and equipment had been revealed. In the two battles, Coral Sea and Midway, American torpedo performance was dismal and it was apparent that the Devastator was obsolete. In 108 effective sorties, 95 torpedoes were dropped resulting in just ten hits for two ships sunk. The Japanese Type 91 Mod 3 air torpedo carried by the B5N2 Type 97 'Kate' had proven itself a reliable and effective weapon, giving the Japanese superior ship killing capability.

American and Japanese dive-bombing capabilities were comparable, but the US held the edge. The US General Purpose 500lb and 1,000lb bombs proved far more destructive than the Japanese 551lb SAP. The SBD Dauntless could carry twice the load of the Aichi D3A1 'Val'. The 'Val' also lacked armour and self-sealing tanks, making it more vulnerable to damage.

In terms of fighter defence and escort, both sides were deficient. The Japanese CAP system with no radar for early detection and no radio communication was extremely poor. American CAP and the integration of radar was far more effective, but enough problems still existed to prevent it from being a truly effective defence.

Japanese fighter escort was stingy but the Zero with its superior range could accompany all strike packages. The F4F Wildcat on the other hand had a radius of action of just 175 miles. The Dauntless with a 500lb had a radius of action of 325 miles, which meant that the F4F would never be able to escort it for a full mission at long range.

The IJN was still a formidable force and far from beaten. And it still outnumbered the US Pacific Fleet with six carriers (two fleet carriers, two converted carriers of Junyo class, and two light carriers) against four American fleet carriers. In the months ahead, the battle of attrition would continue, but America's industrial might was gathering steam. The first of the new Essex class and *Independence* were only a few weeks away from launch. In June 1942 the first production Vought F4U-1 Corsair took flight and on July 30 the Grumman XF6F-3, powered by the Pratt Whitney 2800 engine made its maiden flight. Carrier anti-aircraft defences were also improved with more 20mm guns and the addition of quad mounted 40mm Bofors in place of the 1.1in machine cannon.

BATTLE OF THE EASTERN SOLOMONS, AUGUST 1942

After the Battle of Midway the arrival of *Wasp* from the Atlantic gave the US Pacific Fleet four carriers – *Wasp, Hornet, Enterprise* and *Saratoga*. All their air groups had been rebuilt following the heavy losses at Midway and in addition the Grumman TBM-1 Avenger torpedo bomber replaced the obsolete TBD-1 Devastator. AA defences had also improved. *Saratoga's* 8in guns were replaced with four new twin 5in/38 mounts; *Enterprise* had all but one of its 1.1in mounts replaced by four of the new quad 40mm Bofors. As the Americans moved swiftly to improve their AA defence with more and better guns, Japanese carrier AA defences stagnated and would remain ineffective until the end of the war.

The Japanese did make some changes to their carriers however. To bolster fleet defence the number of fighters on the fleet carriers was raised to 27 Zeros and the number of D3A1 dive-bombers was increased to 27. Radar was also added with the *Shokaku* being the first to receive the Type 21 early warning radar.

On August 7, 1942 US Marines landed unopposed on Guadalcanal. They quickly captured the Japanese airfield, renaming it Henderson Field. Both F4F Wildcats and SBD Dauntlesses were quickly flown in. Covering the landings were the carriers *Enterprise, Wasp* and *Saratoga*. Rabaul based Japanese bombers and fighters struck back with disastrous results. To challenge the US ships 27 G4M1 'Betty' bombers escorted by 17 A6M2 Zeros were sent from Rabaul. Unable to find the American carriers they went after a cruiser. American Wildcats and AA fire shot down five bombers and two Zeros for the loss of eight Wildcats.

The next morning the 26 torpedo armed G4M1s returned, escorted by 15 Zeros. Again, no carriers were spotted. Running in at wave top level they went for the cruisers and were met by a ferocious AA barrage. Eight were shot down and only a few managed to drop their torpedoes. As the survivors withdrew the F4F Wildcat CAP fell on them. Four more went down in flames. In the end only five severely damaged G4M1s survived the attack.

As the land-based IJN bombers engaged the Americans, the Japanese carriers prepared for a counteroffensive. Of the three American carriers available in the South Pacific, only two would see battle – *Enterprise* and *Saratoga*. *Wasp* was refuelling to the south and too late to see action. By August 24 the carriers *Zuikaku* and *Shokaku* and the light carrier *Ryujo* commanded by Admiral Nagumo entered the waters off Guadalcanal. Nagumo placed *Ryujo* well ahead of the two main carriers and 200 miles north of Henderson Field. With no reports of the American carriers, *Ryujo* launched a strike on the island. At 1110 hours Admiral Fletcher received a report placing *Ryujo* 245 miles away. At 1340 he therefore launched a strike on *Ryujo* with 29 SBDs and seven of the new Grumman TBF-1 Avenger torpedo bombers. As the strike made its way towards *Ryujo* a Japanese floatplane sighted the American carriers at 1425 hours. With a CAP of just seven Zeros the *Saratoga* strike force made short work of the *Ryujo*, scoring three 1,000lb bomb hits and a single torpedo hit with no losses.

The Japanese response was swift. At 1602 hours American radar detected the incoming strike 88 miles out. *Shokaku* and *Zuikaku* launched a two-wave strike of 54 dive-bombers escorted by 24 fighters. To meet the incoming raid were 54 Wildcats. As the Japanese arrived, *Shokaku's* dive-bombers were tasked to attack *Enterprise*. Fifteen 'Vals' dove on *Enterprise* scoring three hits. Three others attacked the escorting battleship *North Carolina*. *Zuikaku's* dive-bombers were given *Saratoga* as their target,

but the Wildcat CAP forced them to attack the closer *Enterprise* group. Just three dove on the *Saratoga* and four tried to hit the *North Carolina*, all missed. At 1648 hours the attack was over. Japanese losses had been heavy with 18 'Vals' and six Zeros shot down. Damage control parties had *Enterprise* operational shortly after.

Fortune was on the Americans' side. The entire Japanese second strike approached the US carriers but never located *Enterprise*. It was a missed opportunity. A last strike of 11 dive-bombers and eight torpedo bombers was launched from *Enterprise* but they were unable to find the main Japanese carriers. At the end of the battle, Fletcher still didn't know how many carriers he faced or where they were. The only American aircraft to attack the Japanese fleet carriers were two scout SBDs that attacked the *Shokaku* (these two SBDs sighted the Japanese carriers early, but the information never reached Fletcher).

ANALYSIS

The Americans never did find the Japanese fleet carriers. Their carrier- and land-based scout planes did nothing wrong – there was simply a breakdown in communication that allowed the carriers to escape detection. Had a report been received, Fletcher was ready with a medium-sized strike force.

This was also the first time US carriers had been assigned different roles. *Saratoga* was the strike carrier while *Enterprise* handled CAP as well as search and anti-submarine patrols.

Radar played an important role too, giving the CAP fighters time to climb to altitude, but there were still problems. While the Wildcats and AA fire shot down 24 of the attacking force, the results could have been better. The estimated altitude of the incoming Japanese strike was off by 4,000ft. And the lack of Identification Friend or Foe (IFF) systems in American aircraft meant carrier radar could not discern friendlies from bandits.

Fighter direction also suffered from poor radio discipline. Excessive chatter and lack of clarity jammed up the frequencies, negating the vital flow of information .

This was also the first time the Japanese used radar. Though capable of early warning, it was not used for fighter direction.

THE BATTLE OF SANTA CRUZ, OCTOBER 1942

By October 1942 the Americans were firmly in control of Henderson Field and the expanding perimeter around it. However, the Japanese then launched a major ground offensive on the island, coordinated with their naval operations. After the capture of Henderson Field by Japanese troops, the IJN moved in to destroy the US naval units supporting the marines on shore.

The Japanese carrier strike force outnumbered the Americans with the carriers *Junyo* and *Hiyo* forming the Advance Force and the carriers *Shokaku*, *Zuikaku* and *Zuiho* of the 1st Carrier Division. The *Hiyo*, however, was forced to retire due to an engine room fire on October 21. Even without the *Hiyo* the Japanese still had an impressive force of 203 carrier aircraft. The carrier group was commanded by Vice Admiral Nagumo. Incorporated into the battle plan was the Vanguard Group. Centred on the battleship *Hiei*, this group was positioned 70 miles ahead of the carriers and was intended to soak up US strikes before they got to the flattops.

To counter this threat the Americans had only two carriers, *Enterprise* and *Hornet* with 153 aircraft. *Saratoga* was torpedoed by a Japanese submarine on August 31 and was out for repairs and *Wasp* was sunk by a Japanese submarine on September 15. Both *Enterprise* and *Hornet* were operating at maximum capacity and most of their Wildcat fighters were fitted with two 58 gallon drop tanks, effectively doubling their range. Commanding the two carrier task forces TF-16 and TF-17 was Rear Admiral Thomas Kinkaid. In terms of intelligence, both sides were blind, but both knew carriers were in the area and for the Americans that they were outnumbered in carriers and in aircraft.

Even before the battle began the Americans suffered their first losses. On October 25, Kinkaid ordered a 'reconnaissance in force' of 16 Wildcats, 12 Dauntless and seven Avengers. They were ordered to fly out to 150 miles. If nothing was found, they were to return. The commander of the flight, in his zeal, passed the 150 mile mark. That decision meant they would have to land in the dark. The result was one Wildcat, four Dauntless and three Avengers lost, either ditched or damaged beyond repair.

BELOW: Taken from the cruiser *Pensacola*, this photo shows four Japanese B5N2 torpedo bombers flying through a barrage of exploding 5in shells heading toward the carrier *Yorktown* during the battle of Midway.
US NAVAL HISTORICAL CENTER

ABOVE: After dropping their torpedoes two B5N2 'Kates' pass the *Yorktown* surrounded by exploding AA fire. Moments later two torpedoes hit *Yorktown* with devastating results. During the war, torpedoes were the true ship killers and every time a US carrier was hit by a torpedo during the battles of 1942, the carrier ended up sinking. US NAVAL HISTORICAL CENTER

In the early morning hours of October 26, PBYs found the Japanese carriers about 200 miles from Kinkaid's carriers, but the report never reached Kinkaid. At 0645 hours American carrier scouts found the Japanese carriers. Minutes later at 0658 hours a 'Kate' search plane found and reported the position of TF-17. Both sides now raced to launch their first strike.

A full deck load of 55 aircraft from *Hornet* was launched, with an improvised strike of 20 aircraft from *Enterprise*. All aircraft were off by 0747 hours. At the same time the first wave of 21 Zeros, 21 'Vals' and 20 'Kate' torpedo bombers headed for the US carriers.

At 0740 hours first blood went to the Americans. Two scout SBDs from *Enterprise* found Nagumo's carriers and attacked. One 500lb bomb hit the flight deck of *Zuiho*, knocking her out of action. At 0840 hours *Shokaku*'s new radar detected *Hornet*'s strike at 78 miles out. *Hornet*'s first wave of 15 SBD-3, six TBF-1 and eight F4F-4s began their attack at 0927. Fighting through the Japanese CAP of 23 fighters, *Hornet*'s dive-bombers hit the *Shokaku* with three 1,000lb bombs, shattering her flight deck and causing severe fires. *Shokaku* was now out of the fight.

Hornet's six Avengers from the first wave failed to find the carriers, expending their torpedoes on the Vanguard Group instead. *Enterprise*'s small strike force was spotted an ambushed by the escort Zeros from *Zuiho*'s strike group heading for the American carriers. Unable to find the Japanese carriers *Enterprise*'s remaining aircraft also attacked the cruisers of the Vanguard Group for no results. Finally, *Hornet*'s last strike of nine SBDs and ten TBFs, all armed with bombs, hit the cruiser *Chikuma* with three bombs. The American results were a disappointment. Air group fragmentation and poor communications led to a waste of bombs and torpedoes. Losses included five Wildcats, two Dauntless and two Avengers.

At 0855 hours the Japanese strike was detected at 40 miles. Thirty-seven Wildcats were assigned to CAP and despite the extremely heavy anti-aircraft fire put up by the carriers and escorts, the Japanese would launch their best and most destructive coordinated carrier strike of the war. It would also be their last.

In a brilliant coordinated torpedo and dive-bombing attack the first wave selected *Hornet* as its target. *Zuikaku*'s dive-bombers scored three hits. At 0914 hours *Shokaku*'s torpedo aircraft crippled *Hornet* with three hits – bringing the ship to a stop. Japanese success came at a heavy price though. The combined CAP and improved AA defence resulted in 62 aircraft shot down, leaving only 15 aircraft to return to their carriers.

ABOVE: During the battle of Midway the Japanese carrier Hiryu suffered four bomb hits and was left a burning wreck, sinking on June 5. The forward elevator was blown off and lies against the island. US NAVAL HISTORICAL CENTER

At 1015 the second wave commenced its attack on the undamaged *Enterprise*. The time difference between the *Shokaku's* dive-bomber group and *Zuikaku's* torpedo bombers meant a coordinated attack was impossible. Nineteen dive-bombers from *Shokaku* scored two hits and a near miss. *Zuikaku's* torpedo bombers followed. Attempting an anvil attack, they missed completely. The last to attack were the 17 dive-bombers from *Junyo*. Eight of them targeted *Enterprise* and scored a glancing flow off the bow. The remaining eight damaged several escorts including the battleship *South Dakota*. Seven torpedo bombers also attacked the *Enterprise*, but without success. Japanese losses were heavy with 10 'Vals' and eight 'Kates' shot down.

Both sides had been bloodied, but the Japanese had *Shokaku* and *Zuiho* operational. Kinkaid, with the damaged *Enterprise*, was forced to retire with 41 Wildcats, 33 Dauntless and 10 Avengers. *Zuikaku* and *Junyo* would launch three more strikes – hitting the immobile *Hornet* with a single 1,760lb bomb, one 551lb bomb and a final torpedo hit. *Hornet* proved a tough nut to crack though, absorbing an amazing amount of punishment: three torpedo hits, five bomb hits and two crashed aircraft in total. Early on October 27 it was finally sent to the bottom with a salvo of torpedoes from a Japanese destroyer. The last carrier battle of 1942 was over.

ANALYSIS

At the end of 1942, the Japanese still had five carriers – *Shokaku, Zuikaku, Junyo* and *Zuiho,* but they were not combat ready. *Shokaku* remained under repair until March 1943 and *Zuiho* wasn't ready until January 1944. As for the rest, there was insufficient aircraft and aviators to man them – 148 aircrew having been lost during the battle. With the obvious exception of Midway, the *Kido Butai* had performed generally well.

The American carriers had also put in an admirable performance, but at a price. Of the six carriers ready in 1942, four had been sunk. But Japanese expansion had been reversed at Coral Sea and Midway, allowing the Americans to begin their own offensive at Guadalcanal.

Both sides now understood how vulnerable carriers really were. In the first two carrier battles, fleet air and anti-aircraft defences were generally ineffective. The only solution was more fighters, and better fighter direction. By Santa Cruz American fighter direction techniques had improved and the introduction of more and newer antiaircraft weaponry on both carriers and escorts made Japanese attacks a costly affair.

The Japanese were shocked by the damage inflicted by AA fire, as a staff officer aboard *Junyo* relates: "We searched the sky with apprehension. There were only a few planes in the air in comparison to the number launched several hours before. We could see only five or six dive-bombers. The planes lurched and staggered onto the deck, every single fighter and bomber bullet-holed. Some planes were literally flying sieves. As the pilots climbed wearily from their cramped cockpits they told of unbelievable opposition, of skies choked with anti-aircraft shell bursts and tracers."

For 1942, US naval gunners were credited with 228 aircraft shot down in the Pacific.

IJN air defence on the other hand remained poor. Radar had been introduced but only for early warning of an incoming raid – not fighter direction. During the clash at Santa Cruz it gave *Shokaku* ample warning to empty its avgas pipes and fill them with CO_2, and probably saved the ship.

Offensively Japanese carriers, their aircraft, weapons and tactics were deadly. The accuracy of the B5N2 Type 97 torpedo bomber

BELOW: A Japanese 'Val' dive-bomber trails smoke as it dives toward USS *Hornet* (CV-8), during the morning of October 26, 1942. This plane struck the ship's stack and then her flight deck. A B5N2 'Kate' is flying over *Hornet* after dropping its torpedo, and another 'Val' is off the bow. Note the 5in AA shell bursting between *Hornet* and the camera, spraying the sea with shrapnel. US NAVAL HISTORICAL CENTER

LEFT: Crewmen aboard *Enterprise* fight fires in the ship's starboard after 5/38 gun gallery after it was hit by a Japanese bomb during the Battle of the Eastern Solomons, August 24, 1942. Note the hole in the flight deck at the bottom of the photo, the result of another bomb hit. NARA

RIGHT: USS *Wasp* (CV-7) burning and sinking, south of San Cristobal Island. Torpedoed by a Japanese submarine on September 15, 1942 *Wasp* was hit three times. With the crew unable to contain the damage, the carrier was finally sent to the bottom by three torpedoes from the destroyer *Lansdowne*.

ABOVE: US carriers not only faced Japanese carrier bombers, but land-based ones as well. Here three G4M2 'Bettys' make a low- level run against US Navy ships manoeuvring between Guadalcanal and Tulagi in the morning of August 8, 1942. US anti-aircraft ship defences made these attacks extremely costly for the Japanese.
US NAVAL HISTORICAL CENTER

and its effective Type 91 aerial torpedo made it a true ship killer. In contrast, Japanese dive-bombers were unable to sink an American carrier on their own. The Japanese practice of massing their carriers in a single group and their superior control and flexibility gave them greater destructive power. By combining squadrons from different carriers, large strikes were routinely mounted.

Conversely, American carriers operated in separate task groups – single carriers, separated by five to ten miles – and were never able to duplicate this feat. Each carrier sending its own strike force at different times led to uncoordinated attacks and a diluting of force. This practice led to poor results during the last two battles of 1942.

As the Japanese struggled to rebuild their carrier force and train new air crews, the US Navy was in the process of reinventing itself. By mid-1943 the new Fast Carrier Task Force would transform naval warfare in the Pacific. ∎

CHAPTER 3
TOOLS OF THE TRADE

★

New weapons and equipment

ABOVE: *Essex* (CV-9) under way during May 1943. The 24 SBD dive-bombers parked aft clearly show how much deck space they take-up without having folding wings. Forward are 11 F6F Hellcats and 18 TBF/TBM Avengers.
US NAVAL HISTORICAL CENTER

SPECIFICATION

★ ESSEX (CV-9) ★
Displacement: Full load 36,380 tons
Dimensions: Length 872ft, beam 93ft, draught 27.5ft
Maximum speed: 33kts
Radius: 15,440 nautical miles at 15kts
Aviation ordnance: 625.5 tons
Crew: 3,448 (service)

The slogging carrier battles of 1942 had altered Japan's well thought-out plan to fight a defensive battle against the Americans in the Pacific. Japan's war strategy focused on capturing the vital resources of Southeast Asia first and then establishing a defensive perimeter stretching from the Aleutian Islands, through the Central Pacific, Solomons, Bismarck Islands, New Guinea, the Netherland East Indies and all the way to the border of India.

With their large surface fleet and newly acquired string of airfields and anchorages the Japanese planned for a coordinated defensive battle. As American naval forces headed west, Japanese submarines and flying boats would be tasked with picking off US surface ships. Once it had been weakened, the US Pacific Fleet would be destroyed by the IJN's combined fleet of carriers and battleships in one decisive battle.

American strategy against the coming war with Japan was well thought out and had been developed over several decades before the conflict. With remarkable prescience, the US military produced War Plan Orange. The crucial thrust of the plan centred on a full out maritime war against Japan in three phases. In Phase I the Americans predicted the Japanese would seize US possessions in the Pacific, including the Philippines and territory in Southeast Asia. Phase II would be the American response with a naval offensive to capture islands in the Carolines, Marshalls and Gilberts. With secure bases and supply lines the recapture of the Philippines would be possible. Phase III would target islands closer to Japan. This would tighten the blockade around Japan and provide bases for the aerial bombing of the Japanese homeland.

The Japanese knew that a short victorious war was their only hope, while the American plan envisioned a step by step campaign that would take years rather than months.

By the end of 1942, the US Navy had lost four fleet carriers: *Lexington* (CV-2), *Yorktown* (CV-5), *Wasp* (CV-7) and *Hornet* (CV-8), leaving just *Enterprise* and the damaged *Saratoga*. Japanese losses included: *Shoho*, *Akagi*, *Kaga*, *Hiryu*, *Soryu* and *Ryujo*. To bolster its carrier force the US requested that the British carrier HMS *Victorious* be transferred from the British Home Fleet to the Pacific.

In February 1943, US forces on Guadalcanal achieved America's second major victory of the war. After six months of fighting the Japanese were forced to evacuate and surrender the island. Guadalcanal and Tulagi were turned into major air and naval bases in support of the continued Allied advance further up the Solomon island chain.

The Japanese were now clearly on the defensive and scrambling to mount a cohesive and effective defence. As American air power grew the Japanese were forced to send their precious carrier air groups to reassert air superiority over the Allied air forces. In April, Yamamoto launched Operation *I-Go*. After five heavy raids against Guadalcanal, Port Moresby and adjacent airfields the Japanese claimed success and shortly afterwards the offensive was called off on April 16. But the Japanese had failed to do any serious damage – sinking just one destroyer, a corvette, a tanker and two cargo ships. Just 25 aircraft had been shot down.

The use of carrier air groups from shore bases had been only moderately successful. It did, however, set a precedent for the future deployment of carrier air groups in land-based operations.

The IJNAF was now committed to a grinding battle of attrition which it was ill-equipped to win. In the dogfights over the Solomon Islands and Rabaul, the IJNAF sacrificed far too many squadron leaders and experienced pilots. Many of those losses were at the hands of Marine Corps pilots flying the new F4U Corsair. Unacceptable for carrier operations, the Corsair was given to the Marines where it became the most important American fighter during the Solomon campaign. These losses had a direct effect on the Japanese carrier fleet's effectiveness and would be evident in the last carrier battle of the war.

ENTER THE *ESSEX*

The Americans knew a war with Japan would be a long one and that early defeats would be inevitable, but hopefully not disastrous. Well before the attack on Pearl Harbor the US Navy had plans for a powerful new fleet of aircraft carriers. The first new carrier in the class, CV-9, was ordered as part of the Naval Expansion Act of 1938. It's design roots can be found in the prewar 20,000-ton *Yorktown* class design. From the outset designers knew the next generation of aircraft would be heavier and larger and would require more deck space. Increased armour protection and more endurance would be vital for fighting a war in the Pacific.

The new *Essex* also incorporated a mid-ship deck edge elevator. This allowed aircraft to be lifted from the hangar deck to the flight deck without having to use the centreline elevators. Aircraft could be struck below or brought up to the deck without disrupting flight operations. In June 1940 three more carriers were ordered and after the dramatic victory of Germany over France in May 1940 seven more were added to the list. After the attack on Pearl Harbor yet another two were ordered, with ten more in 1942 and three more in June 1943. *Essex* (CV-9) was launched on July 31, 1942, several months ahead of schedule. At

> *"The Essexes won the great Pacific battles that broke the Imperial Japanese Navy."*
>
> Norman Friedman, naval aviation historian

ABOVE: USS *Intrepid* (CV-11) at speed and ready to launch Hellcats and Avengers over the Philippine Sea in November 1944. This photo clearly shows the spacious flight deck of the Essex class, the two catapults and extensive anti-aircraft armament on the port side. Note F6F-3 Hellcat fighter parked on an outrigger forward of her island.
US NAVAL HISTORICAL CENTER

ABOVE: USS *Hancock* (CV-19) May 1944 while wearing camouflage pattern 32/3a. These deceptive camouflage patterns were used to confuse the enemy as to the speed and direction of a ship when spotted.
US NAVAL HISTORICAL CENTER

27,500 tons design standard displacement, she was the largest American carrier yet built, with the exception of the two *Lexington* class carriers. These ships would be the most well equipped and heavily armed carriers of the war.

Five shipyards would be involved in the *Essex* building programme. Given top priority and matched with the efficiency of American shipyards, one *Essex* took just 18 and a half months to complete.

As with previous carriers the flight deck was not armoured, but the new *Essex* did offer better protection. Triple-bottomed, the *Essex* had four layers of torpedo protection. The main deck (hangar deck) armour of 2½in was designed to withstand a hit from a 1,000lb general purpose bomb dropped from 10,000ft. The side armour was designed to resist 6in cruiser shells. The armoured belt was between 4in and 2½in thick and protected an area of 508ft including the ship's machinery, magazines and aviation fuel storage.

Four sets of Westinghouse steam turbines drove four propellers generating 150,000 shaft horse power. Fuel oil storage of between 6,161 and 6,331 tons gave the *Essex* enormous range – up to 17,250 nautical miles.

ANTI-AIRCRAFT DEFENCE

The *Essex* class were the most heavily armed carriers of the war. Long range guns consisted of twelve 5in/38 calibre guns: four in single weapon open mounts, two forward, two aft on the port side of the flight deck, while the remaining eight were in four twin turrets located fore and aft of the island on the starboard side. Range was 10 miles with a rate of fire of 15 rounds per minute. When firing the revolutionary VT fused shell, it was one of the most effective heavy anti-aircraft gun of the war.

VT PROXIMITY FUSE

One of the most important scientific developments in the AA battle was the introduction of the VT fuse. Built around a miniature radio transmitter and receiver, the VT fuse overcame the major disadvantage of the mechanically set timed fuses and was capable detecting its target in flight and detonating within 30ft of it. In 1943 the number of 5in AA shells needed for a shoot-down numbered 508

> *"The spectacular increase in the effectiveness of naval anti-aircraft armament was one of the great tactical revolutions which occurred during the course of the war."*
> **US Navy Bureau of Ordnance**

per aircraft. The VT fuse decreased that to just 155 rounds per bird.

The 5in guns were controlled by two Mark 37 fire control directors with FD Mark 4 tracking radar. Unable to distinguish low-level attacks from surface clutter the Mark 4 radar was replaced with the Mark 12 radar and Mark 22 height-finder radar combination.

Backing up the 5in guns was the superb 40mm Bofors AA gun. As many as 17 quadruple mounts were fitted, depending on the modernisation of the individual ship. Fire control for the 40mm Bofors was matched with the Mark 51 Director. Incorporating the Mark 14 gunsight gave the 40mm an effective range of 3,000 yards. And finally, 65 single-mount 20mm Oerlikon cannon were fitted along both sides of the flight deck.

> "Maximum combat efficiency of individual ships and task organisations can best be attained through full utilisation of all available sources of combat intelligence. By the evaluation of all available information by trained personnel, such data can be quickly disseminated to the flag and commanding officers, to other control stations concerned over interior communication circuits, and to other ships and aircraft via exterior communication facilities."
>
> CIC Manual 1944

RADAR

American carriers possessed a major advantage over their Japanese counterparts and that was radar. From a tactical point of view, it was probably the most revolutionary development for carriers during the war and acted as a force multiplier.

The Essex class was originally equipped with the SK long-range search radar, but this was later replaced with the improved SK-2 radar (range 100 miles against targets at 10,000ft). The back-up air search radar, the SC-2 had a range of 80 miles against targets at 10,000ft.

The air search radars could not determine the height of an incoming aircraft, essential for an effective intercept. To address the problem the SM height-finder was introduced for fighter control and had a range of 50 nautical miles out to 10,000ft. All this radar information would be displayed in the Combat Information Centre (CIC). Radar also gave the fleet the ability to manoeuvre at high speed. The plan position indicator (PPI) radar display, as part of the CIC, allowed a multi-carrier task force to maintain formation at high speed, at night and in heavy seas. The deck reckoning tracer (DRT) aided navigation and surface ship tracking.

Aircraft and ships were also equipped with identification-friend-or-fore (IFF) transponders. This allowed for the quick identification of hostile ships and aircraft. But all this information would be useless without effective radio communication and here again the US Navy was technically superior. By 1943 radio communication was vastly improved by the use of four-channel very high frequency (VHF) radio. VHF used channel variation which prevented enemy interception and allowed for simultaneous radio contact with other ships and aircraft.

Commanding all this electronic hardware was the fighter director officer (FDO), one of the most important officers on the ship. In the coming battles, the FDO working in the CIC would transform carrier air defence from its primitive state during the carrier battles of 1942 to a state of the art air defence system.

AIR GROUP COMPOSITION – AIRCRAFT HANDLING

When first commissioned, the *Essex's* planned air group was to consist of 36 F3F-4 fighters, 36 SBD-5 dive bombers and 18 TBF-1 torpedo bombers.

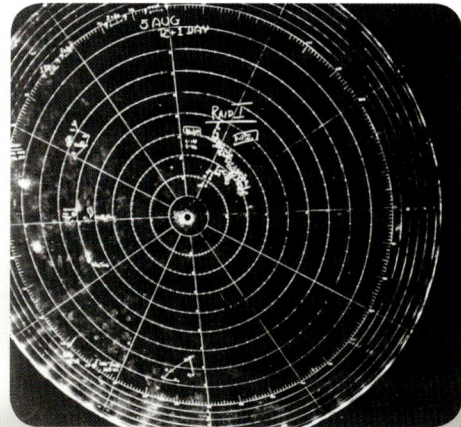

ABOVE: This radar plotting screen was taken aboard *Hornet* on August 5, 1944. Operating off Bonins island, which is noted on the left of the display, a Japanese air-raid is also noted, middle right. Radar was a force multiplier and gave the fast carrier task force a high degree of protection from conventional Japanese air attacks. US NAVAL HISTORICAL CENTER

By 1944 the SBD scout bomber squadron was no longer needed. As a result, the dive-bomber squadrons were combined into one 24 aircraft unit. The number of fighters grew to 54

BELOW: *Yorktown* (CV-10) launching an F6F-3 using the side catapult. The open deck hangar design for the Essex class allowed for the installation of a double action catapult mounted in the forward hangar bay. It was intended to offer tactical flexibility but proved impracticable and all were eventually removed. NARA

ABOVE: A twin mount 40mm Bofors anti-aircraft gun with the Mk 51 director aboard the escort carrier *Santee* (CVE-29). The 40mm Bofors was arguably the best medium AA gun of the war. During 1945 the 40mms of the US Fleet fired 718,699 rounds and shot down 476 aircraft for a rate of 1,508 'rounds per bird'. NARA

RIGHT: USS *Intrepid's* forward 5in/38 twin mounts trained on the starboard bow prepare to fire. During 1945, 108,516 5in gun shells were expended, shooting down 173 aircraft for a 'rounds per bird' of 627.

launch. The Essex class had one forward flush deck catapult with an 18,000lb capacity – and this proved its worth. Without having the entire task force turn into the wind, a carrier could launch a strike independently, saving time and fuel. The cycle time for a catapult launch was 45 to 60 seconds. By the end of the war almost half of carrier bomber launches were made using the catapult.

and included radar-equipped night fighter and photo reconnaissance fighter aircraft. As the kamikaze threat grew, the number of fighters again expanded to 73 in December 1944 with the number of strike aircraft reduced to just 30 (15 dive-bomber, 15 torpedo). At the beginning of 1945 two air groups discarded their Helldivers in favour of 93 fighters (45 fighters – 45 fighter-bombers) and just 15 torpedo bombers.

In 1942 carrier air groups were assigned numbers, the first being Air Group 9. By June 1944 air group designations were changed to reflect the type of carrier they were flying from. Essex class carrier air groups were designated CVG and the light carrier *Independence* class were designated CVLG.

One of the key advantages of the Essex class was the ability to handle large air groups efficiently. By 1945 most fleet carriers carried 108 aircraft and used the continuous deck park system.

The flight deck was 108ft wide and 862ft long, equipped with three large elevators: one centreline forward, one offset to starboard near the island and the deck edge elevator positioned on the port side amidships. Elevator cycle time was 45 seconds, including time to load and unload aircraft.

The large open hangar deck allowed aircraft to be warmed up prior to takeoff, speeding launch times. The time required to launch a full deck strike was relatively short, around 10-20 seconds per plane.

First off would be the lighter fighters, followed by the dive-bombers and the heavier torpedo aircraft. The large fleet carriers had the speed and deck space to launch without the need for a catapult

STRIKE DOCTRINE

The US Navy strike doctrine of 1942 was ineffective and lacked coordination. The practice of each carrier launching independent strikes, with each squadron heading to their target individually, reduced potential striking power. And with American carriers operating in separate task forces the lack of coordination was even greater. By 1944, strike cohesion had improved, but was still based on carriers launching their own strikes, independent of the other carriers in the task group.

LOGISTICS

America's fast carrier task force was only as effective as the logistics supporting it. Without a constant supply of oil, aviation fuel, aircraft, food and millions of other items the planned air and naval campaign in the Pacific would have been impossible.

Together with the debut of the Essex and Independence class carriers a sophisticated mobile logistics capability was developed. Using forward fleet anchorages and a fleet of 34 dedicated oilers, the US Navy Fast Carrier Force was able to operate for months at a time using underway replenishment. This operational flexibility allowed for high tempo operations. American carrier task forces now had the ability to project power on a sustained basis rather than just mounting raids as the Japanese carrier forces had done early in the war.

ROUNDING OUT THE FLEET

As the war unfolded in Europe, America continued to ramp up its preparations for the coming conflict. President Franklin D. Roosevelt, having been Assistant Secretary in the Navy during the First World War, was concerned by the fact that the new Essex class carriers wouldn't join the fleet until 1944. To bridge the gap, the president suggested using some of the Cleveland cruiser class light cruisers for conversion into light carriers. Interestingly the Navy rejected the idea stating that the new carrier would be too small

ABOVE: *Enterprise* (CV-6) in March 1942 off Hawaii during gunnery exercises for the recently installed 20mm batteries. The Oerlikon 20mm cannon was adapted by the US Navy in 1941 and proved a reliable weapon with a high rate of fire of 450 rounds per minute. NARA

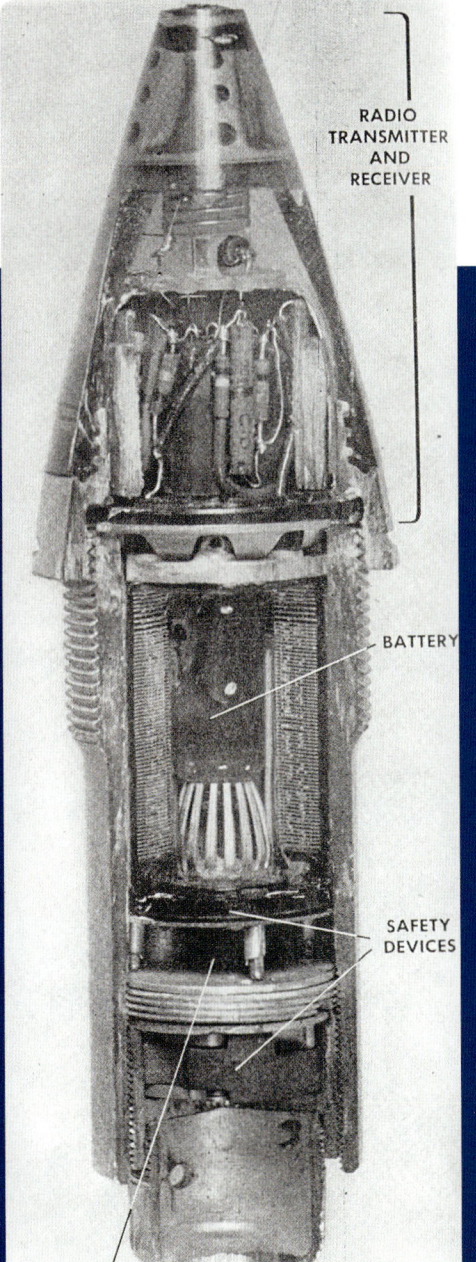

ABOVE: The inner workings of a 3in/50 VT fuse head. During 1945 the 3in/50 gun using the VT fused shell shot down 30.5 aircraft for a 'rounds per bird' of 359. US NAVAL HISTORICAL CENTER

ABOVE: *Lexington* at Puget Sound Navy Yard, February 1944, showing the various radar antennae. US carriers were well equipped with the latest radar and electronic navigation equipment giving the fast carrier task force a major tactical advantage over the Japanese. US NAVAL HISTORICAL CENTER

CARRIER STRIKE 39

and conversion using the cruiser hulls involved too many operational compromises. Fortunately for the Navy, Roosevelt pushed back and ordered a new study.

Eventually the US Navy agreed that by accepting the design limitations of using a cruiser hull, a light carrier conversion could be completed more quickly. The first conversion was ordered in January 1942 and by June 1942 nine more hulls were added to the programme.

Christened the Independence class (CVL), the new carriers had a short, narrow flight deck which was further restricted by an Island.

The lead ship in the class was USS *Independence*, commissioned in January 1943. Armament included two quadruple 40mm mounts, eight twin 40mm and fourteen 20mm guns. In October 1943 the mix of aircraft consisted of 12 F6F-3 Hellcats, nine SBD-5 Dauntless, and nine TBF-1 Avengers. In 1944, *Independence* became one of the first carriers assigned as a night carrier with an air group of 19 F6F-5N Hellcat night-fighters and eight TBM-1D Avenger night bombers. Like the *Essex* class, the new light carriers were fitted with the standard set of radars, radios and electronic navigational aids.

The new *Independence* class had a top speed of 31kts. While not equal to the *Essex* class, it was sufficient for fleet work.

The quick conversion of nine *Independence* Class ships was a major achievement and provided an insurance policy. Representing the equivalent of four *Essex* fleet carriers, the new light carriers gave the fleet carriers a greater degree of flexibility and offensive power. They could now devote all of their air power to

ABOVE: One of the primary jobs of the CVE escort carrier was the transport of aircraft and equipment. Here *Long Island* (ACV-1) has a deck load cargo of partially assembled aircraft, complete airframes and equipment.
US NAVAL HISTORICAL CENTER

ABOVE: USS *Independence* (CVL-22) in San Francisco Bay, California, on July 15, 1943. On deck are nine SBD dive-bombers parked amidships and aft, and nine TBM torpedo planes parked amidships and forward.
US NAVAL HISTORICAL CENTER

SPECIFICATION
★ INDEPENDENCE CLASS ★
Displacement: 14,300 tons full load
Dimensions: Length 622.6ft, beam 71.5ft, draught 26ft
Maximum speed: 31kts
Radius: 8,325 nautical miles at 15kts
Crew: 1,569 in service.

offensive operations, leaving fleet air defence and anti-submarine patrols to the light carriers.

COMBUSTIBLE, VULNERABLE AND EXPENDABLE – THE ESCORT CARRIER

Like the light carrier, the escort carrier was a ship the Navy didn't want. Once again, the driving force behind the idea was President Roosevelt. Long before the attack on Pearl Harbor he directed the chief of naval operations to acquire a merchant ship for conversion into a small carrier.

After acquiring two C-3 type merchant ships for conversion the USN was still reluctant and stated it would need 18 months to convert the ships into carriers. Unimpressed, Roosevelt gave them three months. The first escort carrier conversion was completed on June 2, 1941 and commissioned as *Long Island* (CVE-1). Following the construction of four *Long Island* class carriers the *Bogue* Class was introduced.

Based on the same C-3 merchant hull the *Bogue*s had a longer flight deck, a second elevator and additional anti-aircraft guns. This was followed by a small number of *Sangamon* Class escort carriers based on a tanker hull. Just four were built. The next class returned to the smaller merchant hull. The first *Casablanca* Class was ordered in July 1943 and, incredibly, by July 1944 fifty ships were finished. Last in the class was the *Commencement Bay*. Only a few of those built saw action in the Pacific.

Because their small size – flight deck and hangar space – the escort carriers were limited in the number of aircraft they could carry. The standard fighter was the Grumman FM-2 Wildcat. Designed specifically for escort duty, it was lighter and equipped with a more powerful engine making it ideal for small carrier decks. The F6F Hellcat was also used, but only on the larger *Sangamon* class ships. The standard compliment on the *Bogue* and *Casablanca* class ships consisted of 16 FM-2 fighters and 12 TBM Avengers.

To be effective escort carriers were organised into carrier divisions of four ships. Their role was to provide CAP and ASW protection during major amphibious operations as well as ground attack support for the troops ashore. While the escort carriers were used in the combat role their primary, and often overlooked, tasks were training and aircraft replenishment. By the end of the war the CVE fleet delivered 31,701 aircraft, including 4,500 for the Fast Carrier Task Force.

A total of 77 escort carriers were commissioned into the USN with the majority serving in the Pacific. Their contribution in concert with the US Navy's light carriers greatly enhanced the fighting power of Fast Carrier Task Force. Without them the war in the Pacific would have lasted much longer.

SPECIFICATION
★ CASABLANCA CLASS ★
Displacement: 10,902 tons full load
Dimensions: Length 512.3ft, beam: 65.2ft, draught: 22.5ft
Maximum speed: 20kts
Radius: 10,240 nautical miles at 15 kts
Crew: 916

BELOW: USS *Cahaba* (AO-82) refuels USS *Iowa* (BB-61) and an unidentified aircraft carrier in the Pacific, 1945. Underway replenishment at sea was a real gamer changer. The side-by-side method allowed for shorter and heavier hoses which meant faster refuelling. Not only was fuel transferred, but ammunition, personnel, food, water and mail could be exchanged too. US NAVAL HISTORICAL CENTER

ON FOLDED WINGS – US NAVY AIRCRAFT

During the war the US Navy and Marines were equipped with fighters and bombers that were rugged, well-armed, versatile and capable of carrying heavy loads. In terms of performance the F4U Corsair, F6F Hellcat and TBF Avenger were the stand out performers.

The Hellcat and Corsair were arguably the most versatile fighters of the war (fighter-bomber, night-fighter, photo reconnaissance), performing equally well afloat and ashore. During a multi-service (Navy, Marine, Air Force, RAF, FAA) conference in 1944, the Corsair was named the best all-round fighter-bomber in the Allied inventory. And with the best trained aviators of the war, the US Navy possessed an exceptional air fighting force.

CHANCE VOUGHT F4U CORSAIR

In February 1938 two of the Navy's most advanced fighters were undergoing flight tests. The Brewster XF2A (Buffalo) and Grumman XF4F-2 (Wildcat) would later enter production and become the US Navy's first monoplane carrier fighters. During the testing the Bureau of Aeronautics sent out a request to the American aviation industry for a new carrier fighter with superior performance to the existing Brewster and Grumman. The new requirement called for a fighter capable of 350mph, armed with four machine guns, and with a low stall speed of 70mph for safe carrier operations.

In April 1938 the Chance Vought Corporation submitted its design to the Bureau of Aeronautics. Designed around the new Pratt & Whitney XR-2800 Double Wasp engine, delivering 1,850hp, the Vought team produced the XF4U-1 prototype. The aircraft was a powerful streamlined design and to accommodate the large, 13ft diameter Hamilton Standard propeller, the design team came up with the ingenious inverted gull wing.

On May 29, 1940 the XF4U-1 made its first flight. On October 1, it became the first American fighter to surpass 400mph, clocking in at 405mph. On June 30, 1941 the US Navy ordered 541 F4U-1s and the new fighter was christened 'Corsair'. During carrier trails in August 1941 the XF4U-1 demonstrated a disturbing tendency to drop the port wing when approaching stalling speed, making it very dangerous during a carrier landing. In combination with combat reports from Europe, the Bureau of Aeronautics requested Vought make a number of changes. More guns and amour plate were added along with moving the fuel tanks from the wings to a larger tank installed in the fuselage between the cockpit and engine. This lengthened the fuselage and pushed the cockpit back.

In June 1942 the first F4U-1 was delivered. Powered by a 2,000hp Pratt &Whitney R-2800-8 with a two-stage supercharger the F4U-1 was capable of 417mph. Carrier trails were disappointing, however. Poor visibility over the nose and an ongoing tendency for the port wing to suddenly stall without warning made it completely unsuited for carrier operations. Until these problems could be addressed the US Navy had no choice but to assign the Corsair to the US Marines for land-based operations. In April 1944 the F4U was finally cleared for carrier use. The first carrier borne Corsairs would be four F4U-2 night-fighters of VF(N)-101 aboard USS *Enterprise* in January 9, 1944.

Variants

- F4U-1/FG-1 – the first Corsair was easily recognised by its bird cage canopy. The FG-1 designation was given to those fighters produced by the Goodyear Aircraft Company. Armed with six .50cal M2 machine guns (2,350 rounds total) the F4U-1 had 150lb of armour plate and was powered by the Pratt & Whitney R-2800-8 radial engine.
- F4U-1A/FG-1A – the F4U-1A replaced the bird cage canopy with a new wider canopy with only two frames. The pilot's seat was raised 7in, offering better visibility over the nose. These Corsairs introduced a 6in long stall strip just outboard of the gun ports on the right wing leading edge.
- F4U-1C – this was armed with four AN-M2 20mm cannon with 231 rounds per gun. The -1C wing was also fitted with four zero-length rocket launchers to carry four rockets.
- F4U-1D/FG-1D – the ultimate Corsair sub-type was the D model. It was the first Corsair variant to

ABOVE: The Vought XF4U-1 with gear and flaps down, April 1941. The prototype featured the 'birdcage' canopy and was armed with two .30in machine guns in the nose firing through the huge Hamilton Standard propeller and a .50in machine gun in each wing. NARA

SPECIFICATION

★ VOUGHT F4U-1D ★
CORSAIR

Displacement: One
Armament: Six wing-mounted M2 Browning .50cal machine guns with 2,350 rounds
Maximum Speed: 417mph at 19,000ft
Range: 1,015 miles

serve aboard US carriers in squadron service. The F4U-1D did away with the outboard internal wing tanks, relying on the 160-gallon belly tank instead. The Ds were powered by the Pratt &Whitney R-2800-8W with water injection for emergency power. Two pylons were added on the underside of the inner wing between the fuselage and landing gear. These pylons could carry a 1,000lb bomb or a 150-gallon drop tank.
• F4U-2 – a total of 32 F4U-1s were converted into night-fighters with the installation of the AN/APS-4 airborne intercept radar.

GRUMMAN F6F HELLCAT

Like the Corsair the F6F Hellcat's first clash against IJN fighters was between land-based units in the Solomon Islands. The Hellcat's introduction to combat occurred on September 6, 1943 when F6F-3s from US Navy squadron VF-33 shot down their first Zero-sen. Introduced a full six months after the Corsair's combat debut, the Hellcat's arrival couldn't have come at a more critical or opportune time. Up to this point the only qualified carrier fighter was the F4F-4 Wildcat. As mentioned before, the Corsair was not suitable as a carrier fighter. Fortunately for the Americans and those who had to fly it, the Hellcat arrived just in time.

The design of the Hellcat is best described as evolutionary rather than revolutionary. Unlike the Corsair, the Hellcat did not begin from a clean sheet of paper. As early as February 1938, Grumman designers were looking at putting a larger engine on the new XF4F-2 Wildcat. This led to the Model G-33 design showing the Grumman XF4F-2 modified to carry the big Wright R-2600 radial engine. Grumman designers believed the XF4F-2 with the R-2600 engine would not differ in appearance or dimensions from the smaller-engined design. The Bureau of Aeronautics was sceptical about Grumman's approach however. With the new heavy engine, larger propeller, altered centre of gravity and higher landing speeds, a number of major modifications would be required.

In September 1940, Grumman realised that more horsepower meant design changes would indeed have to be made. Their new Model G-50, powered by a Wright R-2600-10 engine, using a two-stage supercharger with 1,700hp had an increased wingspan and lengthened fuselage, but still looked like a larger F4F.

The bureau was still not impressed. Based on combat reports from Europe, they now realised a carrier fighter with a speed of 400mph, a range of 1,500 miles, heavy armament, armour protection and folding wings was needed. The Bureau requested several design changes and Grumman followed suit, making significant modifications to the Model G-50 design.

Wing mounted landing gear replaced the fuselage units, allowing for a larger diameter propeller. The wing was moved from the mid position to a new low wing configuration. The G-50 design also placed the cockpit high above the low wing and the nose sloped downward, giving excellent forward pilot visibility. Designated as the XF6F-1 the US Navy ordered two prototypes on June 19, 1941. Powered by the 1,700hp Wright R-2600-10 engine the XF6F-1 did not meet all the US Navy's performance requirements. Grumman was instructed to equip the second XF6F-1 with the more powerful 2,000hp R-2800-10 engine.

The modified airframe was designated XF6F-3 and flew for the first time on July 30, 1942. It was the perfect fit of aerodynamic design and engine power. Remarkably just three months later the first production F6F-3 made its first flight. ➤

BELOW: Early F4U-1 Corsairs of VF-12 on a training flight in the US in late 1942. VF-12 was the first US Navy unit to receive the new gull winged fighter. AUTHOR'S COLLECTION

"*Only fighters can keep our aircraft carriers afloat.*"

Lieutenant Commander John Thach

ABOVE: The Grumman XF6F-3 with the larger Double Wasp R-2800 engine. Top speed increased to 375mph at 17,000ft. NARA

ABOVE: The Pratt and Whitney R-2800 engine was a war-winning power plant and was not only fitted to the Hellcat, but the F4U-1 and P-47 Thunderbolt as well. Aviation mechanics aboard *Lexington* work on a Grumman F6F-3 during a lull between strikes on Mili and Kwajalein, circa early December 1943.

The new F6F-1 Hellcat was rugged, well-armed, reasonably fast, easy to fly and easy to maintain. It was a masterpiece of carrier aircraft engineering and design and its record speaks for itself. The Hellcat would prove superior to the Zero in almost every respect, save low speed

SPECIFICATION

★ GRUMMAN FM-2 ★

Crew: One
Armament: Four M2 Browning .50cal. machine guns with 450 rounds per gun
Maximum speed: 320mph at 18,600ft
Range: 900 miles

manoeuvrability, which Grumman had considered the least important aspect of aerial combat.

The Hellcat was the best carrier borne fighter of the war and was America's premiere 'ace maker' with 307 pilots credited with five or more kills.

Variants

• F6F-3 – the Hellcat was a large fighter, some 60% heavier than the lighter F4F Wildcat. Entering combat in September 1943 the Hellcat stood in sharp contrast to the light, nimble Zero-sen. In armament and armour, the Hellcat was vastly superior. Its armament of six M2 Browning .50cal machine guns was more than adequate and only required a short burst to shred a Zero. The Hellcat was well armoured with extensive protection. The pilot was provided with face-hardened armour to cover his head and shoulders. A sheet of armour plate was placed just ahead of the instrument panel, along with a bullet resistant windscreen to guard against head-on attacks. All the fuel tanks were self-sealing, and the oil tank and oil cooler had a section of frontal armour plate.

• F6F-5 – after building 4,402 F6F-3s, Grumman shifted production to the F6F-5 version. Powered by the Pratt & Whitney R-2800-10W with water methanol injection, the engine could produce 2,200hp of emergency power. Spring tabs were also added to the ailerons to improve the rate of roll above 200mph. The F6F-5 was also configured for fighter-bomber missions. A Mk 51 bomb rack was installed under the inboard section of each wing, capable of carrying a 1,000lb or drop tank each. Finally, three Mk 5 zero-length rocket launchers were fitted to the outer lower wing panels to carry the 5in High Velocity Aircraft Rocket (HVARs).

• F6F-3N/F6F-5N – this was the dedicated night fighter version of the Hellcat. Equipped with the AN/APS-6 airborne intercept radar (APS = Airborne Pulse Search), mounted on the Hellcat's right wing, a good Hellcat pilot could pick up a target at a maximum of four miles. The F6F-5N was armed exclusively with four 20mm cannon.

• F6F-5P – photo reconnaissance version fitted with a K-14 camera mounted behind the pilot facing out the fighter's port side. Armament remained six .50cal machine guns.

GRUMMAN FM-2 WILDCAT

Until the arrival of the F6F Hellcat and F4U Corsair the US Navy relied on the rugged F4F-4 Wildcat. After a year of intense combat, the Wildcat's results were impressive and it still had plenty of useful life left in it. Flying exclusively from escort carriers (CVE) the FM-2 performed a number of roles including CAP, close air support, spotting naval gunfire and anti-submarine operations.

ABOVE: An early production F6F-3 in flight. Grumman had production of the F6F-3 in full swing just three months after the first flight of the XF6F-1.

LEFT: An F6F-5N Hellcat shows the unique twin 20mm cannon armament fitted exclusively to a small number of night-fighter Hellcats. Despite the heavy firepower many night-fighter units experienced jamming problems with their cannon and most units kept the standard six-gun .50cal armament. NARA

SPECIFICATION

★ GRUMMAN F6F-5 ★ HELLCAT

Crew: One
Armament: Six wing-mounted M2 Browning .50cal. machine guns with 400 rounds each
Maximum Speed: 380mph at 23,400ft
Range: 1,085 miles (1,620 miles with drop tank)

The FM-2 began life as the XF4F-8 with two prototypes constructed. To improve take-off performance from the shorter escort carriers it was powered by the supercharged Wright R-1820-56 engine of 1,350hp. Armed with four .50cal machine guns the FM-2 was also equipped with two wing racks for 250lb bombs and Mk 5 zero length rockets launchers for 3 HVARs per wing.

Distinguished by its taller vertical stabiliser and rudder, the US Navy took delivery of the new Wildcat in December 1942.

CURTISS SB2C-1 HELLDIVER

The destruction of Japanese carriers in 1942 was due exclusively to the Dauntless SBD divebomber. Dependable, easy to fly, and a stable platform in a dive, the SBD was well liked by the crews who flew it. Its only deficiencies were its slow speed and maximum bomb load of 1,000lb.

Well before the Pacific war began, the US Navy was looking to upgrade its dive-bombing capabilities with a more potent aircraft. In August 1938 a specification was issued for a new monoplane scout bomber with an internal bomb bay, folding wings, arrestor hook, and catapult hooks. It also had to carry a 1,000lb bomb load farther than the Dauntless.

With its long history of building divebombers, the Curtiss Aircraft Company of Buffalo, New York was given the job. The challenge for Curtiss was to produce an aircraft with an internal bomb bay and a large fuel load that was still so small that two could fit on a carrier elevator as the same time. So great was the need for a new dive-bomber, the US Navy hastily ordered 370 of the new SB2C-1 before a prototype had taken flight. The conflicting requirements and the rush to production led directly to a long and painful gestation period.

The XSB2C-1 first flew on December 18, 1940. In early February 1941 it crashed due to failure of its Wright R-2600 Cyclone engine. When flight testing resumed a rash of problems followed with directional instability and structural weakness being the most serious.

Hundreds of design changes were made to fix the problems. This slowed production further and it wasn't until December 15, 1942 that the first SB2C-1 was delivered to the fleet. And yet despite all this effort the Helldiver was still unfit for carrier operations. It wasn't until early 1943 that the SB2C-3 Helldiver was finally approved for fleet service. The Helldiver never met its performance expectations, but it did prove to be an accurate dive-bomber. In June 1945 Assistant Secretary of the Navy for Air Artemus L. Gates said this of the Helldiver: "When we needed the SB2C neither we nor it was ready. Thanks to the spirit of our people and our airplanes, we won a war with our mistakes as well as with our victories."

Variants

- SB2C-1 – powered by a 1,700hp Wright 2600-8 engine, the SB2C-1 made its maiden flight on June 30, 1942. Early carrier trials were disastrous, leading to the modified SB2C-1C. It wasn't until November 1943 that the Helldiver made its combat debut.

SPECIFICATION

★ CURTISS SB2C-3 ★ HELLDIVER

Crew: Two
Armament: One 2,000lb of bomb, four 500lb bombs, one 1,600lb armour-piercing bomb, two 350lb depth charges, two forward AN-M2 20mm cannon with 800 rounds per gun, aft mounted twin .30cal machine guns
Speed: 294 at 12,400ft
Range: 1,200 miles with a 1,000lb bomb

ABOVE: The Grumman XTBF-1 made its first flight on August 7, 1941 and exactly one year later provided carrier-based air support for the marine landings on Guadalcanal in August 1942. NARA

ABOVE: Curtiss SB2C-1C aboard *Intrepid* October 1943. From 1943 through to 1945 some 30 Navy bombing squadrons deployed with SB2Cs on combat tours. NARA

- SB2C-2 – this was an experimental seaplane version and never entered production.
- SB2C-3 – the 'Dash 3' was easily identified by the lack of a propeller spinner. Early versions of the Helldiver were chronically underpowered for their size. The newer version was upgraded to a Wright R 2600-20 engine developing 1,900 horse power and a new four bladed propeller was fitted. Aircraft fitted with the APS-4 sea search radar were designated SB2C-3E.
- SB2C-4 – new perforated dive brakes were fitted that addressed a buffeting problem when diving and low-speed handling improved. Rails for eight HVARs were fitted. Over 2,045 were built.
- SB2C-5 – entering production in February 1945, only a small number of the 'Dash 5s' reached operational squadrons by August 1945. Just 970 were built.

GRUMMAN TBF/TBM AVENGER

As previously mentioned the TBF replaced the Devastator as the US Navy's sole torpedo bomber after the Battle of Midway. Reliable, versatile and able to take a tremendous amount of damage, the Avenger was a huge success in both the torpedo and conventional bomber roles.

Variants

- TBF-1 – the first production version built by Grumman (TBF-1) and the Eastern Aircraft Company as the TBM-1. For lend lease aircraft supplied to the Royal Navy, it was designated TBF-1B.
- TBF/TBM-1C – this version replaced the single .30cal cowl mounted gun with two-wing mounted .50cal machine guns and bullet resistant glass was added to the rear turret.
- TBF/TBM-1D – TBF/TBM-1 airframes were converted into night capable bombers with the addition of a wing mounted radome containing ASD-1 radar.
- TBM-3 – built exclusively by Eastern Aircraft, 4,011 TBM-3s were built and it was the most produced version of the Avenger. To boost take-off performance from the shorter light and escort carrier decks, the Wright 1,900hp Wright R-2600-20 was fitted. Unfortunately, the added weight negated the added power.
- TBM-3D – purpose built night bomber version with ASD-1 radar on the leading edge of the starboard wing.
- TBM-3E – introduced late in the war, this variant had a stronger airframe, improved search radar and no ventral gun.

SPECIFICATION

★ GRUMMAN TBM-3 ★ AVENGER

Crew: Three
Armament: One 2,216lb torpedo, one 2,000lb bomb or four 500lb bombs, eight 5in HVAR rockets, two forward firing M2 Browning .50cal machine guns, one dorsal turret M2 .50cal machine gun and one ventral .30cal machine gun
Speed: 267mph at 15,000ft
Range: 1,130 with torpedo

BELOW: The training flight line at Norfolk, Virginia shows the different types used to create a qualified naval aviator. On the tarmac are six Boeing NS2 Stearmans, three F4F Wildcats and a single TBF Avenger. American airfields in the south and along the Gulf coast provided good weather for year round training. NARA

DEADLY ORDNANCE

MARK XIII TORPEDO

Formally designated as the Mark XIII in August 1930, this was the torpedo that would serve as the US Navy's primary weapon throughout the Second World War. The first successful run of a Mark XIII occurred in March 1932, with the second prototype achieving 30 knots over 6,000 yards.

A total of 156 Mk XIII Mod 0 torpedoes were built, enough to provide two loads for each of the 18 Devastator torpedo bomber squadrons assigned to the pre-war carriers. In 1940 the Mod 0 was replaced by the Mod 1. This version differed in the rudder-propeller arrangement – the Mod 0 was equipped with a rail-type tail with the propellers located in front of the rudders.

For reasons that remain unclear, the Mod 1 entered service with a more conventional tail. The Mod 1 proved to be an unreliable weapon with only 31% running satisfactorily. The Mod 1 also had to be dropped at low and slow speeds – 50ft at 110kts. Despite its obvious faults, the US Navy deemed the weapon fit for combat, going to war with an unreliable torpedo.

After a disastrous 1942, in terms of torpedo attacks and lack of successes, it took another year to make the Mk XIII a reliable weapon. A number of modifications were added: a shroud ring to the tail of the torpedo reduced erratic running when entering the water; a water trip valve was added to start the torpedo only after it had entered the water and finally, a shroud or drag wing made of plywood was placed over the warhead to help absorb the shock of entry. All these modifications allowed the Avenger to drop its weapon at close to 270mph and 800ft high.

BOMBS

Fortunately for the US Navy their bombs were far more reliable then the Mk XIII torpedo. The four Japanese carriers sunk at Midway were dispatched by 500lb and 1,000lb general purpose (GP) bombs alone. During the Pacific campaign the US Navy would use both general purpose and armour piercing bombs of various weights.

General purpose or demolition bombs had thin metal walls and a large explosive charge. These were used against ground targets and unarmoured ships. Against carriers, 500 and 1,000lb GP bombs were fused to detonate after just 0.1 seconds in order to rip up carrier flight decks.

The most widely used GP bombs included: AN-M57 250lb, AN-M64 500lb and AN-M65 1000lb.

Against heavily armoured battleships and heavy cruisers, dive-bombers were armed with armour piercing bombs (AP). These bombs had thick steel cases with a relatively small explosive charge, typically just 5% of the total weight. A delayed fuse allowed the bomb to penetrate before detonating. In May 1942 the US Navy introduced the new AP AN-Mk 1 bomb. Weighing 1,600lb, its explosive content was 240lb. Both the Avenger and Helldiver were the only aircraft capable of lifting such a large bomb and it was rare for an *Essex* class carrier to have more than 20 Mk 1s in its magazine.

In October 1942 the US Navy introduced the AN-Mk 33 1,000lb AP bomb, which contained 144lb of explosives. It would be the most widely used AP bomb in the Pacific war. When dropped from a dive-bomber in a 300mph, 60-degree dive it was capable of penetrating 5in of deck armour.

HVAR ROCKET

The 5in high velocity aerial rocket (HVAR) was one of the most spectacular weapons used during the war. HVARs were an immediate success, giving the Hellcat, Corsair, Avenger, Helldiver, and to a lesser degree the FM-2 Wildcat the explosive power of a destroyer broadside. Entering service in July 1944, two versions were built, one general-purpose high explosive with base and nose fuses, and one with a semi-armour piercing warhead. The HVAR used a modified 5in/38 AA common projectile. Effective range was 400 yards.

SPECIFICATION
★ MARK XIII TORPEDO ★
Length: 13ft 9in
Warhead of 603lb of TNT, 606lb of TPX or 600lb of HBX
Speed: 30 knots with a range of 5,700 yards

SPECIFICATION
★ HVAR ROCKET ★
Weight: 134lb including 24lb of propellant and a 45lb payload with a 7.8lb warhead
Length: 66 in
Velocity: 950mph

THE IJNAF REBUILDS

At the beginning of 1943 the Japanese carrier force was unable to launch any offensive operations. Lack of aircraft and crews prevented the quick re-establishment of carrier air groups. Attrition had outstripped supply and Japan's inability to match the US capacity for mass production limited its options. The Mitsubishi Zero was a prime example. Switching to a new design meant a loss of production which the Japanese could ill afford. In order to sustain production quantities, the Zero remained in service to the end of the war.

New aircraft were, however, introduced, but in small numbers. Both the Aichi D3A1 and Nakajima B5N2 had proven their worth in the battles of 1942 but were ready for replacement.

YOKOSUKA D4Y1 'JUDY'

The 'Judy' was a replacement aircraft for the 'Val'. Early versions were powered by the liquid-cooled Atsuta engine, a version of the German 1,400hp DB 600 series engine built under licence by Aichi. Problems with the Atsuta engine led to the radial

ABOVE: A Yokosuka D4Y1-C reconnaissance variant with drop tanks prepares for take-off in Marianas Islands, 1944. NARA

SPECIFICATION

★ YOKOSUKA ★
D4Y1 'JUDY'
Crew: Two
Armament: Two forward-firing 7.7mm Type 97 machine guns, one rearward-firing 7.92mm Type 1 machine gun
Maximum speed: 342mph
Range: 910 miles

engine D4Y3 version fitted with the air-cooled Mitsubishi Kinsei 1,560hp engine.

Dimensionally, the 'Judy' was no larger than a Japanese fighter. It possessed remarkable speed in all its models but lacked armour protection for the crew and self-sealing fuel tanks.

The 'Judy' was the fastest carrier-borne dive-bomber of the war and one of the most versatile – serving as a light bomber, night-fighter and reconnaissance aircraft. Many would be modified for kamikaze missions, making it also one of the most feared aircraft of the war.

NAKAJIMA B6N1 'JILL'

The B6N1 made its combat debut as a land-based torpedo bomber in November 1943 at Bougainville. Designed as a replacement for the B5N 'Kate', work on the new IJN specification began in 1939. Powered by a 1,870hp Nakajima Mamori engine, the first prototype flew in March 1941.

In early 1943 the B6N1 was approved for production and by August a small number had been sent to reinforce the land based IJNAF aircraft at Rabaul. By June 1944 approximately 78 B6N1s were embarked on the carriers *Shokaku*, *Taiho*, *Hiyo*, *Junyo* and *Zuikaku* in preparation for the Battle of the Philippine Sea.

In that same month production of the B6N2 powered by the 1,850hp Mitsubishi Kasei engine began. The B6N2 was an impressive performer – top speed was 299mph with a 1,764lb torpedo. Just 1,266 B6N1s and B6N2s were built.

MITSUBISHI ZERO

The Mitsubishi A6M Zero was arguably the best carrier fighter in the opening phases of the war. The Zero's early success was due in large part to the well-trained pilots who flew it. Flying experience of JNAF pilots at the time of Pearl Harbour averaged about 800 hours, many with combat experience. As the war progressed the

ABOVE: A B6N2 Tenzan 'Jill' being serviced by ground crew on an airfield on Saipan circa 1944. The 'Jill' slowly replaced the B5N2 'Kate' as the IJNAF's premier carrier-borne torpedo bomber starting in late 1943. NARA

Zero's fighting abilities began to deteriorate and so did the quality of its pilots.

By early 1943 the Zero's poor performance against newer fighters like the F4U Corsair was clear to both the Allies and Japanese. Promises of a new interceptor did not materialize and the Japanese were forced to modify the existing Zero fighter to keep pace.

The Zero was the most numerous fighter employed by the IJN in the Pacific. It was also the mostly widely used aircraft in the kamikaze role. Even with the F6F and F4U's superior performance, in the hands of an experienced pilot, the Zero remained an extremely dangerous opponent.

Variants
- A6M5 Model 52 – the Model 52 was designed to simplify and speed production and increase its diving speed. Wingspan remained the same as the square tip Model 32, but modifications included the elimination of the wing tip folding mechanism. To increase diving speed, heavy gauge wing skin was added, and the exhaust collector ring was replaced with straight individual stacks. This directed high velocity exhaust gas backward for additional thrust. Powered by a 1,130hp Sakae 21 engine, maximum speed was 351 mph at 19,000 feet. The A6M5 Model 52 was the most widely used model with 1,701 manufactured.
- A6M5a Model 52a – heavier gauge wing skin was added to increase diving speed to 460mph, just 20mph slower than the F4U Corsair. This was to be the highest diving speed attained by any Zero variant. Firepower

SPECIFICATION

★ NAKAJIMA ★
B6N1 'JILL'
Crew: Three
Armament: One 7.7mm Type 92 machine gun in rear cockpit and one Type 92 firing through ventral tunnel
Maximum speed: 299mph
Range: 1,892 miles

was improved with the addition of new Type 99 Model 2 Mk 4 20mm cannons. Mitsubishi produced 391 examples.
- A6M5b Model 52b – CO_2 fire extinguishers were built into the fuel tank areas of the fuselage and around the firewall. Pilot protection was increased with the addition of a 2-inch bullet resistant windshield and firepower was increased for the first time. One of the two Type 97 7.7mm fuselage machine guns was replaced by a larger Type 3 13mm machine gun. Mitsubishi produced 470 examples.
- A6M5c Model 52c – increased firepower, more fuel and pilot protection. Firepower was increased to three Type 3 13mm machines guns and two 20mm cannon. Armour plate was installed for the first time behind the pilot's seat along with a 37-gallon self-sealing fuel tank. Mitsubishi produced 93 examples of the 52c.
- A6M6c Model 53c – the Sakae Model 31 A engine with water-methanol injection was fitted, but it proved erratic and performance suffered as a result. Mitsubishi produced only one Zero 53c.
- A6M7 Model 63 – this was the fighter-dive-bomber variant of the Zero. Armament was the same as the 52c and in place of the normal centerline drop tank Mitsubishi developed a bomb rack capable of carrying a 500lb bomb.
- A6M8c Model 54c – for only the second time in the war the Zero was fitted with a more powerful engine – Mitsubishi Kinsei 62, developing 1,340-horse power. Maximum speed was 356mph at 19,685 feet. Test pilots agreed it was the best model of the Zero yet produced and the fastest of all Zero variants. Only two were completed.

SPECIFICATION

★ MITSUBISHI A6M2 ★
ZERO MODEL 21
Crew: One
Armament: Two 7.7mm Type 9 machine guns with 500 rounds per gun, two 20mm Type 99-1 Mk.3 cannon with 60 rounds per gun
Maximum speed: 331mph at 14,930ft
Range: 1162 miles

ABOVE: This photograph captures the A6M5's clean and compact lines. The Zero was the most manoeuvrable fighter of the Pacific campaign thanks to its large wing area and generously proportioned ailerons. Above 15,000ft and at speeds above 250mph, however, the Zero lost its exceptional manoeuvrability. AUTHOR'S COLLECTION

'DO NOT DOGFIGHT WITH THE ZEKE 52!"

The importance of avoiding close-quarters turning combat with the Zero was a lesson learned the hard way during the air battles of 1942 between the A6M2 Model 21 Zero aka 'Zeke' and the Grumman F4F-3 and F4F-4 Wildcat. In the hands of an experienced pilot the Wildcat gave as good as it got and was able take on the Zero with revised tactics – particularly avoiding close-in manoeuvring combat – rugged construction and heavy armament. When the F4U Corsair and F6F Hellcat entered service, the same rules of combat applied.

In October 1944 the Technical Air Intelligence Center tested a newly capture A6M5 Model 52 Zero – the latest version – against a Grumman F6F-5 Hellcat, a Vought F4U-1D Corsair and a Grumman FM-2 Wildcat. The results were not surprising.

"Speed runs were made at full available power every 5,000 feet from sea-level to 30,000 feet, the F4U-1D, F6F-5 and FM-2 using War Emergency Power. Rolls, turns, dives, manoeuvres, mock combat and general characteristics were tested at various altitudes. Pilots were rotated in their assignment to aircraft in order to obtain a better cross section of opinion. All the airplanes were loaded to their 'standard fighter' weights.

"The Zeke was powered by a Nakajima SAKAE 31A engine, not equipped with water injection. The plane was easy to fly, except for excessively high control surfaces at high speeds. At speeds around 160 knots the controls tightened, and at speeds over 200 knots the control forces became objectionably heavy, especially in the ailerons."

In almost every category the American fighters, with the exception of the FM-2, were superior.

"Zeke 52 vs. F4U-1D. The best climb of the F4U-1D was equal to that of the Zeke 52 up to 10,000 feet, about 750ft/min better at 18,000 feet, and about 500 ft./min better at 22,000 feet and above."

At sea-level the Corsair was 48mph faster than the Zero, at 5,000ft it was 42mph faster, at 10,000ft 58mph faster, 15,000ft 70mph faster, 20,000ft 78mph faster and at 25,000ft an incredible 80mph faster, dropping to 74mph faster at 30,000ft. Top speeds attained were 413mph at 20,400ft for the F4U-1D and 335mph at 18,000ft for the Zero.

The Hellcat wasn't quite so superior, however. the Zero climbed about 600ft/min better up to 9,000ft, after which the advantage fell off gradually until the two aircraft were about equal at 14,000ft. Above that altitude the F6F-5 had the advantage, varying from 500ft/min better at 22,000ft to about 250ft/min better at 30,000ft. Like the Corsair, the F6F-5 was much faster than the Zero at all altitudes. Top speeds attained were 409mph at 21,600ft for the F6F-5 and 335mph at 18,000ft for the Zero.

Sheer speed and climbing potential did not win turning dogfights, however. The suggested tactics for both the Corsair and Hellcat were the same: "Do not dogfight with the Zeke 52. Do not try to follow a loop or half roll with pull-through. When attacking use your superior power and high-speed performance to engage at the most favourable moment. To evade a Zeke 52 on your tail, roll and dive away in a high-speed turn."

It was a different story with the Wildcat – which had neither the speed to escape from a Zero nor the manoeuvrability to out-turn it. In fact, the Zero was progressively faster than the Wildcat above 5,000ft. The Wildcat was 6mph faster at sea-level, then 4mph slower at 5,000ft, 12mph slower at 10,000ft, 8mph slower at 15,000ft, 19mph slower at 20,000ft, 22mph slower at 25,000ft and 26mph slower at 30,000ft.

Top speeds were 321mph at 13,000ft for the Wildcat and 335mph at 18,000ft for the Zero.

Suggested tactics for the Wildcat pilot were: "Do not dogfight with the Zeke 52. Maintain any altitude advantage you have. To evade the Zeke 52 on your tail, roll and dive away in a high-speed turn."

PAC-10 – THE GAME CHANGAR

The Fast Carrier Task Force that was about to advance through the Pacific was not the fleet of prewar plans. The prewar US Navy, like the British and Japanese, was battleship-centric. Concentrated together the large battleships would manoeuvre as a unit, seizing objectives and destroying the enemy capitols ships when the opportunity presented itself. By early 1943, the introduction of the Fast Carrier Task Force gave the Navy a more effective fighting organisation. The carrier task force and their independent task groups demonstrated their ability to form a powerful striking force, capable of decisive action on their own.

By late 1942, the sea battles around Guadalcanal and the four major carrier battles had revealed flaws in the US Navy's prewar approach to the development and dissemination of tactical doctrine. The large fleet carriers and supporting ships were going into battle without proper indoctrination and tactical cohesion, limiting their effectiveness. A new approach was needed.

In June 1943, a new tactical manual, *Current Tactical Orders and Doctrine, US Pacific Fleet,* known as PAC-10, was issued to the fleet. PAC-10 provided the Navy with a common set of tactical principals for the cooperation of both small and large forces and detached units in battle.

With PAC-10 in place, ships could now move between task groups seamlessly without reequipping them with lengthy new instructions. Each ship knew its role, how the other ships in the fleet operated and how to respond when under attack. The manual's introduction stressed the importance of this new doctrine: "PAC-10 is intended… to obviate necessity for… special instructions under ordinary circumstances and to minimise them in extraordinary circumstances. The ultimate aim is to obtain essential uniformity without unacceptable sacrifice of flexibility. It must be possible for forces composed of diverse types and indoctrinated under different task force commanders, to join at sea on short notice for concentrated action against the enemy without exchanging a mass of special instructions."

The US Navy entered mid-1943 with the hallmarks of victory firmly in place. The shipyards and aircraft factories were churning out aircraft and ships at an unprecedented rate. The emphasis on "decisive offensive action, reliance on individual initiative of ship commanders and development of decentralised command" in combination with some of the best war fighting naval technology, sound doctrine and excellent leadership meant the long bloody struggle ahead would end in victory.

Admiral Nagumo, the victor at Pearl Harbor and defeated at Midway, knew that war with America meant everything had to go Japan's way: "This battle was a tactical win (Santa Cruz October 1942), but a shattering strategic loss for Japan. Considering the great superiority of our enemy's industrial capacity, we must win every battle overwhelmingly in order to win this war. This last one, although a victory, unfortunately, was not an overwhelming victory."

CHAPTER

CARRIER STRIKES 1943

"Hit hard, hit fast, hit often."

ABOVE: Task Group 38.3 (TG-38.3) as they enter Ulithi Anchorage after strikes against the Japanese on Luzon, Philippines. In line are *Langley* (CVL-27), *Ticonderoga* (CV-14), *Washington* (BB-56), *North Carolina* (BB-55) and *South Dakota* (BB-57). NARA

On May 9, 1943 the new Navy arrived in the Pacific. Dropping anchor at Pearl Harbor On May 9, 1943 the new Navy arrived in the Pacific. Dropping anchor at Pearl Harbor was the new *Essex* (CV-9) fast carrier with Air Group 9 equipped with 36 F6F-3 Hellcats, 36 SBD-3 Dauntless and 18 TBF-1 Avengers, plus an additional SBD for liaison duties and nine reserve aircraft, three of each type. This was followed by *Yorktown* (CV-10) on July 24 with Air Group 10, *Lexington* (CV-16) on August 9 with Air Group 16 and the light carriers *Independence* (CVL-22) arriving on July 22 and *Princeton* (CVL-23) on August 9. With the surviving original carriers *Enterprise* (CV-6) and *Saratoga* (CV-3) the US Navy possessed five fleet carriers and two light carriers with more on the way.

The hard lessons of 1942 forced the US Navy to revise its carrier doctrine. The pre-war practice of operating only one or two carriers in a task group was abandoned. With the *Essex* and *Independence* class carriers up to four separate task groups were formed in 1943 alone, all under the leadership of the Commander, Fast Carrier Force Pacific. Each task group consisted of a mix of fleet and light carriers (usually three fleet and two light carriers). Escort was provided by a division of fast battleships (two to four), four cruisers, and ten to twelve destroyers. To provide the best AA defence, while steaming in formation, the carriers were placed in the centre of a four-mile radius circle of escort vessels.

As the US Navy added to its quantitative advantage it also possessed a qualitative one as well. US Navy pilots were considered the best trained in the world and they had to be. Having the guts and ability to land an aircraft on a pitching, rolling deck separated the Navy flyer from all others. By 1943, Navy aviators entered their assigned squadrons with 350 flying hours. For Hellcat pilots that number would 500 by the time they entered combat. In comparison the average Japanese aviator in 1944 entered service with less than 200 hours.

At the outset of war, the Japanese placed little emphasis on expanding their pilot training programme. As America's carrier force expanded, the Japanese were forced to sacrifice their trained naval aviators in the defence of Rabaul and the Solomons. With their carriers lying at Truk or in home waters during 1943, their air groups were repeatedly sent south to reinforce the depleted JAAF. It was a futile exercise.

By the end of 1942 just 2,300 Japanese pilots had been trained, in sharp contrast the US Navy added more than 5,000 pilots and another 12,000 followed in 1943.

In terms of fighter pilot skill, the US Navy was the only air force that taught proper aerial gunnery from the outset. Not only were shooting skills emphasised, but naval aviators were taught the difficult art of deflection shooting. Their fighter tactics were also well honed. They knew never to 'dogfight' with the Zero and to keep the battle in the vertical plain, using dive and zoom tactics to counter the Zero's manoeuvrability. The US Navy training booklet emphasised: "Altitude is your wealth. Never spend it unless it buys you speed or an advantageous firing position."

In the coming air battles Hellcat pilots would rack up impressive scores. Over a 24 month period F6F pilots would be credited with some 5,200 enemy aircraft destroyed for the loss of 450 aviators.

By mid-1943 the war in the Pacific had entered a new phase. The Pacific Fleet, under the command of Admiral W. Nimitz, had defeated the Japanese in the attritional struggle for Guadalcanal and damaged the IJN carrier force to such a degree that it was forced regroup and repair.

It was now time for the new carrier task forces to seize the opportunity and start a strategic offensive aimed at breaking the Japanese defensive perimeter on the road to Japan itself. The prime objective of the new offensive would be the Central Pacific. Both sides recognised the strategic importance of the Marshall, Caroline and Marianas island groups. Directed by the Joint Chiefs of Staff (JCS), Nimitz was ordered to develop a plan to attack the Japanese strongholds and beyond. Nimitz's plan, codenamed GRANITE, set out two specific operational goals – firstly a rapid pace of operations to pressure the Japanese continuously and keep the offensive initiative and secondly to draw the Japanese fleet into a decisive battle.

Before the offensive could begin however, the new carrier force needed some combat experience and a chance to work out doctrine and procedures. To keep the Japanese guessing, a series of hit-and-run raids were ordered to begin at the end of August.

On August 23, 1943 the newly formed Task Force 15 set sail from Hawaiian waters. Their destination was Marcus Island, 2,720 nautical miles away. Leading the way were the new *Essex* (CV-9), *Yorktown* (CV-10) and *Independence* (CVL 22) carriers escorted by the battleship *Indiana*, two cruisers and nine destroyers.

Marcus island was a Japanese weather station, with an airfield and seaplane facilities but with little strategic importance to the US Navy. It would, however, provided the baptism of fire for the new *Essex* and *Independence* light carriers, the Grumman F6F Hellcat and the numerous first time dive-bomber and torpedo bomber crews.

In order to achieve total surprise, a predawn launch was ordered. On August 31, at 0415 hours *Yorktown* was the first to launch. At 0520 hours *Essex* began launching its aircraft with Hellcats from VF-5 and VF-9 leading the way. At 0605 hours the Avengers from *Yorktown* released their 500lb bombs and incendiaries over the airfield.

Several Avengers armed with 2,000lb bombs added to the destruction. As AA fire filled the air the Hellcat pilots responded with strafing attacks to silence the guns. Next in were the SBDs. Diving from 9,000ft they aimed their 1,000lb bombs at the fuel storage tanks and buildings. As the Hellcats continued with their strafing, several G4M 'Betty' bombers were spotted and quickly destroyed.

After losing a TBF and Hellcat to AA fire the first strike returned just as the second began their attack on the island. After ten hours of bombardment and strafing the island was left a smoking wreck. VF-5 lost two Hellcats and *Yorktown* lost an Avenger to AA fire. For the Hellcat pilots the mission was a bit of a disappointment. No Japanese fighters rose to defend the island, leaving the eager aviators to make simple strafing runs. With guns fired and bombs dropped the inexperienced aviators had their first taste of battle with more to come.

That evening Task Force 15 set course for Hawaii and a new mission. Arriving on September 7, the *Essex* and *Yorktown* were ordered to act as glorified transports but with a precious cargo. Heading for San Francisco both carriers embarked hundreds of Air Force personnel and marines going home for much needed R&R. For the return trip, on September 13, the carriers were loaded with 2,000 men each and flights deck packed with aircraft and equipment. By the 19th they were back at Pearl.

The Hellcat's first air-to-air victory was not long in coming. On the following day, September 1, the light carriers *Princeton* (CVL-23) and *Belleau Wood* (CVL-24) were assigned to cover the landings on Howland and Baker Islands. Hellcats from VF-22, VF-23 and a detachment from VF-6 provided the CAP. Shortly after twelve noon a division (four aircraft) of VF-6 Hellcats, led by Lt Richard L. Loesch was vectored to an incoming bogey at 7,000ft. The intruder was a Kawanishi H8K 'Emily' flying boat. Attacking from head on, Loesch and his wingman fired about 300 rounds each, concentrating on the cockpit and inbound engines. The 'Emily' fell away in a right hand 180 degree turn, crashing into the sea.

Tarawa in the Gilberts was the next target. In mid-September the new fleet carrier *Lexington* (C-16) led the *Princeton* (CVL-23) and *Belleau*

ABOVE: The flight deck of *Essex* (CV-9) looking aft from the carrier's island during its shakedown cruise, March 20, 1943. On the deck are F6F-3 fighters with wings folded and SBD-4 scout bombers. Without folding wings fewer SBDs could be carried and they took up more deck space. NARA

ABOVE: Hellcat fighters of VF-5 fly escort to mixed formation of Hellcats and Avengers as they head to Marcus Island on August 31, 1943. US NAVAL HISTORICAL CENTER

BELOW: *Yorktown's* (CV-10) shakedown cruise in the spring of 1943. An F6F-3, fully chocked, warms up prior to take-off.
US NAVAL HISTORICAL CENTER

Wood (CVL-24) for a two-day strike. No aerial opposition was encountered and like the Marcus Island raid, Tarawa was left a fiery wreck.

For the next ten days the carriers returned to Pearl Harbor to replenish with ammunition, food and fuel, the three 'Bs' – bombs, beans and black oil. By this time the Pacific carrier fleet stood at an incredible eight fleet carriers, seven light carriers and 24 escort carriers. In sharp contrast Japan's Third Fleet Striking Force consisted of just six carriers – the veteran *Zuikaku* and *Shokaku*, and the light carriers *Zuiho, Hiyo, Junyo* and *Ryuho*.

On September 29, the *Essex* set sail from Pearl Harbor as the flagship of Task Force 14. It was a powerful force of 40 ships including three fleet carriers (*Essex, Yorktown*, and *Lexington*) and three light carriers (*Belleau Wood, Cowpens*, and *Independence*). Aircraft carried amounted to 351 – 171 F6Fs, 99 SBDs and 81 TBFs.

Their target was Wake Island, 2300 miles to the west. Wake consisted of three small islands in the shape of a wishbone. Each island was about four miles long with an airfield at its southeast end. On October 4 Task Force 14 turned towards Wake and began their high-speed run. As the Task Force approached the island, *Independence* and *Belleau Wood* were dispatched to a position northeast of Wake. Their job was to intercept any Japanese reinforcements flying up from the Marshalls. *Essex, Yorktown, Lexington* and *Cowpens* provided the offensive punch.

Thirty minutes before sunrise on October 5, Task Force 14 turned into the wind. 100 miles east of Wake Island the carriers *Essex, Yorktown, Lexington* and *Independence* launched three fighter divisions. In the early light of dawn, 47 F6F-3 Hellcats formed up and turned west towards their target. On the dark sea below, *Essex* and *Yorktown* launched some 70 SBD-5 Dauntlesses and TBM-1C Avengers loaded with bombs. At 0445 hours the first strike headed for Wake. This was followed by the second strike at 0537 made up of 45 fighters, dive-bombers and torpedo bombers.

As the Hellcats approached and before the sun was fully up, Japanese radar detected the inbound strike about 50 miles out. Twenty-seven Zeros (most likely a mix of A6M3 Model 32s and A6M3 Model 52s) from the 252 Kokutai rose to the attack. In addition, five G4M 'Betty' bombers were scrambled to attack the carriers. The first to engage the Zeros were the pilots of VF-5.

A short, sharp dogfight ensued with the pilots of VF-5 claiming three Zeros and one 'Betty' shot down. At roughly the same time the *Essex* Hellcats of VF-9 tangled with a formation of Zeros over Wake. As the Hellcats dealt with the intercepting Zeros the first wave of Avengers dropped their bombs as the first anti-aircraft guns were finding their range. The SBDs were next, diving down from 12,000ft. After the first encounter with the Hellcats, the 252nd Kokutai had just three Zeros ready for a second mission, losing 16 fighters in 15 minutes of combat. Three more Zeros fell to the guns of VF-6 south of Wake.

The damage inflicted after two days of strikes was considerable – 22 of Wake's 34 Zeros were destroyed. The intercepting Zeros managed to shoot down six planes, with AA fire bringing the total to 12 US aircraft lost in combat. Wake Island was an important Japanese base and the damage inflicted was considerable. It would be a long time before it would be useful to the Japanese again. After two days of strikes Task Force 14 sent over 730 sorties against the little island leaving over 60 enemy aircraft destroyed either in the air or on the ground.

For the young Hellcat pilots it was a moment of triumph and one of great significance. The first major encounter between the A6M2 Type 52 Zero and F6F-3 Hellcat clearly demonstrated the Hellcat's superiority over the famed Zero. While the combat had been brief, the dogfights clearly showed that their tactical doctrine was sound: maintain high speed in the combat zone, keep the fight in the vertical trading height for speed in diving attacks, fight in pairs, and avoid the Zero's low-speed turning advantage.

Most of the combats took place below 12,000ft, highlighting the F6F's superior speed and its ability to outrun the Zero. While the Zero had a better rate of climb at these altitudes, some IJNAF pilots attempted to escape by initiating a climbing turn. It wasn't enough. The Hellcat pilots were able follow and shoot them down with ease. The short dogfight also revealed the IJNAFs fatal flaws: gunnery was extremely poor and their habit of fighting as individuals and not in pairs greatly reduced their combat effectiveness. Having blown the tape off their guns the Hellcat pilots returned to their carriers full of confidence in their new fighter.

FORTRESS RABAUL

In 1942 Rabaul became the focus of Japanese expansion in the Southwest Pacific. Located on the eastern end of New Britain its long, wide, deep water harbour made it an ideal naval base. Simpson Harbour was also protected on three sides by volcanic mountains. On January 22, 1942 the Japanese landed on New Britain taking Rabaul the next day.

As Japanese plans for expansion unfolded, Rabaul was perfectly placed to project both air and sea power towards northwest Australia. From Rabaul's airfields, Lae and the Admiralty Islands were just 400 miles away; Port Moresby on New Guinea just 500 miles, and Guadalcanal, at the southern end of the Solomons, was 650 miles away.

After the loss of Guadalcanal in February 1943, the Japanese were now firmly on the defensive. By the start of 1943 Rabaul was garrisoned with 100,000 troops and airmen and ringed with five airfields. It was now a massive fortress that needed to be neutralised before victory in the Southwest Pacific could be achieved.

After the Wake Island raid, the Fast Carrier offensive in the Pacific increased in momentum. In late October, American Marine and Army forces were preparing to invade Bougainville in the Northern Solomons. On November 1, Operation Shoestring began. With naval units in the South Pacific theatre diverted for operations in the Central Pacific, American forces were stretched to the limit. Admiral William Halsey, commander for the South Pacific Area, had just four Cleveland Class light carriers and eight Fletcher Class destroyers to cover the landing fleet.

As American troops landed at Cape Torokina in Empress Augusta Bay on Bougainville the Japanese reacted quickly by sending 1,000 Special Landing Force troops on five destroyers at Rabaul to make a counter landing. Escort for this force consisted of two heavy cruisers, two light cruisers and six destroyers. Spotted by an American submarine, the element of surprise was lost. With the submarine report in hand,

ABOVE: The bombing of Marcus Island, August 31, 1943. Bomb craters can be clearly seen on the runways. During the raid two Hellcats and one Avenger were shot by AA fire. NARA

the Americans evacuated most of the troop transports and landing craft to the south.

On the evening of November 2 the Japanese ran into US Task Force 39, which consisted of three light cruisers and seven destroyers. At 0230 ▶

BELOW: SBD-4s prepare for takeoff from *Yorktown* (CV-10) for strikes against Wake Island October 5-6, 1943. NARA

RIGHT: Hellcats and SBDs on the forward deck of the new *Lexington* (CV-16) of Air Group 16 on their way for a two day strike on Tarawa Atoll in the Gilbert Islands during mid-September 1943. NARA

ABOVE: AN-M65 1,000lb bombs chalked up in preparation for loading aboard *Cowpens* (CVL-25) prior to the Wake Island raid, October 5, 1943. The AN-M65 had an explosive weight of 530lb. NARA

LEFT: A full deck strike prepares for take-off from *Yorktown* (CV-10) headed for Wake Island, October 1943. NARA

hours an opening salvo of torpedoes from both sides was launched followed by radar directed gun fire from the US light cruisers. The Japanese replied with optically controlled-gunnery and scored a number of hits on the US cruisers. As the Japanese cruiser fire became heavier and more accurate, the American cruisers manoeuvred behind a smoke screen – negating the Japanese optically sighted guns. At 0320 hours with daylight approaching and the fear of being caught by American aircraft, the Japanese broke off the attack. For one US cruiser sunk and one destroyer damaged the Japanese lost one light cruiser and one destroyer sunk, with another cruiser and two destroyers damaged.

As the defeated force entered Rabaul harbour at dawn on November 5 they were met by the sight of seven heavy (*Takao, Maya, Atago, Suzuya, Mogami, Chikuma* and *Chokai*) and one light (*Noshiro*) cruisers and several destroyers ready to renew the attack. When combined with the cruisers *Myoko* and *Haguaro* already in harbour the Japanese had a force capable of overwhelming the American cruisers. Admiral Halsey was aware of the Japanese presence and knew he did not have the forces available to protect the invasion fleet. He sent a flash message to Admiral Nimitz at Pearl Harbor and requested emergency help.

The only carriers close by were *Saratoga* and *Princeton* (CVL-23) of Task Force 38 commanded by Admiral Frederick Sherman. Both had provided air cover for the invasion. Nimitz coolly ordered both carriers to attack Rabaul. At the same time, Task Force 50.3, with the carriers *Essex, Bunker Hill* (CV-17) and *Independence* under the command of Rear Admiral Alfred E. Montgomery sortied from Pearl Harbor.

Up to this point in the war, no successful attack against a well-defended land target had been made by US carrier aircraft. Rabaul was a hornet's nest of defences with up to 300 aircraft which included 150 Zeros (a mix of A6M2 'Zekes' and A6M3 'Hamps') from the 1st Koku Sentai (Air Flotilla) (Zuikaku, Shokaku and Zuiho air groups) and the 11th Koku Kantai (Air Fleet) (2101st, 204th, 251st and 253rd Kokutais). In 1943 the highest priority was given to Rabaul's anti-aircraft defences. A total of 367 guns were assigned to its defence which included 118 heavy guns (75mm, 120mm and 120mm) 212 light guns (25-20mm) and 37 13.2mm heavy machine guns. Add the numerous AA guns from the warships in Simpson Harbor and Rabaul was one of the most heavily defended bases outside of Japan.

With little time to plan the attack (orders were received on November 4 to attack on the 5th) only one strike was put on. Racing at 27 knots, Task Force 38 turned into the wind 57 miles northwest of Cape Torokina at 0900 hours on November 5. Ninety-seven aircraft from both carriers rose to the attack: 52 F6F-3 Hellcats from *Saratoga's* VF-12 and *Princeton's* VF-23, 23 TBF-1C Avengers from both carriers and 22 SBD-5 Dauntlesses from *Saratoga's* VB-12. As the strike force headed for Rabaul, CAP over the carriers was provided by land-based F6F units VF-33, VF-38 and VF-40 from Vella Lavella and Barakoma.

At 50 miles out Rabaul came into view. With little hope of surprise the strike force was met by nearly 60-70 Zeros. Expecting the American formation to split before attacking, the Japanese missed their best opportunity to intercept. As the SBDs and TBFs held formation through the heavy AA fire, the Zeros were reluctant to follow. Instead they stood out of range, feinting attacks in the hope of drawing the Hellcats away from the bombers.

As the attack went in, the SBD and TBF pilots were greeted by the sight the Japanese fleet anchored and taking on fuel. Both shore based and AA guns afloat sent up a wall of flak for little effect. The *Maya* was hit by a single bomb. The *Atago* took three near misses with *Takao* and *Mogami* taking one bomb hit each. *Chikuma* was damaged by a near miss. Light cruisers *Agano* and *Noshiro* were also hit along with two destroyers, one hit by a dud torpedo.

It was only after the SBDs and TBFs had finished their runs that the Zeros pounced in earnest. Five SBDs were shot down by Zeros and AA fire with two F6F Hellcats shot down by ground fire and three lost in air-to-air combat. VF-12 and 23 claimed 21 victories between them with the TBFs and SBDs adding seven more. Actual Japanese losses totalled two Zeros, one D4Y1 'Judy' and one G4M1 'Betty'.

For the Japanese the battle was not over. An hour later, 27 B-24 Liberator heavy bombers and 58 P-38 Lightnings from the US Army Fifth Air Force added to the destruction. It was fine example of inter-service flexibility and cooperation and one the Japanese were never able to emulate.

For the Japanese the two strikes were a crippling blow. Five of their six cruisers were damaged, several severely. With back to back

ABOVE: Wake Island takes a pounding. After two days of strikes by Task Force 14, 61 enemy aircraft as well as barracks, shipping and airfield installations had been destroyed, October 1943. NARA

ABOVE: Two TBF-1 Avengers from *Coral Sea* (CVE-57) fly near Butaritari Island, Makin Atoll, as US landing craft approach the invasion beaches, November 20, 1943. NARA

defeats in just three days, the Japanese were forced to withdraw their warships to the relative safety of Truk, never to return.

With the combined efforts of Task Force 38 and the Fifth Air Force heavy bombers, a follow up strike on Rabaul was quickly put on to finish the job. After three days at sea Task Group 50.3 dropped anchor south of Guadalcanal on November 11. The next day the aircrews learned that they, along with Task Force 38, would make a second strike against Rabaul. At the time of the attack most of the heavy cruisers had left, returning to Truk or the Home Islands for repair. Only *Maya* remained along with several light cruisers and numerous destroyers.

Rabaul would now be attacked by three fleet and two light carriers, one of the largest fast carrier strikes of the war up to that point. It would also be the Curtiss SB2C-1 Helldiver's combat debut. The Navy's third operational F4U-1A Corsair squadron, VF-17, based in the Solomons would participate too. Ironically, in April 1943 the pilots of VF-17 became the first carrier qualified F4U unit in the fleet. By that time, however, the Navy was equipping all its carrier-based fighter units with the F6F Hellcat exclusively, leaving the Navy F4U units ground based.

At dawn on November 11, Task Force 38 turned into the wind. Operating under the cover of weather they launched a strike of 55 Hellcats, 25 Avengers and 21 Dauntlesses. When they arrived Simpson Harbour was almost completely covered in cloud and rain. Through the breaks in the clouds the bombers found three cruisers, hitting one. Seventy Zeros rose to intercept – chasing the bombers in and out of the clouds, shooting down two and damaging five more. The Hellcat pilots of VF-12 scored only one victory. Weather washed out a second strike and with aircraft recovered Task Force 38 retired to the south without being detected.

Positioned 165 miles southwest of Rabaul, *Essex*, *Bunker Hill* and *Independence* launched their strike at 0945 hours. The 185-aircraft strike force included 33 new SB2C-1s (each carrying four 500lb AP bombs) from VB-17 from *Bunker Hill*. Fully alerted the Japanese sent a dozen Zeros to intercept the first formations well before the target. The Zero pilots tried to lure the Hellcat escorts away from the bombers, but the Navy pilots stuck to their charges.

Once over the target, the *Essex* strike found Rabaul free of intercepting Zeros. The remaining Japanese warships were caught as they desperately tried to leave the harbour. As a barrage of bombs and torpedoes rained down 68 Zeros finally joined the fray. *Bunker Hill's* Air Group 17 followed *Essex's* strike. In the wild dogfights that followed the Hellcats of VF-6, VF-9, VF-18 and VF-22 claimed 30 Zeros shot down but in reality just 11 Zeros had gone down for the loss of nine US aircraft shot by fighters and flak – four Avengers and five Hellcats. Four Hellcats, two Helldivers and one Avenger returned to the carriers but were so badly damaged they ditched beside the carriers rather than landing on them.

While aircraft losses had been light on both sides, the Japanese navy suffered heavy losses.

Both the light cruiser *Agano* and destroyer *Naganmai* were hit by torpedoes. One bomb hit the destroyer *Suzunami* while it was loading torpedoes, causing a secondary explosion which shattered its hull. Three other ships were slightly damaged, including the heavy cruiser *Atago*.

As the strike aircraft did their work, air cover for the carriers of Task Force 50.3 was provided by the shore-based F4U-1A Corsairs of VF-17 'Jolly Rogers' and F6F-3 Hellcats of VF-33. During their patrols, both squadrons were allowed to bring their fighters aboard – VF-17 landing on *Essex* and *Bunker Hill*, with VF-33 refueling aboard *Independence*. Much to their delight, the ground-based aviators were treated to hot showers and lunch in the wardroom.

RIGHT: The pilot's view of the LSO. Here the LSO appears to be signalling 'cut'. "This is a mandatory signal. Pilot cuts throttle immediately. He takes his eyes off the signal officer for the first time and looks at the deck for alignment." NARA

BELOW: Landing a damaged aircraft onto a carrier (*Lexington* CV-16) was fraught with danger. Aircraft performance was unpredictable and the potential for disaster was great. Returning from the Wake strike a damaged Hellcat makes its final approach. The LSO on the right appears to be signalling to the Hellcat pilot that he's 'too high' or he's in the process of giving him the 'wave off'. US NAVAL HISTORICAL CENTER

As the carriers began launching a second strike, poor weather over the target scrubbed the follow up blow. Shortly after lunch *Essex's* radar plotted an in-coming raid. Hellcats from VF-33 were scrambled to investigate while the remaining Hellcats and Corsairs were made ready for take-off. Twenty minutes later the VF-33 Hellcat pilots reported the bogey only 40 miles from the task group. The bogey was in fact 67 Zeros, 27 Val dive-bombers, 14 Kate torpedo bombers and a handful of G4M1 'Betty' bombers. More fighters were scrambled. Twelve Hellcats of VF-33 and the 24 Corsairs from VF-17 intercepted the incoming raid. Fighter direction was the responsibility of the *Essex* and *Independence*, but as radio control over the fleet broke down mistakes were made. The first intercepts were against the Zeros and not the deadly Vals and Kates. Four divisions of fighters were vectored far from the battle only to find that the 'incoming bogies' were actually 12 Hellcats from the aborted second strike.

For the next three quarters of an hour the Corsairs of VF-17 and Hellcats of VF-33 had much of the early combat to themselves. The remaining Hellcats were rearmed, refuelled and scrambled as quickly as possible. Fighter direction over the fleet was quickly overloaded. Confused fighter pilots were either given the wrong vector instructions or unable to understand what they did hear. Most headed towards the bursting flak over the fleet. Others found themselves instantly engaged shortly after take-off.

BELOW: USS *Lexington* (CV-16) Aircraft return to the carrier during the Gilberts operation, November 1943. Crewmen in the foreground are sitting on the wing of an SBD-5, as a Hellcat lands and a TBF-1 taxies to a parking place on the forward flight deck. USN landing cycle time was about one plane every 20-50 seconds. Landing times could be higher depending on deck crew training and landing conditions.

The 'Vals' and 'Kates' that managed to evade the fighters found the American AA fire both accurate and deadly. Through skillful manoeuvring the carriers avoided all the bombs and torpedoes dropped.

The American fighter pilots and AA gunners claimed more than 90 Japanese aircraft shot down. Like the claims over Rabaul they were excessive, but the Japanese suffered a terrible defeat nevertheless with 17 'Vals', 14 'Kates' and four D4Y1 'Judys' shot down along with two Zeros. US losses amounted to two Hellcats shot down, two Corsairs ditched due to lack of fuel, one Helldiver on patrol that disappeared and one Avenger that was destroyed in an accident.

In the months that followed, Rabaul was relentlessly pounded by USAAF, Marine and Navy aircraft. In October 1943 when the Allied air offensive started, Rabaul had 300 aircraft. By mid-February 1944 all airworthy aircraft (89) departed for Truk leaving the Japanese waiting for an invasion that never came. In the end the air battles in the Southwest Pacific proved a graveyard for the IJNAF and its carrier air groups. While the carrier battles of 1942 accounted for over a quarter of its elite pool of aviators, they paled against the casualties in the Solomons. Between April 1942 and April 1943 the IJNAF lost 2,817 aircraft destroyed.

After the Rabaul raids, Task Force 50 was and organised into four task groups.

TASK GROUPS

★ **TASK GROUP 50.1** ★
Yorktown (CV-10)
Lexington (CV-16)
Cowpens (CVL-25)

★ **TASK GROUP 50.2** ★
Enterprise (CV-6)
Belleau Wood (CVL-24)
Monterey (CVL-26)

★ **TASK GROUP 50.3** ★
Essex (CV-9)
Bunker Hill (CV-17)
Independence (CVL-22)

★ **TASK GROUP 50.4** ★
Saratoga (CV-3)
Princeton (CVL-23)

After the Rabaul raids, the four groups of Task Force 50 were now assigned to the first operation in the Central Pacific – Operation Galvanic, the invasion of the Gilbert Islands. Located 1,500 miles east northeast of Rabaul and 2,400 miles southwest of Hawaii, the Gilberts are a string of islands stretching some 500 miles. The targets for the invasion were the Makin and Tarawa Atolls.

To protect the landing force and prevent Japanese reinforcements from arriving, the carrier task groups were deployed over a wide area. They were also joined by eight escort carriers which provided CAP, ASW and ground support for the Marines.

D-Day for Tarawa was set for November 20. Task Group 50.1 – *Yorktown*, *Lexington* and *Cowpens* – was given the most important combat assignment. Positioned between the Gilberts and Marshalls, its job was to intercept any Japanese attacks while mounting strikes against airfields in the Marshalls. With no aerial opposition the three carriers launched strikes against Jaluit and Mille, two of the largest airfield in the eastern Marshalls on November 19. Strafing Hellcats and glide bombing Avengers left the airfields smoking wrecks. Task Group 50.2 – *Enterprise*, *Belleau Wood* and *Monterey* – formed the Northern Group striking Makin and the Marshalls while Task Group 50.3 – *Essex*, *Bunker Hill* and *Independence* – formed the Southern Group around Tarawa.

At Truk, the Japanese Combined Fleet under the command of Admiral Kogo reacted to the invasion with what little they had. The sustained naval and air losses in the defence of Rabaul robbed them of any real offensive power. Just 16 G4M1 'Betty' bombers were launched for a dusk attack. As they approached *Bunker Hill's* VF-18 CAP was vectored to intercept. Six bombers were quickly shot down, with AA gunners accounting for three more, but not before they dropped their Type 91 torpedoes. One found its mark, hitting *Independence* in her stern. After emergency repairs, *Independence* steamed to Funafuti for more repairs before sailing to Mare Island Navy Yard in San Francisco.

The Japanese knew attacking the American carrier task groups in daylight was questionable. More and more they turned to dusk and night attacks. Through the night of November 20-21, a number of nocturnal attacks were launched. One 'Betty' was shot down shortly before dawn by a VF-2 Hellcat from *Enterprise*. To combat these nocturnal raiders, and prior to Galvanic, a carrier-based night-fighter system had been developed.

ABOVE: Preparation for the Rabaul attack was meticulous. Here two intelligence officers build a relief map of Rabaul's Simpson Harbor, New Britain, for training naval aviators prior to the attack. US NAVAL HISTORICAL CENTER

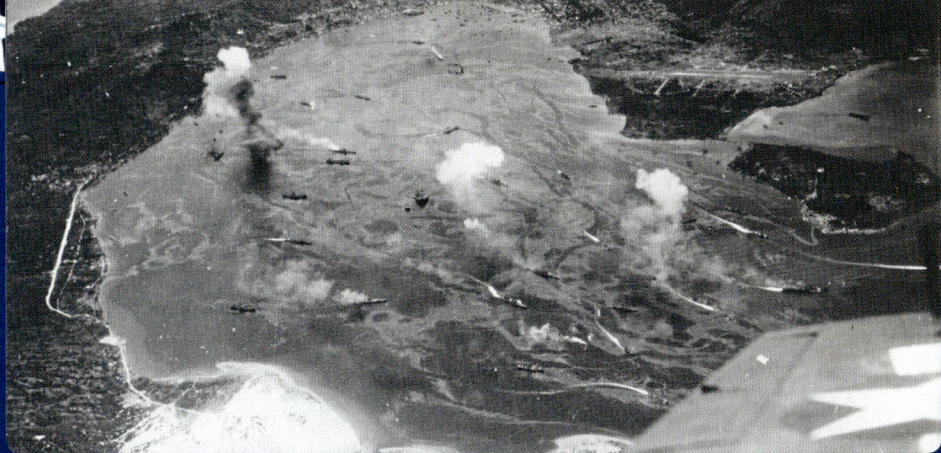

ABOVE: Carrier strike on Rabaul, November 5, 1943. Japanese ships under carrier plane attack in Simpson Harbor. On the left the cruiser *Maya* is hit causing a big fire. Several other cruisers are among the ships heading for sea, to the right. NARA

ABOVE: Following the Rabaul carrier strike of November 11, 1943 the Japanese struck back. Here a Japanese bomber explodes on the water just astern of *Essex* (CV-9), after being shot down by anti-aircraft fire. *Independence* (CVL-22) can be seen just to the right. NARA

ABOVE: Rabaul's harbour and airfields bristled with both heavy and light anti-aircraft guns, the most numerous being the Type 96 25mm gun in single, double and triple mounts. The Type 96 suffered many deficiencies. Its small fifteen-round magazine required frequent reloading, reducing its overall rate of fire. NARA

'Butch' O'Hare, commander of Enterprise's Air Group Six, had organized and trained what were called 'bat teams'. These were three-aircraft formations with two Hellcats and one TBF Avenger equipped with radar to find airborne targets. Working in conjunction with shipboard fighter directors, the radar-equipped Avenger would be vectored towards an incoming bogey. When in radar range the Avenger would lead the Hellcats into a position for a visual identification. At that point the Hellcats would close the distance and shoot the bomber down.

The Navy's first night-fighter kill was actually achieved by an Avenger but ended in tragedy. Just after sunset on November 26, O'Hare and Ens Warren Skon (seven victories) were teamed with Lt Cdr John Phillips, skipper of VT-6 flying his Avenger. Fifteen 'Bettys' were reported inbound. After launch the two Hellcats had trouble finding the Avenger. The FDO also had trouble guiding the Avenger towards the incoming raid. Finally, O'Hare and Skon found the Avenger, but were positioned behind the aircraft. After 30 minutes, Phillips and his radar operator found two 'Bettys' but the Hellcats couldn't make visual contact. Not wanting to miss the opportunity, Phillips shot down both bombers using his wing mounted .50cal machine guns.

As more 'Bettys' appeared, Phillips called for a rendezvous to reorganize and renew the attack. As they moved into attack positions a brief, but confusing nocturnal shout-out broke out. The TBF gunner and one or more of the 'Bettys' exchanged fire with O'Hare being caught in the crossfire. The best evidence has O'Hare between the TBF and one of the 'Bettys' as he was hit by

BELOW: SBD-5s from Task Force 38 – *Saratoga* and *Princeton* – head towards Rabaul on November 5, 1943.

machine gun fire from a 'Betty' above and behind him. Seconds later he slid out of formation, vanishing into the dark. On November 29, the Navy's first and most famous ace was listed missing in action.

The 'bat team' was not the operational answer to nocturnal raiders. Two months later the more effective purpose-built radar equipped F4U-2 Corsair night-fighters of VF(N)-1 became operational on *Enterprise*.

The nocturnal raiders, while small in number, were a serious threat to the carrier groups. The 'bat teams' couldn't stop every raider, so to neutralise the threat Task Groups 50.1 and 50.2 were ordered to strike the Japanese bases on Kwajalein. Rendezvousing on December 1, Task Force 50, commanded by Admiral Pownall planned for a dawn attack on December 4. Steaming at full speed and undetected the six carriers began launching their strikes at 0630 hours. Thirty minutes later 250 fighters and bombers were heading towards their target. There they found 30 ships in the lagoon, including two cruisers.

Once again, the Japanese were taken by surprise. The small number of Zeros that did get airborne were quickly dispatched. Next in were the SBDs armed with 1,000lb bombs, taking aim at the vessels in the lagoon. This was followed by the TBFs, some armed with 2,000lb 'block busters'. As the bombers went in, the Hellcats strafed the seaplanes and parked aircraft on the airstrip. The Hellcat pilots from VF-2 were credited with four Kawanishi H8K 'Emily' flying boats and 11 A6M2-N 'Rufe' floatplane fighters destroyed.

In the lagoon the SBDs and TBFs sank three freighters and damaged four more. As the strike force departed four VF-5 Hellcats from *Yorktown* were attacked by 20 Zeros. The enemy pilots were good, but their gunnery skills were lacking. Two F6Fs were shot down, with one pilot bailing out and being picked up by a destroyer. The aircraft action report summarised: "Why they didn't shoot us all down is a mystery. We would have destroyed them if the situation had been reversed. The one thing we did learn was that they weren't as good gunners as we are."

In the dogfights over the atoll that day Hellcats claimed a total of 28 Zeros for three F6Fs. At the conclusion of the strikes, Hellcat pilot Lieutenant Commander Edgar Stebbins, spotted close to 60 'Betty' bombers untouched on an airfield on Roi. He quickly radioed for second strike but was overruled by Admiral Pownall. It was a mistake.

By noon the Japanese responded with a formation of 15 'Kate' torpedo bombers. Seven were shot down by the CAP and anti-aircraft fire and no torpedoes found their mark. Flying low under the radar, another formation of 'Kates' arrived. Intercepted by the CAP, four still managed to attack *Yorktown* with no hits and four were shot down by its AA gunners.

At 1300 hours the planned Wotje island strike was launched. As the carriers headed north, the strike force inflicted heavy losses on the Japanese: three transports sunk, one cruiser damaged and approximately 40 aircraft destroyed.

At 1945 hours the first of 37 'Betty' bombers left behind at Roi were spotted on radar. Now, under a full moon, wave after wave of enemy aircraft dropped flares and launched torpedoes. *Essex* reported the attack as, "the longest sustained night torpedo attack of the war to date". For seven-and-a-half hours the 'Bettys' pressed the attack. Anti-aircraft fire was intense and accurate. *Yorktown's* AA cruiser escort *Oakland* (CLAA-95) shot down no fewer than 12 'Bettys' in 30 minutes.

At 2237 hours the fleet's luck ran out. After manoeuvring at high speed and sending up walls of anti-aircraft fire a torpedo hit *Lexington* in the stern – jamming its rudder. By midnight damage control parties had rigged up a temporary steering mechanism. Steaming at 20kts, *Lexington* left the area headed for Pearl Harbor.

For the Japanese the last four months of 1943

ABOVE: Target approach photo of Kwajalein, December 1943 prior to the December 4 raid. USN aircrew were supplied with the best intelligence available. Aerial reconnaissance was essential prior to any attack. NARA

ABOVE: Target approach photo of Kwajalein, December 1943 prior to the December 4 raid. USN aircrew were supplied with the best intelligence available. Aerial reconnaissance was essential prior to any attack. NARA

ABOVE: In this dramatic photo a Japanese Nakajima B6N2 'Jill' has its tail blown off by a 5in shell during the Gilbert Island assault, December 4, 1943. US NAVAL HISTORICAL CENTER

LEFT: Catching the wire didn't necessarily mean a safe landing. This F6F-3 has its tail ripped off after a hard landing aboard *Belleau Wood*, August 1943. The aircraft plunged over the side, killing the pilot. Life as a carrier pilot was challenging and unforgiving. The smallest error could result in disaster. NARA

had been a disaster. American carriers had operated with impunity, surprising the Japanese and attacking at will. Even when the Japanese were alerted and able to intercept incoming strikes with 50 or 60 Zeros, the results were dismal. While equipped with air-search radar, the Japanese had no fighter direction in place to guide their formations to the right height and place to intercept.

Once they were airborne the pilots were on their own, relying on their eyeballs to detect an incoming strike. The numbers tell a sobering story. During four carrier strikes and the invasion of the Gilberts, carrier-borne and ground-based Hellcats accounted for nearly 230 Japanese shot down for a loss of fewer than 30.

The Americans wouldn't leave unscathed, however. While Japanese airpower was largely ineffective, its submarine force was still active and dangerous. On November 24, the escort carrier USS *Liscome Bay* (CVE-56) was torpedoed by Japanese submarine I-175. Fifty three officers and 591 enlisted men went down with the ship. ∎

BELOW: A Hellcat from VF-12 is signalled for take-off aboard Saratoga (CV-30) during the Rabaul raid on November 5, 1943. NARA

CHAPTER 5

OPERATION HAILSTONE

The Truk Lagoon raid and how it revolutionised naval air warfare 1944

ABOVE: With flaps down a VF-9 F6F-3 Hellcat is given the signal for takeoff from *Essex* (CV-9) on the first day of operations against Truk February 17, 1943. US NAVAL HISTORICAL CENTER

"It was our superior pilots and superior tactics [that] gave us victory over the Japs. Sometimes they just kept coming at us and they must know they will be knocked down."

Hellcat pilot Herb Houck

On January 10, 1944 the brand-new carrier USS *Intrepid* (CV-11) arrived at Pearl Harbor. Rear Admiral Marc A. Mitscher boarded Yorktown on the 13th and took command of the newly formed Task Force 58 (TF-58). It was an impressive force consisting of six fleet carriers: *Intrepid, Enterprise, Yorktown, Essex, Bunker Hill* and *Saratoga* and five light carriers: *Belleau Wood, Cabot, Monterey, Princeton* and *Cowpens*, embarking more than 500 Hellcats, Dauntlesses, Helldivers, and Avengers. The carriers were also equipped with night-bombing Avengers and F6F-3N and F4U-2 night-fighters.

Supporting the carriers were an additional eight escort carriers, seven new battleships, six cruisers and 36 destroyers, plus fleet tankers and associated service vessels. All told the combined fleet, light and escort carriers could launch more than 750 combat aircraft. The new Pacific Fleet was now far stronger than it had ever been. So strong in fact, that the earlier carrier strategy of hit and run raids used in the autumn of 1943 and the Gilberts campaign no longer applied. Individual task groups could now position themselves off any enemy base and maintain air and naval superiority for as long as required.

With the Gilberts once again in American hands, the next target in the US Navy's campaign in the Central Pacific was the Marshall Island chain. With the loss of the Solomons and the irreparable damage done to Rabaul the Japanese knew their continued presence in New Guinea was just a matter of time. For the Japanese high command, the Marshalls now became expendable, but not before they were reinforced. By January 1944, 28,000 troops had been assigned to defend the Marshalls.

The invasion was code named Operation Flintlock. On January 28, TF-58 arrived and began bombarding the string of atolls and the islands Kwajalein, Jaluit, Wotje and Maloelap. Kwajalein was invaded on January 31 and by February 3 was declared secured.

The taking of Kwajalein, Eniwetok and Majuro

ABOVE: The model A6M5 Model 52 was designed to simplify and speed up production and increase its diving speed. Heavy-gauge wing skinning was added, and the exhaust collector ring was replaced with straight individual stacks. Maximum speed reached 351mph at 19,000ft. AUTHOR'S COLLECTION

atolls transformed fast carrier operations in the Pacific. With TF-58 based out of Pearl Harbor, the travel time to and from a target meant offensive operations were limited to approximately one strike a month. By the end of February, all three lagoons were ready to support new offensive operations. With fuel and supplies closer to the front, several strikes a month could be mounted at multiple targets.

To maintain offensive momentum and with the quick success of Flintlock, Admiral Nimitz decided to accelerate the invasion of Eniwetok Atoll. Eniwetok was crucial as a staging base for the planned advance into the Carolinas and Mariana islands. To ensure success, the major base at Truk had to be suppressed and prevented from interfering with the Eniwetok operation.

In July 1942, the Japanese Combined Fleet headquarters was based at Truk and was a major staging area for war material destined for the south Pacific. It was also a vital base for replacement aircraft assigned to Rabaul.

For the Americans Truk was considered the 'Gibraltar of the Pacific' shrouded in mystery. Many thought the base impregnable and for the first two years of the war there was little or no intelligence available on it. On February 4, 1944 two Marine PB4Y-1 Liberators of VMD-254 flew a photo-reconnaissance mission 850 miles from Bougainville. Intelligence officers began the process of mapping out the base and the various anchorages in the lagoon. The planning for Operation Hailstone had begun.

Once the Marine planes left, Admiral Mineichi Koga – commander of the Combined Fleet, knew the Americans would return. Koga ordered the fleet to withdraw to Palau, leaving two light cruisers, eight destroyers, a number of auxiliaries and a large number of transports. In terms of air defence, Truk was not as robust as Rabaul. Just 40 heavy and light AA guns protected the base and with the small number of warships in harbour, the number of barrels available was small. But there was no shortage of aircraft. A few days before the American attack a large number of new A6M5 Model 52 Zeros were flown in, some bound as reinforcements for Rabaul. In addition there were approximately 64 Zeros from the 201st, 204th, 251st, 501st and 902nd Kokutais ready for combat. Some published sources put the number of Zeros available at 161. For offensive operations the IJNAF had another 180 aircraft of various types with approximately 100 operational 'Betty', 'Kate' and 'Jill' bombers.

ABOVE: Truk was not as heavily defended by AA guns as was Rabaul. The Japanese Army Type 98 20mm gun was one of the types used to defend the base. With a rate of fire of 120 rounds per minute, the Type 98 proved to be a hard-hitting weapon. NARA

ABOVE: The Japanese had numerous Type 93 13.2mm twin AA guns both on ships and on the ground. Limited in its effectiveness and range, it could only engage very low flying aircraft. NARA

CARRIER STRIKE 61

IJNAF UNITS ON TRUK

★ 4TH KONKYOCHITAI (NAVAL BASE FORCE)
902nd Kokutai: 25 Aichi E13A Navy Type 0 'Jake' Seaplane. Unknown number of Nakajima A6M2-N Navy Type 2 'Rufe' Seaplane Fighters and Mitsubishi F1M Navy Type 0 'Pete' seaplanes.

★ 22ND KOKU SENTAI (AIR FLOTILLA)
755th Kokutai: 8 Mitsubishi G4M Navy Type 1 'Betty' bombers
552nd Kokutai: 15 Nakajima B5N2 Navy Type 97-3 'Kate' torpedo bombers

★ 26TH KOKU SENTAI
204th Kokutai: 31 Mitsubishi A6M3 'Zero' fighters
201st Kokutai: 8 Mitsubishi A6M3 'Zero' fighters
501st Kokutai: 25 Mitsubishi A6M3 'Zero' fighters
251st Kokutai: 9 Nakajima J1N1-S 'Irving' night-fighter
582nd Kokutai: 10 Nakajima B6N1 'Jill' torpedo bomber
(Zeros consisted of a mix of A6M3-Model 22, Model 32, and an unknown number of A6M5-Model 52s flown in prior to the attack)

★ 23RD KOKU SENTAI
753rd Kokutai: 10 Mitsubishi G4M Navy Type 1 'Betty' bombers

★ 28TH KOKU SENTAI
551st Kokutai: 14 Nakajima B6N1 'Jill' torpedo bombers

By January 1944, the power of the US Navy's Fast Carrier Task Force was truly impressive. For the attack on Truk, Task Force 58 assigned three of its Task Groups to the operation. Task Group 58.4 with the carriers Saratoga, Princeton and Langley were assigned to support Operation Flintlock, the landings on Eniwetok.

TASK FORCE 58

★ TASK GROUP 58.1

Enterprise/Air Group Ten
VF-10: 32 F6F-3 Hellcats
VB-10: 30 SBD-5 Dauntlesses
VT-10: 18 TBF-1 Avengers
VF(N)-101: 4 F4U-2 Corsair Night-fighters

Yorktown/Air Group Five
VF-5: 36 F6F-3 Hellcats
VB-5: 36 SBD-5 Dauntlesses
VT-5: 18 TBF-1 Avengers

Belleau Wood/Air Group 24
VF-24: 26 F6F-3 Hellcats
VF-6: 12 F6F-3 Hellcats
VC-22B: 8 TBF-1 Avengers

★ TASK GROUP 58.2

Essex/Air Group Nine
VF-9: 36 F6F-3 Hellcats
VB-9: 36 SBD-5 Dauntlesses
VT-9: 17 TBF-1, 2 TBM-1 Avengers

Intrepid/ Air Group Six
VF-6: 36 F6F-3 Hellcats

VB-6: 36 SBD-5 Dauntlesses
VT-6: 14 TBF-1, 5 TBM-1 Avengers
VF(N)101: 4 F4U-2 Corsair Night Fighters

Cabot/Air Group 31
VF-31: 26 F6F-3 Hellcats
VT-31: 8 TBM-1, 1 TGB-1 Avengers

★ TASK GROUP 58.3

Bunker Hill/Air Group 17
VF-18: 37 F6F-3 Hellcats
VB-17: 31 SB2C-1 Helldivers
VT-17: 19 TBF-1, 1 TBM-1 Avengers
VF(N)-76: 4 F6F-3N Hellcat Night Fighters

Monterey/Air Group 30
VF-30: 25 F6F-3 Hellcats
VT-30: 5 TBF-1, 4 TBM-1 Avengers

Cowpens/Air Group 25
VF-25: 24 F6F-3 Hellcats
VT-25: 9 TBF-1 Avengers

In terms quantity and quality, the Navy Air Groups had the clear advantage. By this time most of the VF Hellcat squadrons had combat experience, many with aces. The air battles in the autumn of 1943 had proven the Hellcat as the superior fighter. When matched with well-trained pilots and the tactics devised to combat the Zero, the Hellcat was a killer. While most agreed the Zero was the superior fighter at slow speeds (200mph), able to turn inside the Hellcat, it lost that edge at higher speeds. The Hellcat was faster in level flight and in a dive. It could also out climb the Zero at low and medium altitudes. It was also far more rugged. Even when caught in the sights of a Zero its chances of survival were good. The Zero's armament of two 7.7mm machine guns and two slow firing 20mm cannon meant an accurate two or three second burst produced too few rounds to be effective. The Aircraft Action Report for VF-16 dated December 4, 1943 revealed the stark differences between the two fighters, "as far as armament, armour and general ruggedness of the airplanes were concerned, the F6F again shows itself immeasurably superior to the Zero".

Japanese ace Saburo Sakai said after the war: "Our 20mm cannon were big, heavy and slow firing. It was extremely hard to hit a moving target. Shooting down an enemy aircraft was like hitting a dragonfly with a rifle! It was never easy to score... our opponents were tough."

For Zero pilots to have any hope of success they needed the element of surprise, approaching unseen and firing at close range. However, the quality of Japanese pilot training by 1944 was poor with the vast majority receiving little if any aerial gunnery training. Their flying skills were also vastly inferior. An Aircraft Action Report from VF-9 dated February 26, 1944 confirmed, once again, the sorry state of Japanese fighter ability: "Zeke still very vulnerable to our fire from F6F-3 when hit in area of wing roots or engine. Enemy VF pilots encountered in this action seemed to be outstandingly stupid and poorly trained in VF tactics.

"Evasive manoeuvres on part of Zeke pilots almost nil. One Zeke pilot attempted to slug it out with an F6F by making head on run. Zeke came out second best."

Hellcat tactics were simple. Dive, shoot and climb back to altitude. It was extremely hard for the Zero pilots to counter. At this point in the war American fighter pilots discovered that the less manoeuvring you did while in combat the better your chances of success and survival. Using speed and the height advantage were key.

Hellcat units were continually revising their tactics. For the Truk raid, Admiral Mitscher borrowed a fighter technique used by the Luftwaffe during the Battle of Britain in 1940. Instead of flying close escort for the bombers, German Bf 109 fighters flew ahead of the formations in sweeps or 'Freie Jagd' (free hunt) ranging far ahead, clearing a path for the bombers. The Truk strike would begin with a dawn fighter sweep of 70 Hellcats.

In terms of air defence and intercepting tactics the IJNAF failed to counter US Navy methods. Instead of adopting the 'fighter four' and fighting pair method of combat, Japanese squadrons continued to use the three aircraft shotai as their standard tactical formation. This loose formation consisted of the shotai leader and two wingmen flying behind at different altitudes. When attacking, the shotai leader would signal for individual passes in line astern or line abreast. The practice of trading altitude for speed was a universal maxim in aerial combat. While Japanese pilots were taught to exploit the turning capability of their fighters, they also sought the altitude advantage; diving on an enemy, firing a quick burst and pulling out below the target.

Compounding the Zero's inability to effectively intercept incoming raids was the complete lack of radio communications both air-to-air and air-to-ground. Japanese radios were badly designed and broke down at a very high rate. By 1944 the harsh field conditions and lack of spare parts made the failure rate so high that Zero pilots simply removed them to save weight. With no way to communicate between formations, the Japanese found themselves at a major tactical disadvantage.

Just before dawn on February 16, 1944 Task Force 58 turned into the wind. Ninety miles east of Truk the first Hellcats began their short take-off runs into the clear, cool morning air of the Pacific. Seventy-two Hellcats would be launched with each VF squadron assigned to a specific altitude.

From top to bottom, 22 Hellcats from VF-18 were assigned top cover at 25,000ft, 12 Hellcats from VF-6 and 11 from VF-9 covered the medium altitudes and low-level was assigned to the 12 Hellcats from VF-10 and 12 from VF-5.

The Hellcats of the four light carriers, *Belleau Wood*, *Cowpens*, *Monterrey* and *Cabot*, provided CAP for the fleet and acted as a reserve. This would become standard practice and a source of frustration for the CVL pilots who resented not being assigned to the juicer missions with a chance to score.

Japanese radar picked up the incoming raid about 30 minutes out. Fortunately for the Americans, the Japanese order to scramble was delayed and not all the defending fighters got off in time. As dawn's light brightened over Truk the biggest air battle of the Pacific War up to that time began. At 0800 hours Lieutenant-Commander William Kane, Air Group 10 commander and flight leader of the sweep arrived over Moen island. Arriving at 8,000ft Kane and the Hellcats of VF-10 spotted a large number of Zeros clawing for altitude. As they fell on the Japanese formation of 40-50 Zeros a wild dogfight broke out. In a matter of seconds Zeros began falling out of the sky in twos and threes. Four Zeros attempted a poorly executed pass against Kane and his wingman, Lt Vernon Ude, and each shot one down. In less than five minutes, Kane and Ude had downed five Zeros. All told, the pilots of VF-10 claimed 14 aircraft shot down with five more destroyed on the ground while expending "19,800" rounds of .50cal ammunition.

The squadron's Aircraft Action Report No 9-44 revealed insights into their success: "Comparative Performance, Own and Enemy Aircraft. Zekes burned quickly indicating unprotected tanks. F6F can manoeuvre with Zeke for a short time but will eventually be out manoeuvred if Zeke has experienced pilot. F6F has more speed and can dive away. Zekes encountered at Truk seemed to have no armour for pilot.

"Rufe is very manoeuvrable for float plane but slightly slower than Zeke. One pilot found Rufe out climbing and out turning F6F. Rufe burned like Zeke after good burst from .50cal. guns, indicating unprotected tanks. No comparative performance on Tojo as two shot down were taking off when encountered and both burst into flames and crashed. No indication of protected tanks."

ABOVE: Eten Island was struck many times during the raid. Seen here on the first day of strikes the damage is extensive. Dublon Island and town is in the middle background, with several merchant ships offshore, and one large tanker tied to the fuel pier in left centre. US NAVAL HISTORICAL CENTER

ABOVE: Captured B5N2 'Kate' equipped the Type H6 airborne radar. The antennae can clearly be seen along the rear fuselage and leading edge of the wing. This airframe and radar went under 35.9 hours of test and evaluation at NAS Anacostia, starting in November 1944. NARA

BELOW: Japanese shipping under air attack in Truk Lagoon on the first day of raids, February 17, 1944. Dublon Island is at left, with Moen Island in the background. Four ships appear to have been hit by this time. US NAVAL HISTORICAL CENTER

ABOVE: Eten Island Airfield, Truk, photographed from a *Yorktown* (CV-10) plane February 17, 1944. A large number of Japanese planes can be seen on the field, and numerous bomb craters are evident, but the field looks to be operational. Dublon Island is in the background, at top.
US NAVAL HISTORICAL CENTER

As the dogfights swirled above them the pilots of VF-5 headed for the seaplane base at Dublon. With four Hellcats as top cover the strafing began. Five flying boats were claimed destroyed – three Kawanishi H6Ks 'Mavis' and two Kawanishi H8Ks 'Emily'. After their runs they joined the melee above claiming three Zeros, three 'Rufes' and a single 'Pete' for the loss one Hellcat to AA fire.

The Hellcats of VF-6 and VF-9 went in next. Fifteen minutes before they reached the lagoon they began their climb from 1,000ft to 14,000ft. As the two squadrons headed to the Moen Island airfield they could see the Hellcats of VF-5 and VF-10 below. Ten aircraft from VF-6 spiralled down to begin their strafing runs and just as they did Lt Alexander Vraciu and his wingman Ens Louis Little caught sight of a number of Zeros 2,500ft above them.

As the Japanese fighters came down, Vraciu and Little turned into the attack, forcing the formation leader to break off. Reacting quickly Vraciu dispatched two Zeros and a Rufe with Little adding a Zero. Seconds later Vraciu spotted a Zero heading into a cloud: "I noticed one Zero skirting in and out of clouds and as I made a pass at him, he promptly ducked back into them. I played cat and mouse with him for several minutes until I climbed into the sun to let him think I had retreated. When I came down on him for the last time, he never knew what hit him as his wing tanks and cockpit exploded. I ended up splashing four Zeros that day to bring my total aerial victories up to nine kills. Little did I know that within in six months I would more than double that score."

The strafing runs proved extremely destructive with VF-6 claiming 24 aircraft destroyed on the ground, 11 in the air for the loss of one pilot due to AA fire.

The most successful squadron of the day belonged to the pilots of VF-9. Assigned as top cover for the strafing Hellcats below, the three divisions (four aircraft per division) fought separate battles. As each division arrived over the target separately the squadron's third division was the first to be attacked. As tracers flashed past their canopies, Lts Charles Moutenot, Bill Bonneau and Eugene Valencia were forced to break hard. With Zeros all around each was caught up in their own dogfight. Moutenot dispatched one Zero with Bonneau splashing one Zero and three 'Rufes'.

Forced to dive from 14,000ft to low over the water, Valencia found himself boxed in by six to eight Zeros, firing at him continuously. Fortunately, their marksmanship was extremely poor. Taking the initiative, Valencia racked his big Hellcat around and made a head-on attack, shooting down one Zero. Hauling his fighter into a tight turn, he shot down two more. The other three dove away.

At the same time, VF-9's second division found itself tangled in a series of twisting dogfights lasting 30 minutes. Several formations of Zeros pounced on the division, forcing the formation into violent evasive manoeuvres. The Japanese pilots did a good job of breaking up the division, first into sections and then into individual Hellcats. The fighting was so intense that Lt H. A. Schiebler was shot down, most likely by another Hellcat.

For Lt Cdr Ed Owens of VF-5 the intense, confusing battle left a lasting impression: "We arrived over the target area with every advantage that could be desired: at dawn, in tactical formation and with the enemy caught by surprise with his aircraft on the ground.

"As we started to strafe airfield, quite a melee developed as the Japs began getting into the air. Actually, there were so many Japs aeroplanes moving that it was almost confusing to select a target and stay with it until it was shot down, without being lured to another target just taking-off, or apparently attempting to join up in some kind of formation.

"After a few minutes it was difficult to find uncluttered airspace. Japanese aircraft were burning and falling from every quarter, and many were crashing on take-off as a result of strafing. Ground installations were exploding and burning, and all this in the early golden glow of dawn. I guess it prompted me to recall it as a 'Hollywood movie'. At times it all looked like it might have been staged for the movies."

As FV-9's second and third division battled it out, the commander of VF-9, Lt Cdr Herbert Houck and his first division remained untouched. As the other Hellcat squadrons dealt with the intercepting Japanese fighters, Herbert turned his division for a strafing attack on Moen airfield and seaplane base. After five accurate runs, the four fighters destroyed 10-12 aircraft before setting their sights on the Parem island airfield. There they added another 15 aircraft destroyed in five strafing runs.

To add insult to injury the VF-9 pilots caught several aircraft taking-off and promptly shot them down. Houck claimed a 'Pete' taking off from Moen seaplane base and a 'Kate' over Parem. Lt Louis Menard would add two more 'Petes' over Moen and two 'Kates' over Parem.

Multiple victories were the order of the day. VF-9 led the way claiming 36 confirmed air-to-air victories and another 25-27 destroyed on the ground. Over claiming on both sides was not uncommon and in the confusion of combat it was easy to be over optimistic. In any case

64 CARRIER STRIKE

the damage inflicted by the Hellcats alone was considerable. By 1400 hours they had claimed 204 destroyed in the air and on the ground with 130 being air-to-air kills. Postwar Japanese records, however, confirmed 70 shot down. The Hellcat pilots had accomplished their mission and much more. By early afternoon they owned the sky over Truk and the destruction they had inflicted was considerable.

THE MIGHTY BROWNING

Armed with just six AN/M2 Browning .50cal machine guns the Hellcat pilots had cleared the skies of Japanese fighters and destroyed more on the ground. The reasons for their success were many and varied.

The Browning AN/M2 was a proven, reliable hard-hitting machine gun. Each Hellcat carried 400 rounds per gun (2,400 total). At a rate of fire of 600 rounds per minute the six-gun battery gave the Hellcat pilot approximately 30 seconds of firing time. The M2 fired a cartridge (ball, armour piercing, armour piercing incendiary) with a higher velocity than the 20mm round of the Zero's Type 99 20mm cannon, giving it long range and good penetrative power.

The lightweight construction of the Japanese naval aircraft, their lack of armour plate and self-sealing fuel tanks, and poor pilot training made them easy targets for the Hellcat pilots. A short accurate two or three second burst was usually all it took to down a Zero. This meant Hellcat pilots with their ample ammunition load were able to achieve multiple kills in a single mission. The Hellcat was also a steady gun platform giving the well-trained Hellcat pilots the best chance for success. The F6F Hellcat and its armament of six M2 Browning .50cal machine guns proved itself capable of dominating almost any tactical situation. While its top speed was not as high as the F4U-1 Corsair (386mph compared to 417mph) its speed, rate of climb and diving speed enabled the Hellcat to engage and disengage combat almost at will. Its heavy armament and rugged construction, combined with proven tactics, deprived the more manoeuvrable Japanese fighters of their inherent advantage.

BOMB RUN

As the Hellcats tangled with Japanese fighters from sea level on up to 12,000ft the first strikes against shipping and the airfields began. Commencing at 0443 hours the carriers began 15 minute staggered launches, resulting in a continuous stream of strike aircraft over Truk. The SBDs, TBFs and SB2Cs from the three Task Groups were loaded with a mix of 500lb, 1,000lb and 2,000lb general purpose bombs, M26 fragmentation cluster bombs, incendiary bombs and Mk 13 torpedoes. The bombers from Air Group Ten from *Enterprise* and Air Group Five from *Yorktown* were the first to bomb. They were followed by Air Group Nine from *Essex* and Air Group Six from *Intrepid* with Air Group 17 from Bunker Hill being the last in.

While the majority of the dive-bombers and the torpedo armed Avengers went after shipping, seven TBF Avengers from VT-10 attacked Eten airfield, dropping a mix of fragmentation and incendiary clusters. This was followed by strafing runs. Fifteen minutes later the destruction continued with the arrival of nine TBFs from VT-6. Their target was the Moen seaplane base resulting in one 'Mavis' and 13 'Rufes' destroyed.

In the harbour, high winds hampered the bombers, but many hits were recorded. None of the ships sank outright, but a large number were left smoking and on fire. Japanese AA fire would account for one SBD from VB-6 and one SB2C from VB-17.

Even with the successful morning fighter sweep, several formations of Zeros attempted to intercept the bombers. The escorting Hellcats of VF-6 and VF-10 were quick to pounce. Lt Walter Harmon from V-10 was credited with three Zeros and a single 'Rufe'. Other VF-10 pilots claimed five more destroyed with VF-6 adding another three.

At one hour and 15 minutes later the second bomber strike of the day went in. Coming

ABOVE: A Grumman Avenger flies over the Japanese destroyer *Akikaze* after a strafing run. The vessel's wake clearly indicates evasive manoeuvring while under attack. NARA

BELOW: Japanese ammunition ship explodes following a dive-bombing attack by a US plane. The aircraft that dropped the bomb was caught in the blast and didn't survive. Dublon Island is at right and Eten Island Airfield is in the middle distance. Facilities on both are on fire. US NAVAL HISTORICAL CENTER

ABOVE and RIGHT: These three photos show the desperate manoeuvres by the Japanese destroyer *Maikaze* to avoid a torpedo attack on the morning of February 17. The second photo clearly shows a torpedo's wake as it races toward the ship for the fatal blow. The *Maikaze* sank with all hands. NARA

in at 15-minute intervals the Air Groups this time focused on the ships in the lagoon. As the light cruiser *Katori* and destroyer *Maikaze* tried to make their escape the TBFs of VT-10 scored single torpedo hits on both ships. The Dauntlesses of VB-10, armed with 1,000lb bombs, scored two hits on the 19,200-ton converted whaling ship, blowing off the stern and leaving it to sink. One SBD was shot down to AA fire.

Japanese fighter resistance remained persistent and dangerous. From the damaged airfields more Zeros rose to the attack. As the second division SBDs from VB-10 went in they were met by four Zeros and a 'Rufe'. The rear gunners made their shots count, claiming one Zero and another damaged before making their escape.

A division of Hellcats of VF-10 ran into a determined formation of Zeros. In a battle that lasted 20 minutes the four pilots battled six Zeros. Three Zeros opened the attack with a head on pass. Three more then joined the fray. After downing two Zeros and damaging three, all of the Hellcats returned to *Enterprise*, albeit shot up and lucky to be alive.

Air Group Nine and Air Group Six from *Essex* and *Intrepid* added to the destruction. Air Group Nine consisted of nine TBFs from VT-9, 12 SBDs from VB-9 and an escort of 14 VF-9 Hellcats. Air Group Six added the same number from VF-6, VB-6 and VT-6. This strike package was led by Air Group Nine Commander Philip Torrey. Scouting ahead of the bombers, he spotted a number of ships near Dublon. VB-9, VT-9 and VT-6 were assigned to attack the shipping and VB-6 and three aircraft from VT-6 were sent to bomb the seaplane base at Moen and the airfield at Eten.

Selecting a destroyer and a large freighter near Dublon the SBDs from VB-9 scored single hits on both. The TBFs of VT-9 armed with four 500lb bombs had more luck, claiming two ships sunk and two more severely damaged. As the ships burned, three VT-6 TBMs (General Motors-built Avengers) planted one 2,000lb each on Eten airfield while the others dropped their 500 pounders on shipping. One Avenger was lost,

caught in the explosion of an ammunition ship, and one was shot down by a Zero. The crew ditched and was later rescued.

The SBDs of VB-6 then headed for the seaplane base at Moen. Four aircraft were destroyed and a large freighter was also hit. Japanese fighters managed to slip through the Hellcat escort, shooting down one SBD.

The Japanese had little time to recover as Air Group 17 launched just 15 minutes after Air Group and Air Group Nine. Seventeen Helldivers and nine TBMs escorted by four Hellcats each from VF-18, V-17 and VF-25 headed for Truk. The light cruiser *Katori* was hit again by the TBMs and two SB2Cs. Staggered by several hits, the cruiser slowed to a crawl. The remaining Helldivers scored several hits on a freighter.

Late in the morning and into the early afternoon the third and fourth strikes of the day went in. As Japanese vessels tried to leave Truk Lagoon via the North Pass the SBDs of VB-6 and VB-9 and the TBFs of VT-9 stopped them cold. The light cruiser *Katori* and destroyer *Maikaze* suffered repeated attacks. The Avengers of VT-9, armed with torpedoes, scored three hits amidships on the *Katori*, stopping it dead in the water. The SBDs of VB-9 concentrated on *Maikaze* but only achieved serval near misses. The fourth strike finally caught up with the *Maikaze* when the SBDs of VB-6 hit its bow, bringing the vessel to a dead halt.

Japanese fighter resistance by this time was sporadic, but the anti-aircraft defences continued to be heavy with two bombers from *Intrepid* shot down during the third strike and two Hellcats from VF-6 were listed as missing in action.

On the fifth strike of the day the bombers were directed to attack the shipping in and around the anchorages near Dublon, Fenfan, Eten, Uman and Moen islands and the airfield on Parem. As the Hellcats from VF-10 strafed the airfield at Parem, the bombers scored numerous hits in the harbour – leaving a tanker and several freighters on fire. Following the Hellcats over Parem, the fragmentation bomb-equipped Avengers from VT-9 destroyed five aircraft on the ground.

In response to a small convoy heading for the open sea west of Truk, *Intrepid* launched 12 SBDs from VB-6 and 12 Hellcats from VF-6. The SBDs sank one tanker and damaged a freighter that sank later.

On the sixth and final strike of the day the airfields were targeted with fragmentation and delayed action bombs. Mitscher wanted to neutralise Truk's airfields to prevent any night raids on the fleet.

Air Group Ten bombed the airfield on Moen, dropping 128lb AN/M1A1 fragmentation bomb clusters, followed by the SBDs of VB-10 who targeted revetments and hit nine Mitsubishi G4M 'Betty' bombers. Twelve Hellcats from VF-10 provided escort with five dropping a single 1,000lb bomb each on the runway. Strafing attacks set 11 fighters on fire.

Air Group Five was assigned to the airfield on Parem, plastering it with fragmentation and delayed action bombs. Air Group Nine followed with bombing and strafing attacks on the remaining damaged aircraft. Air Group 17 turned their attention to the airfield on Eten with five Hellcats from VF-25 dropping single 1,000lb bombs. After their run the SB2Cs from VB-17 went into their dives. Running through a wall of heavy AA fire, they dropped their bombs on the service apron along the runway.

The first days' strike on Truk was a complete success. Since early dawn and throughout the day, 30 distinct airstrikes delivered 369 1000lb and 498 500lb bombs, 70 torpedoes and numerous cluster bombs and incendiaries. The early fighter sweep proved highly effective. Initially just 45 Zeros were scrambled, but they were late getting off which gave the incoming Hellcat pilots the advantage. During the course of the battle another 45 Zeros joined the fight. More than 30 Japanese fighters were shot down with 40 more destroyed on the ground by strafing. Most if not all the Japanese fighters shot down would have lost their pilots – all for the loss of just four US fighters.

In the confusion of battle the Japanese warships that did try to escape were sunk by waiting US submarines or surface ships, while others were set upon and blocked in the lagoon by air attack. The light cruiser *Naka* did manage to escape but was caught 35 miles west of Truk. Several waves of SB2C-1s and TBF-1s from *Bunker Hill* and *Cowpens* hit the cruiser with one bomb and one torpedo, breaking it in two with the loss of 240 crewmen (210 were rescued by other Japanese vessels).

Not all the Japanese vessels sunk at Truk fell victim to US Navy carrier strikes. As the battle raged over the lagoon, Vice Admiral Spruance led an 'around-the-atoll cruise' with elements of TF-50.9. This force comprised the new battleships *New Jersey* and *Iowa*, the heavy cruisers *Minneapolis* and *New Orleans* and four destroyers, all covered by a Hellcat CAP provided by the *Cowpens*. Eager to catch Japanese vessels trying to escape and bombarding shore installations along the way, TF-50.9 did catch a small convoy of ships 40 miles northwest of Truk.

Escorted by the damaged cruiser *Katori*, auxiliary cruiser *Akagi Maru* and two destroyers *Maikaze* and *Nowaki*, the convoy was hit by the battleships and cruisers of TF-50.9. Having had forty-six 16in and one hundred and twenty-four 5in shells fired at it, *Katori* finally rolled over and sank, guns blazing as it went under. The destroyer *Maikaze*, after firing a salvo of torpedoes at the *Iowa* and *New Jersey*, was pummelled by heavy fire and sank with all hands. In the confusion the *Nowaki* sped from the scene, escaping the long-range fire of the *Iowa* and *New Jersey* (extreme range of 34,000 to 39,000 yards).

NIGHT STALKERS

On the night of February 17, the IJNAF struck back. Any chance of a daylight attack on the US carriers had been shattered by the day's bombing and strafing attacks. At 1900 hours six or seven B5N2 'Kate' torpedo bombers equipped with Type H-6 air-to-surface radar came after TF-58.

BELOW: A Mark XIII aerial torpedo hits a Japanese cargo ship, during the first day of US Navy carrier air raids on Truk. Note the several torpedo wakes, including a very erratic one that indicates the torpedo missed its target. US NAVAL HISTORICAL CENTER

Night-fighters were launched to stalk the intruders but no contacts were made. Most of the 'Kates' were driven away by the intense AA fire, but at 2211 hours a single intruder – a 'Kate' or a G4M 'Betty' locked on to the carrier *Intrepid* and hit it with a single Type 91 torpedo. With a jammed rudder and large hole in its hull, *Intrepid* was forced to withdraw returning to the US for several months of repairs.

On the morning of February 18 at around 0400 hours the US Navy returned the favour by launching its first ever low-altitude night bombing attack against enemy shipping from a carrier. Twelve radar equipped TBF-1C Avengers from VT-10 launched from *Enterprise* just 88 miles from Truk. Each Avenger was armed with four 500lb bombs. As they approached Truk, the formation split with five Avengers heading for the anchorages around Moen and Eten Islands and the remaining seven TBFs assigned to the large anchorage area west of Moen and Dublon Island. The Avengers went in individually.

Coming in at 1,500ft and using their radar to identify their targets the pilots quickly found their reception hindered by many coral islets. The numerous ships at anchor also caused merged radar echos. After searching for 30 minutes and picking their targets, the Avengers began their runs.

Inaccurate Japanese AA fire ripped across the harbour, desperately searching out the approaching Avengers. The anchored ships held their fire and waited until the gunners could see the blue glow of the Avengers' exhaust flames. Several Avengers were hit as they passed over their target. After 30 minutes the Avengers returned to *Enterprise* with an impressive score. For the loss of a single Avenger to AA fire, VT-10 scored 13 direct hits and seven near misses, resulting in eight ships destroyed and five damaged. After the attack Lt Cdr William I Martin, commanding office of VT-10, remarked: "I believe the 12 planes got 13 ships that were sunk or beached, and we lost one TBF. I'm told the Japanese confirmed after the war that our estimate of damage inflicted was accurate. The great thing, though, was that half our bombs were hits that night. It was more than you normally get during a daylight attack, with attendant high losses."

This success would lead directly to the first dedicated night air group, Air Group 41 operating from the light carrier *Independence* from July 1944 to February 1945. This was followed by Air Group 90, the second dedicated night attack carrier air group that would operate from *Enterprise* in 1945.

As dawn broke on February 18, the second day of strikes began. Turning into the wind the carriers once again launched a fighter sweep of 72 Hellcats. But the mission was an anti-climax for the eager fighter pilots. The previous day's attacks and dogfights had decimated Japanese air power and not one Japanese fighter rose in defence. During the night the Japanese flew the last of their operational aircraft to safer airfields.

Without fighters to contend with, the Hellcats of VF-5 and VF-10 turned their guns on the airfields at Eten, Moen and Parem, strafing any remaining aircraft and anything that moved. After shooting up Moen, the fighters of VF-9 went for shipping targets. This was followed by strike packages of 12 F6F Hellcats and 12 SBDs from each fleet carrier.

Over the next few hours the air groups attacked the remaining ships in harbour. AA fire remained intense and one Hellcat from VF-9 and one TBF from VT-5 were shot down. In each instance the four aircrew from the two aircraft were rescued.

AIR SEA RESCUE

For the pilots and aircrew of the Fast Carrier Strike Force, being shot down or ditching over the sea was a very real and frightening possibility. They also knew that by 1943 a good deal of planning and resources had been dedicated to the finding and rescuing of downed airmen. This included floatplanes such as the Vought OS2U-3 Kingfisher, submarines, destroyers, and land-based PBY Catalinas.

To insure a downed airman had the best chance for rescue they had to be well equipped. Attached to each navy flier's parachute was a one-man AN-R-2A raft equipped with a repair kit, bailing bucket, two paddles, concertina pump, two bullet-hole plugs, sea anchor, can of drinking water, seat pad, and two hand paddles. Aircrew were also equipped with a life preserver, a revolver or semi-automatic pistol and a knife.

US Navy rescuers showed great courage and determination when it came to retrieving their own. During the second day of strikes on Truk, the Hellcats of VF-9 strafed the airfield at Moen and shipping in the harbour. On his last run over the harbour, Lt George Blair was hit by AA fire and forced to ditch his Hellcat within the lagoon. Capture was almost certain, but as he hit the water the rescue call went out. An OS2U-3 Kingfisher was launched from USS *Baltimore*.

While waiting for the Kingfisher to arrive, nine of Bell's squadron mates stood guard, circling above. Each Hellcat stayed for as long as possible, only leaving when their fuel ran low. When a Japanese destroyer spotted Blair's life raft, the Hellcats began strafing the vessel, forcing it to turn away. The running battle lasted 30 minutes and when only two Hellcats were left the Kingfisher arrived with an escort of Hellcats from VF-9. Blair was quickly pulled aboard the Kingfisher and returned to *Baltimore*, exhausted but unharmed.

ABOVE: Aircraft from the *Intrepid* begin their bombing attacks on two merchant ships anchored off Caroline Island. US NAVAL HISTORICAL CENTER

ABOVE: Japanese ships under air attack off the east end of Dublon Island on the first day of the Truk raids. The big ship in the foreground is most likely the converted cruiser *Aikoku Maru*, which was lost in these attacks. US NAVAL HISTORICAL CENTER

ABOVE: Moen Island seaplane base and other facilities burn on the first day of the Truk raids. Moen airfield is in the lower centre. Dublon Island is in the upper left centre, with Eten Island airfield just beyond. Fefan Island is at right. US NAVAL HISTORICAL CENTER

These rescues had a major effect on morale. On the Japanese side, in contrast, there was a surprising disregard for their downed airmen and there was no organised system of aircraft and ships assigned to the task of air-sea-rescue. After the war, combat pilot Commander Masatake Okumiya was interrogated on this point and said: "Pilots generally had parachutes, life preservers and rafts. Seaplanes, subs and destroyers were sometimes used to search for downed fliers. But this depended entirely on the will of the division commander. There was no organised system at all."

During Operation Hailstone, 22 US airmen were rescued by aircraft, destroyer, and submarine. It is estimated that during the entire war, PBYs alone saved some 540 Navy, Marine and Air Force pilots.

The third and last strike of the day targeted remaining airfield structures and the oil storage tanks on Dublon. The oil tanks had been saved for last to avoid pouring smoke over the harbour and cloaking battle space around Truk. No air opposition was met as the SBDs and TBFs of VB-10 and VT-10 shattered the tanks, leaving a giant black column of smoke to mark the end of a very successful operation.

ABOVE: A Zero caught in the gunsight of a US Navy Hellcat. Strikes can be seen on the front cowling and mid-fuselage by the tail plane. The Hellcat squadrons claimed 62 A6Ms shot down on February 17. NARA

BELOW: A Grumman F6F-3 Hellcat from VF-9 flies over the beached Japanese destroyer *Tachikaze* during TF-58's strikes on the enemy naval base at Truk. US NAVAL HISTORICAL CENTER

ABOVE: A Vought OS2U Kingfisher floatplane being hoisted aboard the battleship *Missouri* (BB-63). The Kingfisher was used extensively in the air-sea-rescue role. Powered by just a 450hp R-985-AN-2 radial engine and with the limited space on board, no more than one or two downed airmen could be rescued at one time. US NAVAL HISTORICAL CENTER

RIGHT: Grumman F6F-3 Hellcat fighters of VF-10 landing on *Enterprise* (CV-6) after strikes on the Japanese base at Truk. Folding wings and whirling propeller blades made the flight deck an extremely dangerous working environment. Constant vigilance was required to avoid injury or instant death. US NAVAL HISTORICAL CENTER

As the aircraft departed they left Truk a flaming wreck. Almost every structure on the island had been knocked down and some 17,000 tons of precious bunker oil for the Japanese fleet had been destroyed. In total the two-day strike on the 'Gibraltar of the Pacific' was an unprecedented success. By the time the last aircraft landed aboard the carriers, TF-58 had flown 1,250 combat sorties, dropping 400 tons of bombs and torpedoes on shipping and 94 tons on airfields and land targets.

The IJNAF lost between 250 and 275 aircraft and 75% of its supplies. All of the air units on Truk suffered heavy losses. The 204 Kokutai was the hardest hit, losing 18 of 31 pilots, while the 902 Kokutai was wiped out – losing all nine of its A6M2-N 'Rufe' fighters. Japanese warship losses were devastating. In both day and night attacks, US aircraft and surface vessels sank three light cruisers: *Agano*, *Katori* and *Naka*; four destroyers: *Oite*, *Fumizuki*, *Maikaze* and *Tachikaze*; three auxiliary cruisers: *Akagi Maru*, *Aikoku Maru* and *Kiyosumi Maru*; two submarine tenders: *Heian Maru* and *Rio de Janeiro Maru*; submarine chasers CH-24 and *Shonan Maru* 15; aircraft transport *Fujikawa Maru*; and 32 merchant ships. Damaged ships included two destroyers, two submarines, a repair ship, a seaplane tender, a submarine tender and a freighter.

In sharp contrast, Task Force 58 lost just 25 aircraft shot down or damaged beyond repair and 26 aircrew killed. Of those aircraft shot down, 22 aircrew were rescued by floatplane, submarine or destroyer.

RETURN OF TASK FORCE 58

On April 29, TF-58 returned to Truk for another two-day strike. Primary targets would be Truk's remaining dockside facilities. Japanese radar spotted the incoming raid, giving 30 minutes' warning and sufficient time to launch a good number of Zeros.

The dawn sweep of 84 Hellcats arrived at 0450 hours and was met by 37 Zeros. Like the first raid, the Hellcat pilots tore into the Japanese formations with good results. First off the mark were the Hellcats of VF-23, led by Lt Cdr Eddie Outlaw. During the morning sweep he personally shot down five Zeros (reaching 'ace in a day' status) with the rest of the squadron adding 16 more. The pilots of VF-6 would add 19 more, giving both squadron a total of 35. During the

ABOVE: The Japanese seaplane base on Dublon Island under bombing attack on the first day of raids. In the lower centre of the photo are numerous fragmentation bombs heading for their target. US NAVAL HISTORICAL CENTER

two-day strike 2,200 sorties were flown, of which 467 were F6F fighter-bomber attacks. Bombs dropped totalled 748 tons. Task Force 58 claimed 58 air-to-air kills (including five 'Kates' on patrol) and 34 destroyed on the ground.

During the two-day strike US losses amounted to 22 aircraft: two lost in the initial fighter sweep while 20 were shot down by AA fire and 34 damaged.

The destruction of Truk was a disaster for the Japanese. Their plan for a robust perimeter defence, in the hope of slowing the Americans down while inflicting heavy losses, was in tatters. Both air defence fighters and AA defences proved inadequate and their offensive strike capabilities were forced to operate under the cover of darkness with minor results.

The myth of Truk's impregnability had been shattered and the subsequent US Navy strikes on the Marianas represented a revolution in carrier warfare. Operation Hailstone demonstrated the Navy's Fast Carrier Task Force was capable of multiple simultaneous operations. It had the mobility and striking power to gain air superiority over the target, provide escort for the dive and torpedo bombers, protect the fleet from air attack, conduct night attack and night fighter defence for the fleet, carry out ASW patrols and provide both air-sea-rescue and naval gun fire spotting. Not only could the fast carriers cover American amphibious operations from a short distance away, they could now strike deep into the heart of Japanese territory in a strategic rather than a tactical way.

With Truk neutralised, the seizure of Eniwetok moved forward, paving the way for the upcoming invasion of Saipan. ■

BELOW: On April 23, Admiral Nimitz ordered a second strike on Truk for April 30. During the two day raid a small number of B6N2 'Jills' attacked TF-58.2. Here a B6N2 runs through heavy AA fire as seen from *Monterey* (CVL-26). The 'Jills' failed in their attack, but US losses over Truk amounted to five aircraft lost in air combat and 21 to AA fire over. This was the last time the once vital Japanese base was targeted during the Second World War. US NAVAL HISTORICAL CENTER

CHAPTER 6

THE END OF THE JAPANESE FLEET

The Great Marianas Turkey Shoot and the Battle of Leyte Gulf

Prior to the planned invasion of the Marianas, the US Navy's primary objective was to weaken Japanese defences in the Central Pacific. The man instrument of destruction would be the USN's Fast Carrier Task Force – Task Force 58. With every passing month TF-58 grew stronger. Its ability to attack heavily defended strategic Japanese bases and airfields with near impunity was staggering.

After crushing the IJN's primary anchorage at Truk on February 17-18, 1944, TF-58 turned its sights on the Marianas and Operation Forager. Up to that point the strikes on Truk were the largest of the war and for the Japanese they represented a major shift in the military balance in the Pacific.

On February 22, two task groups from TF-58 attacked airfields and facilities on Tinian, Guam in the Marianas. Next on the target list was Palau. On March 30 and April 1 TF-58 forced the Japanese Combined Fleet to safer waters while sinking 36 merchant ships and auxiliaries for a total of 130,000 tons. In both raids the IJNAF suffered heavy losses both in the air and on the ground. TF-58 suffered no damage, and USN air losses were negligible.

The pressure was relentless. On April 21 and 22, TF-58 provided support for General McArthur's successful landing at Hollandia. By the end of the month, TF-58 had grown to 12 carriers (five fleet and seven light) including 11 escort carriers. To add insult to injury, TF-58 returned to Truk for another two-day strike on April 29. After 2,200 sorties almost 100 Japanese aircraft were destroyed, and any remaining facilities were blasted to rubble. After two smaller strikes on Marcus and Wake Islands, TF-58 returned to the anchorage at Majuro to rest, replenish and prepare for the invasion of the Marianas.

The loss of the Gilberts and Marshalls, and the destruction of Truk as a major Pacific base, led to profound changes in the leadership of the Imperial Japanese Navy. The death of Admiral Koga in a plane crash on March 31 resulted in Admiral Soemu Toyoda being appointed Commander in Chief of the Imperial Japanese Navy.

In April 1944, the IJN reorganised, turning the Combined Fleet into the First Mobile Fleet, composed of the Second and Third Fleets. With the death of Koga, Vice Admiral Jisaburo Ozawa was given command of the Mobile Fleet. His flagship was the brand-new carrier *Taiho*, the first Japanese carrier with an armoured deck. This reorganisation turned Japanese pre-war fleet organisation on its head. Carriers now formed the nucleus of the battle fleet and for the first time in the history of the Imperial Japanese Navy, a carrier admiral was in charge of the battleships.

After 18 months of reinforcement, the addition of new ships and the return of some combat veterans, the IJN now boasted nine carriers. Of the nine flattops, only the *Taiho*, *Shokaku* and *Zuikaku* could be considered somewhat equal to the Essex Class. The *Junyo* and *Hiyo*, the second largest carriers in the fleet, had been converted from passenger ship hulls in 1942 and had a top speed of just 26 knots. Rounding out the fleet were the four light carriers – *Ryuho*, *Chitose*, *Chiyoda* and *Zuiho*.

New aircraft also joined the fleet – the D4Y3 'Judy' dive-bomber and B6N2 'Jill' torpedo

ABOVE and LEFT: Tracking the US carriers and their various task groups proved difficult for the Japanese. Here a Japanese H8K 'Emily' snooper is shot down by Hellcats off the Gilbert Islands, September 1943. NARA

bomber. Both were major improvements over the 'Val' and 'Kate' used at Pearl Harbour, but only the *Taiho*, *Shokaku* and *Zuikaku* were capable of operating them. This forced the remaining six carriers to use the obsolete 'Val', 'Kate' and A5M2 Zero. Slow production of new types like the 'Judy' and 'Jill' forced the Japanese to use a mix of old and new aircraft for their carrier air groups.

To increase the number of bombers, the IJNAF converted a number of older A5M2 Zero 21s into fighter-bombers, armed with a single 550lb bomb. A total of 84 modified Zeros would be deployed on seven of Ozawa's nine carriers. Incredibly, nearly two-thirds of the IJN carrier aircraft ready for battle in June 1944 had entered service before Pearl Harbor.

Another deficit faced by the Japanese was a lack of training. The new bombers had higher landing speeds than their predecessors and were more difficult to fly. During carrier training in March 1944, aircrew from *Zuikaku* and *Shokaku* suffered heavy losses, forcing the suspension of all deck landing training. This meant the skills of the neophyte pilots remained poor and the skills of the more advanced pilots simply stagnated. Of the three Carrier Divisions, only Carrier Division 1 had pilots with six months of training. Carrier Division 3 pilots had only three months and Carrier Division Two's aircrew were barely fit for service with just 100 hours of training.

For the upcoming battle IJN carrier groups could muster nearly 440 carrier aircraft with a further 630 (how many were serviceable remains unknown) land-based fighters and bombers from the Marianas and Truk. Japanese planners confidently calculated that their land base air forces would destroy a third of the TF-58's carriers.

The only key military advantage the Japanese held was the range of their carrier aircraft. American carrier aircraft had a range of between 150-200nm, depending on tactical conditions, bomb load, and weather conditions. Search range for IJN carrier aircraft extended to some 560nm compared to just 325nm for US aircraft. Strike range for IJN aircraft was 300nm. The Japanese could also use their airfields in the Marianas to refuel aircraft to increase their range even further.

The Japanese also had the advantage of weather. The prevailing winds in the Central Pacific in June 1944 were the easterly trade winds, which meant the Japanese could approach TF-58 from the west while moving into

JAPANESE NAVY FIRST MOBILE FLEET

★ THE 1ST AIR FLOTILLA
- **Carriers:** *Taiho, Shokaku* and *Zuikaku*
- **Fighters:** 80 A6M5b Model 52b
- **Fighter-bombers:** 11 A6M2 Model 21
- **Dive-bombers:** 70 D4Y1/Y1-C and 9 D3A2
- **Torpedo-bombers:** 44 B6N2

★ THE 2ND FLOTILLA
- **Carriers:** *Junyo, Hiyo* and *Ryuho*
- **Fighters:** 53 A6M5b Model 52b
- **Fighter-bombers:** 27 A6M2 Model 21
- **Dive-bombers:** 11 D4Y1 and 29 D3A2
- **Torpedo-bombers:** 15 B6N2

★ THE 3RD FLOTILLA
- **Carriers:** *Chiyoda, Chitose* and *Zuiho*
- **Fighters:** 18 A6M5b Model 52b
- **Fighter-bombers:** 45 A6M2 Model 21
- **Torpedo-bombers:** 9 B6N2 and 18 B5N2

---

the wind. This would allow them to launch and recover aircraft while steering straight towards the US fleet. If Ozawa's carriers could stay beyond the reach of USN aircraft, his plan had a chance of success.

The Japanese plan to use the superior range of their aircraft to attack the US fleet, leave it crippled, and allow the battleships of the Second fleet, which included the world's largest battlewagons, *Yamato* and *Musashi*, to finish it off was optimistic at best. Ozawa knew he was also greatly outnumbered. On May 9, Imperial Japanese Naval Intelligence, in a remarkably accurate assessment, put the number of US vessels ready for battle at 16 battleships, eight large fleet carriers, ten light carriers and 20 CVEs.

LEADING THE WAY

The Battle of the Philippine Sea was fought under the strategic direction of Admiral Chester Nimitz. As Commander in Chief, United States Pacific Fleet, Nimitz controlled all of the naval forces in the Pacific. By June 1944, Nimitz had assembled one of the most highly effective command teams in US naval history. When the Fifth Fleet was created in April 1944, Admiral Raymond Spruance was given command. Vice Admiral Marc Mitscher was the commander of Task Force 58. Subordinate commands of the Fifth Fleet included: Vice Admiral R. K. Turner TF-51, Vice Admiral John H. Hoover TF-57 and Vice Admiral Charles A. Lockwood TF-17, the Submarine Pacific Fleet.

On June 6, 1944, 54 carriers, battleships, heavy and light cruisers and destroyers of the US Fifth Fleet set sail from Majuro Atoll. To date, it was the largest American battle fleet to see action in the Pacific. After two and half years of fighting and expansion the US Pacific Fleet was the best in the world. It was well equipped, well trained, and superbly led. USN carrier pilots and aircrew, almost all with combat experience, were far superior to their IJNAF counterparts. Even those who had yet to see action had more than 400 hours' flying hours flying time. Indeed, once a pilot joined his carrier air group, he would spend up to year training with his group before embarking on a carrier and being sent to war.

BELOW: A VF-1 'Top Hatter' F6F-3 fighter is ready for launch from *Yorktown*, to intercept enemy forces during the 'Great Marianas Turkey Shoot' on June 19, 1944. Just below the cowling a deck crewman is hold up a chalk board with last minute target information. VF-1 made 30 sorties and claimed 32 Japanese aircraft destroyed.
US NAVAL HISTORICAL CENTER

The previous carrier strikes in the autumn of 1943 and early 1944 had shown US Navy aircraft to be rugged, versatile and capable of carrying heavy loads. Tactics and operational procedures were refined. Radar equipped night-fighters and night bombing Avengers only increased a task group's lethality. In terms of fighter performance, tactics and pilot training, the F6F-3 Hellcat completely outclassed the A5M2 Zero. The Zero remained a superb dogfighter, but the Hellcat's superior level speed, diving speed, armament, armour plate and self-sealing tanks made it almost unbeatable.

FIGHTER DIRECTION OFFICER – FDO

US Navy anti-aircraft defences had expanded by 1944, making significant and remarkable advances. During the first four carrier battles of the war, the radar, fighter direction and number of fighters available for CAP duties proved unable to properly protect the carriers. In each encounter IJNAF aircraft were able to penetrate the CAP screen, battle through the AA fire and deliver some punishing blows. Both sides realised that the best method to defeat air attacks was to place the CAP well in advance of an incoming raid.

Early American efforts, while better than the Japanese, proved to be a hit and miss affair. Poor radar warning, incorrect altitude placement, jammed radio channels and faulty communication procedures made it difficult to launch fighters and move others already in the battle space. After much trial and error and improved methods, the problem of effective fighter direction was solved. One of the most important jobs in the Navy was that of fighter direction officer (FDOs). These men were hand-picked specialists. The FDO ranks contained a large proportion of bankers, lawyers, teachers, journalist, and stockbrokers. Men who had demonstrated sound management ability and judgement

Clear, efficient communication was critical for an effective intercept. In 1941 the Navy established a clear FDO vocabulary for both FDO and aircrew which was "provided for the passing of orders and information clearly, briefly, and in a standardised manner. No alternatives are to be used".

Each carrier had a FDO aboard along with seven other men – radar operators, plotters and talkers to form a CIC team. Eventually every ship

FLIGHT DIRECTION OFFICER VOCABULARY

Ammo zero: No ammunition left
Bandit: Identified enemy aircraft
Bogey: Unidentified aircraft
Buster: Fly at normal full speed
Chickens: Own fighters
Fishes: Torpedo aircraft
Hawks: Dive-bombers
Pancake hurt: Returning wounded or damaged. Wish to land
Snooper: Low shadowing aircraft (below 2,000ft)
Tallyho: Aircraft sighted and recognised as hostile

ABOVE: By 1944 Japanese pilot training was in steep decline. This Zero goes down in flames during an attack on Palau on March 30-31, 1944. Many Hellcat squadrons reported the Japanese pilots lacked coordinated offensive or defensive tactics, resulting in one-sided clashes. NARA

ABOVE: Fighter contrails over TF-58 during the 'Great Marianas Turkey Shoot' June 19, 1944. Seen from USS *Birmingham* (CL-62). US NAVAL HISTORICAL CENTER

in Fifth Fleet would have one FDO aboard. With radar, IFF and four channel VHF radio, the FDO in 1944 had all the tools necessary to launch and coordinate effective intercepts and CAP patrols.

CIRCLE THE WAGONS

The CAP and fighter defence of a carrier task group wasn't foolproof. However, the Japanese aircraft that did survive faced a wall of airborne steel. A typical task group operated two fleet carriers and two light carriers with a screen of four cruisers and a dozen destroyers. With the carriers in the centre, the cruisers and destroyers were deployed in four-mile circle around the flattops. This forced the Japanese to run a gauntlet of fire before getting close to the carriers. It was a defensive system that proved highly effective and one the Japanese had no real answer for.

OPENING MOVES

On June 11, 200 nautical miles from Guam the first pre-invasion air strikes were launched. Two hundred and eight Hellcats and eight Avengers from TF-58 attacked the airfields on Tinian and Saipan. The Japanese response was sharp and intense. Hellcat pilots claimed 86 aircraft destroyed in the air and another 33 on the ground. Japanese figures put their losses at 36 aircraft. Eleven American fighters were shot down.

In their opening salvo, the Japanese sent ten G4M 'Betty' torpedo bombers from Truk to confront TF-58. They launched their attack during the early hours of June 12. Dropping flares as they went, they failed to hit any ships.

For the next two days, June 12 and 13, three of TF-58's task groups continued to strafe and pound the airfields and installations on Saipan and Tinian. Japanese fighter activity was significant but their numbers were small compared to the day before. The fighters from VF-2 claimed 11 enemy fighters shot down.

CARRIER STRIKE 75

TASK FORCE 58 ORDER OF BATTLE

★ TASK GROUP 58.1
Hornet (CV-12)
Yorktown (CV-10)
Belleau Wood (CVL-24)
Bataan (CVL-29)
Fighters: 127 F6F-3 and 8 F6F-3N night-fighters
Dive-bombers: 73 SB2C-1C and 4 SBD-5
Torpedo-bombers: 53 TBF/TBM-1C

★ TASK GROUP 58.2
Bunker Hill (CV-17)
Wasp (CV-18)
Monterey (CVL-26)
Cabot (CVL-28)
Fighters: 116 F6F-3 and 8 F6F-3N night-fighters
Dive-bombers: 65 SB2C-1C
Torpedo-bombers: 53 TBF/TBM-1C

★ TASK GROUP 58.3
Enterprise (CV-6)
Lexington (CV-16)
San Jacinto (CVL-30)
Princeton (CVL-23)
Fighters: 116 F6F-3, 4 F6F-3N and 3 F4U-2 night-fighters
Dive-bombers: 55 SBD-5
Torpedo-bombers: 49 TBF/TBM-1C

★ TASK GROUP 58.4
Essex (CV-9)
Langley (CVL-27)
Cowpens (CVL-25)
Fighters: 84 F6F-3 and 4 F6F-3N night-fighters
Dive-bombers: 36 SB2C-1C
Torpedo bombers: 38 TBF/TBM-1C

ABOVE: During the day's air battles six Hellcat pilots would make 'ace in a day'. Others like Lieutenant Junior Grade Alexander Vraciu, USNR; fighting squadron VF-16 'Ace', added six more on June 19, 1944.
US NAVAL HISTORICAL CENTER

AIRCRAFT RECOGNITION

During the war aircraft recognition on both sides was more an art than a science. US fighter pilot claims throughout the Pacific were often mistaken as to the exact type with the vast majority of Japanese fighters shot down claimed as Zeros. This was due to a number of factors. The first was overall ignorance of Japanese aircraft. Air combat was swift and intense, often with only seconds to aim and fire, leaving little time to differentiate between a Zero or a JAAF Nakajima Ki-43 'Oscar'. The most egregious claims were made by the American Volunteer Group (AVG), the famous 'Flying Tigers', where every Ki-43 they shot down was said to be a 'Zero'. The IJNAF did not operate Zeros against the AVG.

On the first day of operations the pilots of VF-2 claimed a number of Japanese Army Air Force Kawasaki Ki-61 'Tony' and Nakajima Ki-44 'Tojo' fighters. The IJNAF and JAAF never flew together and there were no JAAF units assigned to the Marianas. The 'Tonys' were most likely D4Y1 'Judys' and the Ki-44s, Zeros. Hellcat pilots also learned that in the heat of combat the F6F's belly tank was a critical recognition item. Once a Hellcat had jettisoned its tank it was likely to be attacked by friendly fighters.

The June air strikes proved devastating, leaving the Japanese land-based units in the Marianas completely decimated. US Naval intelligence learned that reinforcements were on the way with aircraft flying from Japan to the Bonin Islands north of the Marianas. From there they could fly to Guam and to other Central Pacific bases from Iwo Jima and Chichi Jima. Iwo Jima was a crucial way point for the Japanese defence of the Marianas and Central Pacific.

TF-58.1 with *Hornet*, *Yorktown*, *Belleau Wood* and *Bataan* and TF-58.4 with *Essex*, *Langley* and *Cowpens* were ordered to neutralise Iwo Jima. As they sailed north, TF-58.2 and TF-58.3 took the opportunity to refuel. Closing at high speed, TF-58.1 launched the first strikes against Iwo Jima and Chichi Jima at 1345 hours on June 15 (as the strikes were launched two Marine divisions stormed the beaches of Saipan. By the end of the day 20,000 marines were ashore). To meet the raids the Japanese launched more than 80 Zeros from the 252nd and 301st Air Groups. Both units were badly mauled with just half returning to their bases. Strikes on the second day left 63 Japanese aircraft destroyed on the ground for the loss of 12 US aircraft over the two-day strike. On the 16th, the two task groups turned south heading for Saipan.

Surprised by the appearance of TF-58 off the Marianas on June 11, the Japanese were mobilised into action. Shortly after Operation A-Go was activated, land-based air units were ordered to move to the Marianas and the First Mobile Fleet departed Tawi-Tawi.

The Americans knew the enemy was coming. US submarines spotted the First Mobile Fleet on June 13. US signals intelligence, while unable to break the internal text of Japanese IJN messages, gleaned a great deal from message externals. On the 15th they confirmed a major IJN fleet operation was under way. On June 18, all 15 US carriers began launching long range air search patrols. Long range PB4Y Liberators also flew search patrol missions based out of Los Negros.

These missions typically consisted of one Hellcat with either an Avenger or Helldiver. The SBD-5 didn't have the range to be useful. The search required aircraft to fly 380 miles out from the carriers, followed by a 50-mile cross leg and return to the carrier. These flights could last five to six hours and required the most accurate navigation for a safe return.

The Japanese were also in the air, sending their aircraft in search of TF-58. At 0600 hours on the 18th, Japanese 'Jake' floatplanes from the First Mobile Fleet spotted six carriers from TF-58. That afternoon, seven aircraft from Carrier Division 1, flying 420 miles out, found TF-58 with all four task groups together in formation. The Japanese air search results were accurate – giving Ozawa a good assessment of Spruance's intentions. He surmised that TF-58 would maintain its position relatively close to Saipan.

ABOVE: The principal Japanese long-range reconnaissance aircraft was the Aichi E13A 'Jake'. These two photos capture the moment this 'Jake' was intercepted and shot by a TF-58 Hellcat. NARA

This being the case, Ozawa could launch a strike without fear of an American attack. He marked June 19 as the day of battle and to maintain at least 400 nautical miles between his own forces and the Americans he ordered a course change to the southwest at 1540 hours.

At 2020 hours, for the first time in the operation, Ozawa broke radio silence. The message was sent in order to coordinate with IJNAF land-based units on Guam but American radio direction finding detected the transmission – giving them a fairly accurate position for Ozawa's carriers. Ground based units from Yap and Guam mounted a number of raids on the invasion fleet between June 16 and 18. Little damage was done, but over claiming by Japanese aviators stated that three or four carriers from TF-58 had been hit. Ozawa was unaware that his ground-based units were in no fit shape for a battle. Nineteen aircraft were flown into Guam on June 19, bringing the total available for the coming battle to just 50.

OPENING SALVOS

At noon on June 19, TF-58 turned to the southwest keeping station near Saipan in accordance with Spruance's overall orders.

Weather conditions over the fleet were ideal. Wind continued to come from the east, favouring the Japanese. Ceiling and visibility were unlimited. With temperatures in the mid-80s and high humidity, conditions were perfect for the creation of vapour trails. This made the interception of Japanese aircraft easier for American fighters, with some Japanese aircraft being spotted at 35 miles distant.

At 0530 hours TF-58 launched the first CAP, air search and anti-submarine patrols of the day. The opening shots of what would become the largest carrier battle in history rang out shortly afterwards. The Japanese went first, dive-bombers from Guam attacking destroyers from TF-58.7 (TF-58.7 was Spruance's battleship force with seven battleships, four heavy cruisers and 12 destroyers). No damage was inflicted.

At 0630 hours American radar detected increased numbers of enemy aircraft over Guam. Four Hellcats were vectored in to investigate. At 0720 hours the Hellcats arrived just as large number of Japanese aircraft began taking off. More Hellcats were called in and for the next hour the two sides battled it out. Close to 33 Hellcats joined the fray, claiming 30 Zeros and five bombers. This early morning raid successfully disrupted any attempt by ground based Japanese units to support Ozawa's carriers. At 1100 hours, just as the victorious Hellcats returned to their carriers, American radar lit up.

At 0445 hours the Japanese began launching search aircraft from their carriers, battleships and cruisers. First out were 16 Aichi E13A 'Jake' floatplanes. By 0700 hours, after reaching the end of their search legs, they made their turns for home. It was on their homeward track that one of the 'Jakes' spotted northern elements of TF-58.7 and the carriers of TF-58.4.

With the American fleet spotted, Ozawa started launching his strikes. First to launch were the light carriers of the 3rd Air Flotilla with 69 aircraft – 16 A6M5bs, 45 A6M2s with bombs and eight B6N2s with torpedoes. The launch began at 0830 hours some 300 miles from TF-58. Radar operators from TF-58.7 were the first to detect the incoming raid at a range of 125 miles. At that range, the FDO officers had plenty of time to launch fighters. At 1023 hours every loudspeaker on the US carriers blared: "Pilots! Man your planes!" Every available Hellcat fighter from TF-58 was launched.

For Admiral Mitscher, commander of TF-58, the unfolding situation was of great concern.

BELOW: During the 'Great Marianas Turkey Shoot' Commander David McCampbell shot down five D4Y1 'Judy' dive-bombers in the morning and claimed two Zeros over Guam in the afternoon. On October 24, during the Battle of the Philippine Sea, McCampbell and his wingman Lt(jg) Roy Rushing intercepted a formation of more than 60 IJNAF fighters, dive-bombers and torpedo bombers heading for TF-58. After an hour, McCampbell had shot down nine fighters and Rushing added six. He ended the war as the leading US Navy Hellcat ace with 34 victories. AUTHOR'S COLLECTION

ABOVE and BELOW: TBFs and SB2Cs en route to attack the First Mobile Fleet on the afternoon of June 20. The shorter ranged Helldivers suffered heavily during the evening recovery. Of the 51 that set out for the attack, four were shot down in combat and 39 lost operationally, a loss rate of 84%. US NAVAL HISTORICAL CENTER

Because American carrier aircraft were shorter ranged than their Japanese opponents, he had requested the evening before to move Task Force 58 farther to the west to be in a position to strike the Japanese as soon as they were sighted. The previous four carrier battles had clearly demonstrated that the carriers that struck first usually won.

As far as Admiral Spruance was concerned however, the protection of the invasion fleet was of paramount importance and the first task of TF-58. He refused Mitscher's request. As the radar screens filled with incoming Japanese aircraft the carrier commanders braced to the coming action. Could their carriers absorb the first blows and hit back decisively?

Even before the first intercepts were made, the Japanese aircrew from the 3rd Air Flotilla showed how poorly trained they really were. Instead of heading in straight for their attack, they opted to orbit the American carriers at 20,000ft some 70 miles out. This gave the intercepting Hellcats more time to gain valuable altitude.

As the Hellcats reached their interception altitudes of between 17,000 and 23,300ft the incoming Japanese aircraft were spotted. The first Hellcats to intercept belonged to VF-15 from *Essex*. Diving from 24,000ft they tore into the Japanese formation. The intercept, led by Lieutenant Charles Brewer, was near perfect with Brewer and his wingman claiming eight Japanese aircraft shot down. The Zero escorts proved ineffective, leaving the B6N2 torpedo bombers and Zero fighter-bombers to scatter and become easy targets. In all VF-15 claimed 20 kills. FDO officers vectored more fighters to the scene with Hellcats from *Bunker Hill*, *Hornet* and five light carriers eager to finish the job. Fifty Hellcats participated in total, shooting down 25 out of the 69 Japanese aircraft in the first raid. Just three Hellcats were lost with one *Bunker Hill* Hellcat ditching on the way back.

Close to 40 Japanese aircraft survived and continued inbound for the attack. Before reaching any targets however, they were intercepted by the Hellcats of VF-8 from *Bunker Hill*. Sixteen more were shot down. The remaining Japanese aircraft that did reach TF-58.7 scored a hit on the battleship *South Dakota* at 1049 hours along with near misses on the heavy cruisers *Minneapolis* and *Wichita*. In return the Japanese lost 42 aircraft – eight fighters, 32 fighter-bombers and two torpedo bombers.

The next strike would come from Ozawa's

three fleet carriers of Carrier Division 1. This would be the largest raid of the day, flown by the best trained crews from the 1st Air Flotilla. A sizable group of 128 aircraft – 48 Zeros, 53 'Judys' and 27 'Jills' armed with torpedoes began launching at 0856 hours.

As the aircraft climbed for altitude, below the waves the US submarine *Albacore* had the *Taiho* in its sights. It fired a spread of six torpedoes and one found its mark – hitting the *Taiho* starboard, just in front of the island, and jamming the forward elevator. Flight operations were halted, but within 30 minutes damage control teams realigned the elevator and the launch continued.

More trouble followed. After the launch, eight aircraft developed engine trouble and returned. As the formations headed east they flew over the three light carriers, 100 miles in front of the main carrier force. Poor aircraft recognition led to a barrage of friendly AA fire resulting in two aircraft shot down and eight damaged, forced to return. The strike was now down to 109 aircraft.

American radar detected the in-bound raid at 1107 hours, 115 nautical miles from the carriers. Almost immediately *Essex* launched 12 Hellcats from VF-15. The hard-pressed fighter directors vectored no fewer than 162 Hellcats onto the incoming raid. At 1139 hours the Hellcats dove into the attack. Led by air group Commander David Campbell, it was a one-sided fight. Campbell quickly shot down three 'Judys', his wing man claiming two more. As more Hellcats joined the fray, the Japanese formations broke up and were scattered. Close to 70 Japanese aircraft were shot down, leaving close to 40 heading for TF-58.

Twenty were reported in three formations setting up to attack the picket destroyers of TF-58.7, well away from the carriers, at 1145 hours. Fifteen minutes later the battleships of TF-58.7 come under attack. Two torpedo armed 'Jills' attacked *South Dakota* without

ABOVE: Battle of Philippine Sea, June 1944. SBDs, TBFs and F6Fs fly over USS *Lexington* on their way to attack the Japanese carrier fleet. US NAVAL HISTORICAL CENTER

success, two more selected *Indiana* but both missed with one crashing into the waterline of the heavily armoured ship and causing minor damage. *Iowa* and *Alabama* were also targeted but remained unscathed.

Breaking through the Hellcat CAP a group of six 'Judy' dive-bombers rounded on TG-58.2 with four heading for carrier *Wasp*. No hits were scored, but one of the bombs exploded overhead – raining shrapnel over the deck, killing one crewman and wounding 12 others. At 1203 hours the remaining two 'Judys' selected *Bunker Hill* as their target. Two near misses caused minor damage but killed three men and wounded 73 more. Of the six attacking aircraft four were shot down by AA fire.

The last and final attack from the second raid centred on TG-58.3. Starting at 1157 hours, six 'Jills' split into two formations with three attacking *Enterprise* and three the light carrier *Princeton*. All six missed their targets with three destroyed by AA fire.

Ozawa's second and largest strike was a complete failure and a crushing defeat. Of the 109 aircraft intercepted, 97 were shot down by fighters and AA fire. Losses included 32 fighters, 42 dive-bombers and 23 'Jills'. In spite of the strong American defences, a good number of aircraft were still able to deliver their ordnance. However, of those attackers only about ten exercised any discipline in their target selection, but they were still not skilful enough to score any direct hits.

The third Japanese strike was mounted by Carrier Division 2 from the carriers *Junyo*, *Hiyo* and *Ryuho*. This strike comprised just 47 aircraft including 15 A6M2bs, 25 A6M2s with bombs and seven B6N2s with torpedoes. Take off began at 1000 hours and it wasn't long before it began to fall apart. Shortly after launch, the attack group was ordered to proceed based on an updated contact report of the position of TF-58. Few of the aircraft received this new

BELOW: *Intrepid* (CV-11) seen from the rear seat of an SB2C, after taking off to attack the Japanese Fleet in the Battle of Leyte Gulf October 24, 1944.

ABOVE: The battleship *Musashi* leaving Brunei, Borneo possibly on October 22, 1944 heading for Leyte Gulf. US NAVAL HISTORICAL CENTER

information though, leaving 27 aircraft to fly on – guided by an incorrect contact report.

Having found nothing but empty sea they returned to their carriers without loss. The remaining 20 aircraft, armed with the new contact information, spotted two battleships but decided to press on in the hope of finding the carriers. Having failed to locate any, this small force then turned back towards the previously sighted battleships. At 1225 hours, Hellcats from *Yorktown* and *Hornet* intercepted the gaggle of wandering Japanese aircraft. Fourteen were claimed shot down but the actual number was seven. In the confusion, a small number of the Japanese aircraft broke through with one dropping a bomb 600 yards from *Essex*. The third raid was an utter failure. While 40 of the 47-aircraft returned unscathed, the majority survived because they didn't meet any Hellcat fighters.

At 1100 hours Ozawa's final strike of the day was initiated with aircraft from *Junyo, Hiyo, Ryuho* and *Zuikaku* launching at 1100 hours. This strike totalled 82 aircraft – 30 A6M5b fighters, 36 dive-bombers (27 'Vals' and nine 'Judys'), ten A6M2 with bombs, and six 'Jills'. Like the third strike earlier, this one was directed to a nonexistent contact sighting. After finding nothing, the formation broke up into three smaller groups. The largest group of 20 Zeros, 27 'Vals' and two 'Jills' turned for Guam. As they did so, TF-58 radar painted them at 1449 hours. A formation of 27 Hellcats from *Essex, Yorktown* and *Cowpens* were sent after them and the intercept was near perfect. Thirty of the 49 Japanese aircraft trying to land on Guam shot down. Of the 19 that did land, strafing Hellcats caused heavy damage and many wouldn't fly again.

The rest of the attack was piecemeal and uncoordinated. Fifteen aircraft, probably six Zeros and nine 'Judys' headed for Rota but changed course to attack TG-58.2. While detected on radar, the majority avoided the CAP with six aircraft heading towards *Wasp* unmolested. At 1423 hours *Wasp's* AA fire engaged the attackers just as they began dropping their bombs. No hits were scored. Another group of "Judys" appeared and quickly split up with two targeting *Bunker Hill* and one heading for *Wasp*. No hits were recorded and of the nine attackers, eight were shot down by AA fire.

The fourth and final Japanese strike was another dismal failure. Of the 82 aircraft just nine returned to their carriers. Most were likely damaged and unable to carry out further operations. For all that effort the damage inflicted on TF-58 and TF-58.7 was negligible. No ships were sunk or heavily damaged.

The Japanese continued to suffer, however. The single torpedo hit on the *Taiho* proved fatal. The explosion not only jammed the elevator but more importantly cracked the forward aviation fuel tank and tanks holding the volatile Taraken crude oil used for fuel. To stop the build-up of explosive fuel vapour throughout the ship, damage control personnel turned on the ship's ventilation fans. It didn't work. The fumes spread quickly, turning the *Taiho* into a massive floating bomb. At 1532 hours a huge explosion tore through the ship, blowing holes in her hull and sealing her fate.

Sixty miles away from where the *Taiho* was struck, the US submarine *Cavalla* found *Shokaku* recovering aircraft at 1152 hours. At a range of 1,000 yards, *Cavalla* fired a full spread of six torpedoes, with three hitting the carrier. The Pearl Harbor veteran sank at 1501 hours, taking 1,272 crewmen with her.

More CAPs were flown over the Japanese held islands that evening and Japanese Zeros continued to engage, with *Essex* pilots claiming nine more victories.

ABOVE: Crewmen at their duty stations in the ship's Combat Information Center (CIC), aboard *Independence* (CVL-22). The CIC provided vital real time information on the position of both enemy and friendly formations. NARA

ABOVE: Japanese battleship *Yamato* (right) in action with US carrier planes off Samar. Another battleship is in the left distance, steaming in the opposite direction. US NAVAL HISTORICAL CENTER

Of the 403 Hellcat missions flown on June 19, 296 reported engaging a total of 548 Japanese aircraft. In their four carrier strikes the Japanese launched 373 aircraft. Of these, 243 were shot down – the vast majority by Hellcats. Another 50 aircraft from Guam were also destroyed with another 22 aircraft lost with the sinking of the *Shokaku* and *Taiho* for a grand total of 315. American aircraft losses were extremely light with just 13 Hellcats shot down, one to friendly AA fire and six to operational causes.

June 19, 1944 will be forever remembered as the 'Great Marianas Turkey Shoot' and the greatest carrier battle in naval history. It was a triumph of US technology, training, leadership, tactics and logistics.

THE AMERICANS STRIKE

The search for the Japanese carriers began on June 20, with the first search flights launched at 0530 hours. The carrier air groups flew searches all day. For every hour that went by, Ozawa's carriers opened the distance headed for Okinawa. What became clear was that when the Japanese fleet was discovered it would be at maximum range. And when it was found, would the discovery of the Japanese fleet be in time for a daylight attack? To cut the distance, Spruance ordered TF-58 to a westerly course at 23kts. Mitscher detached TG-58.4 to replenish and continue attacks on Guam and Rota.

At 1528 hours, two Avengers from *Enterprise* finally spotted the Mobile Fleet. The original report was garbled, but by approximately 1545 hours Admiral Mitscher signaled: "Expect to launch everything we have. We will probably have to recover at night." He was right. Shortly after his decision was made a final spotting report put the Japanese carriers a further 60 miles distant.

That put the Japanese fleet 275 miles from TF-58 – well past maximum range for a daylight strike and recovery. At 1624 hours the strike was launched. In just 12 minutes, 85 Hellcats (many armed with 500lb bombs) 77 dive-bombers (51 SB2C-1s and 26 SBD-5s) and 54 Avengers (just 12 armed with torpedoes) took off from 11 carriers. After an uneventful flight, the First Mobile Fleet was spotted at 1840 hours. At 1803 hours Japanese radar spotted the incoming raid, allowing time for the launch of approximately 40 A6M5bs and 29 A6M2s. A respectable number considering the heavy losses suffered the day before.

After the long 300 mile flight there was no time for a coordinated attack. The first target was the carrier *Zuikaku*. The air groups from *Hornet* and *Yorktown*, plus ten bomb-carrying Hellcats from *Bataan* dove into the attack. Defended by 17 fighters and with heavy AA fire and good manoeuvring, *Zuikaku* avoided four torpedoes and was hit with just one bomb.

The next to strike was the air group from *Lexington* assisted by Avengers from *Enterprise*, *Yorktown* and *Belleau Wood*. Their target was the carriers *Junyo*, *Ryuho* and *Hiyo*. Defended by 38 fighters, Carrier Division 2 put up a robust defence. At 1904 hours the Dauntlesses from *Lexington* hit the *Junyo* with one or two bombs but the damage was not significant. The light carrier *Ryuho* was next attacked by Avengers from *Enterprise* with bombs at 1910 hours. No hits were recorded, but several near misses caused slight damage.

The only carrier to be hit and sunk during the engagement was the *Hiyo*. After launching two 'Jills' to lay a smoke screen, she was caught behind the main body of the fleet and became vulnerable. SBDs from *Enterprise* were first to score with one bomb exploding above the bridge causing heavy casualties. Another hit the flight deck. Four Avengers from *Belleau Wood* would land the fatal blow with a single torpedo hit on the *Hiyo's* starboard engine room. This would be the only air launched torpedo hit scored by Avengers during the entire attack. After several internal explosions *Hiyo* was ordered abandoned, sinking at 2032 hours.

Escorted by battleships and heavy cruisers, the carriers *Zuiho* and *Chistose* avoided the attention of the attacking Americans. The *Chiyoda* group with battleship *Haruna* as escort did not and felt the full weight of attacking aircraft from *Bunker Hill*, *Monterey* and *Cabot*. Over 20 Helldivers and Avengers with bombs targeted the light carrier, but only one bomb hit *Chiyoda* on the flight deck with minor damage. Dodging another five torpedoes, *Chiyoda* lived to fight another day. *Haruna* was hit by a single 500lb bomb and a near miss was recorded against the heavy cruiser *Maya*.

With fuel running low and daylight fading the aircraft from *Wasp* opted to attack Ozawa's oilers from the Supply Group. Damaged by near misses, *Genyo Marus* and *Seiyo Maru* were later scuttled.

In a series of hurried and uncoordinated attacks the Japanese carriers avoided annihilation. After fighting and winning a tremendous defensive battle the day before, TF-58's strike aircraft were unable to deal a major blow. The Americans lost 20 aircraft with 12 shot down and six to AA fire. Attacking at dusk in the face of a determined Japanese defence resulted in a disappointing return.

With the battle ended, US fliers now faced the long dark return flight to the fleet. It was 270 miles back to TF-58. Most of the pilots had to rely on instruments for reference and some became disorientated in the dark.

Nearly 200 planes headed eastward, engines running on lean, low on fuel. Seventy-five miles out the leading aircraft began to pick-up the task force's ZB-homing signal. The high-pitched hum in their headsets provided a welcome sound and a precise direction in which to steer. The returning aircraft began to return to the carriers at 2045 hours with many running on fumes. Chaos ensued, with aircraft ordered to land on any deck in sight. Panicked cries from aviators ditching into the black sea jammed the airwaves resulting in Rear Admiral Jocko Clark ordering the task group's ships to turn on their lights at 2040 hours. The night sky was now turned into a still more chaotic scene of searchlights, flares and the whine of low flying aircraft.

After numerous deck crashes and ditching aircraft, almost half of the returning aircraft landed on the wrong carrier. After two hours the 'Mission Beyond Darkness' was over. Of the 230 aircraft ▶

BELOW: Japanese battleship *Musashi* is hit during attacks by Task Force 38 aircraft in the Sibuyan Sea.
US NAVAL HISTORICAL CENTER

ABOVE: Japanese battleship *Nagato* firing its main 16in guns at attacking planes during the Battle of Leyte Gulf. US NAVAL HISTORICAL CENTER

ABOVE: While the *Musashi* received the most attention from US carrier aircraft, *Yamato* also came under attack – suffering two 1,000lb bomb hits, one hitting forward of the No.1 turret. US NAVAL HISTORICAL CENTER.

launched only 115 returned to their carriers with the Helldiver units suffering the most. Of the 51 launched just 10 made it back to the fleet. One hundred pilots and 109 crewmen were forced to ditch. After several days of extensive air search and rescue, 16 pilots and 33 crewmen were listed as MIA.

For the Americans the results of the Battle of the Philippine Sea seemed highly unsatisfactory. In the immediate aftermath of the attack, the only confirmed carrier sunk was the *Hiyo*. The submarine attacks on *Taiho* and *Shokaku* would not be confirmed by intelligence until September. In the end the 'Great Marianas Turkey Shoot' – the submarine attacks on June 19 and the air strikes on June 20 – resulted in a clear and decisive victory over the Japanese. Of their nine carriers, three were sunk and two damaged. More importantly, the air groups available for the remaining six carriers were all but shattered. Of the 430 carrier aircraft available at the start of the battle just 35 remained. Overall Japanese losses, (both ground based and carrier aircraft) on June 19-20 amounted to almost 500. With no pilots to fly from its carriers the IJNAF was a spent force with no chance of revival.

After the overwhelming victory during the Battle of the Philippine Sea and the successful invasion of the Marianas in June 1944, the American advance toward Japan began to gather pace. The overall strategy focused on two axes of advance – one through the central Pacific under the command of Admiral Chester Nimitz and the other through New Guinea and into the Philippines with General Douglas MacArthur and his Southwest Pacific Forces leading the way.

In July 1944 the future of the offensive against the Japanese was still undecided. Nimitz and MacArthur had different plans, and each believed his was the best way to proceed. MacArthur's "I shall return" comment after the Japanese victory in the Philippines in 1942 greatly influenced the decision to invade the Philippines. Nimitz and the US Navy favoured the invasion of Formosa. From there US air power could cut Japanese sea lanes, starving Japan of vital war materials. The Navy's plan was bolder, but MacArthur's strategy was more conventional and would be ready in October 1944. The invasion of Formosa wouldn't be ready until January 1945.

To break the deadlock, President Franklin D. Roosevelt met with his two commanders at Hawaii in July 1944. MacArthur's argument won the day. National honour and pride demanded the Philippines be liberated and Roosevelt's re-election chances hung in the balance.

On August 24, Third Fleet Commander Vice Admiral William 'Bull' Halsey replaced Fifth Fleet Commander Vice Admiral Raymond A. Spruance. With the change in command, Fifth Fleet TF-58 became Third Fleet and Task Force 38 (TF-38).

With dates set for the invasion, TF-38 began preparatory strikes against targets in the Philippines starting in early September. The opposition, mostly JAAF units, proved weak and were no match for the combat tested Hellcat pilots. After four days of strikes, US carrier pilots claimed 170 planes shot down and 300 destroyed on the ground. The destruction of the JAAF in the southern Philippines was so complete that the island of Mindanao was now considered low risk and slated to be bypassed. American forces would head for Leyte directly, two months ahead of schedule.

At the time of the invasion the US Navy would assemble the world's most powerful seaborne force to date. Controlled by the Third Fleet under Halsey, its principal operational component was TF-38. This was broken down into its four task groups numbered TG-38.1 through TG-38.4. TF-58 comprised nine fleet carriers, eight light carriers, 18 escort carriers, six new battleships, four heavy cruisers, ten light cruisers and 58 destroyers. Hellcat units began to receive the new Hellcat F6F-5. Faster with a more powerful engine it was capable of carrying two 1,000lb bombs and six 5in rockets. The venerable Douglas SBD-5 Dauntless had also been completely replaced by the more powerful Curtiss SB2C-3C Helldiver, although the number in each dive-bomber squadron had been reduced from 36 to 24.

For the upcoming operation the fast carriers of TF-38 were assigned two roles – support the invasion with a series of pre-landing strikes against Japanese airfields throughout the Philippines and, once the Marines and Army were established on shore, engaged and destroy any Japanese naval and air forces that threatened the landing zone.

SHO-GO (VICTORY OPERATION)

After the devastating battle of the Philippine Sea in June 1944, the IJN's remaining battleships and heavy cruisers retired to Lingga Roads, south of Singapore. Close to their source of fuel oil and free from aerial attack, training for the upcoming battle began in earnest. The remaining carriers retired to Japanese home waters where the IJN set about forming new air groups.

Early Japanese intelligence estimates had the Americans attacking in November. This would give them just enough time to have their new air groups and carriers ready to join the rest of the fleet. In early October, Japanese intelligence had to revise the timetable. The last ten days of October were now identified as the start of the American invasion, leaving the IJN and its carrier force only partially formed.

The battle plan for the defence of the Philippines was called Sho-Go. With possible landings in the Philippines, Formosa-Ryukyus, Honshu-Kyushu and Hokkaido-Kuriles, several versions of the plan were completed. Sho-I was the one designated for the Philippines and was seen by Japanese intelligence to be the most likely to happen.

While Japanese intelligence got some things right, it faltered poorly in other critical areas. The Japanese erroneously believed that IJNAF aviators had sunk 11 carriers, two battleships, three cruisers and a destroyer during the Battle for Formosa Sea, October 10-12, 1944. It was a serious misjudgment and one that would handicap the overall strategy. Armed with this information Commander-in Chief of the Combined Fleet, Admiral Soemu Toyoda formed the Sho-I.

For the upcoming battle the IJN knew its land-based air units and carrier forces available would have little impact. The success of the operation depended largely on heavy surface forces. In this area the Japanese were well equipped. Commanded by Vice Admiral Takeo Kurita the First Diversion Attack Force consisted of seven battleships (including the world's largest: *Yamato* and *Musashi*), 11 heavy cruisers, two light cruisers and 19 destroyers.

These ships were divided into four forces – Centre Force consisted of battleships *Yamato*, *Musashi*, *Nagato*, *Kongo*, *Haruna* and 10 heavy cruisers, two light cruisers and 15 destroyers. Southern Force was made up of the battleships *Fuso* and *Yamashiro*, one heavy cruiser and three destroyers. The smallest force, designated the Second Attack Force, consisted of the two heavy cruisers *Nachi* and *Ashigara*, one light cruiser and seven destroyers.

The fourth and least powerful force was Admiral Ozawa's Northern Force which consisted of one fleet carrier, three light carriers, two battleships that had been converted into two

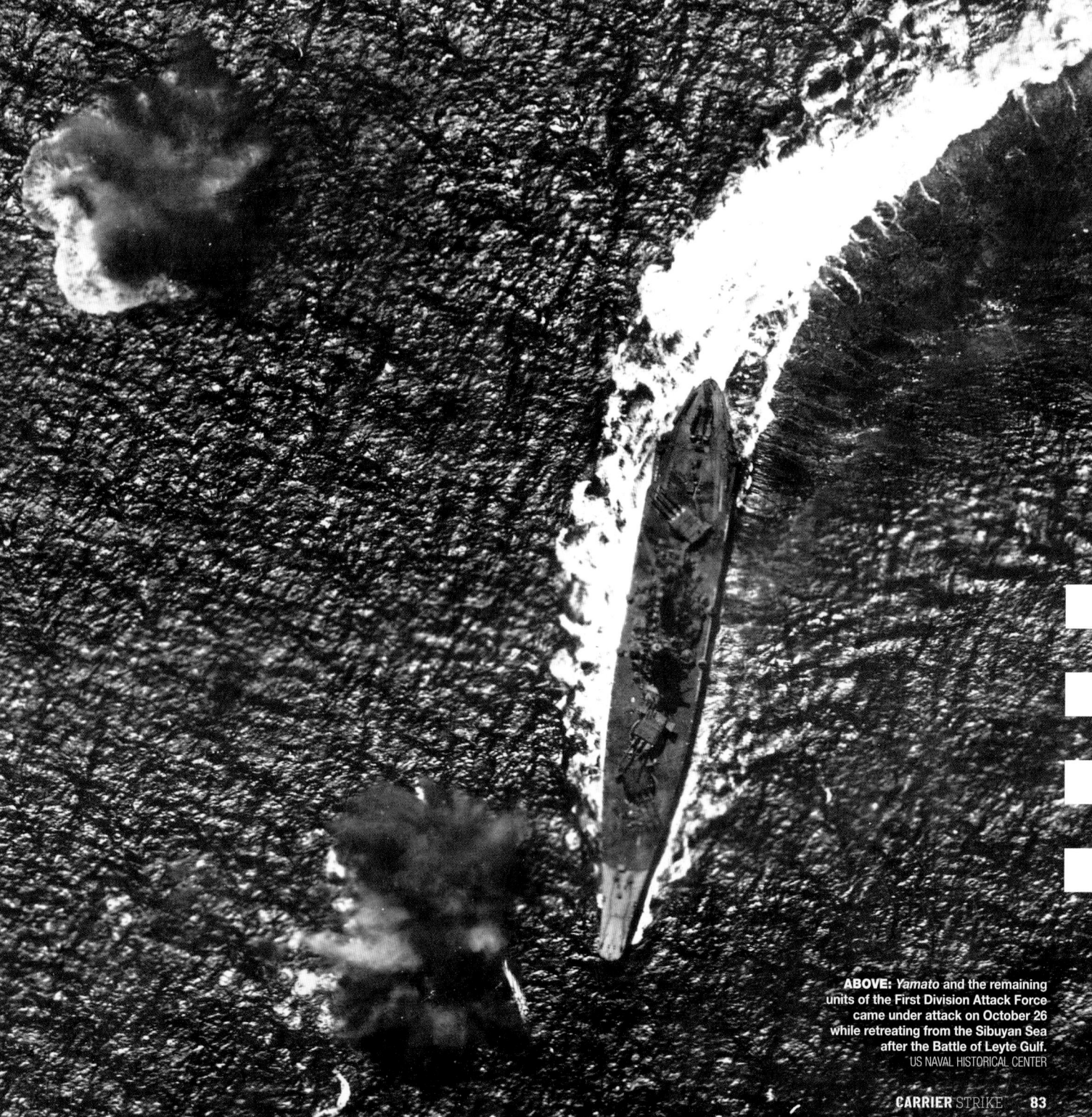

ABOVE: *Yamato* and the remaining units of the First Division Attack Force came under attack on October 26 while retreating from the Sibuyan Sea after the Battle of Leyte Gulf.
US NAVAL HISTORICAL CENTER

ABOVE: *Zuikaku* of Force A came under heavy attack by as many as 50 Avengers and Helldivers but suffered only one bomb hit and survived. Here the *Zuikaku* and its destroyer escort manoeuvre wildly to avoid the rain of bombs. US NAVAL HISTORICAL CENTER

ABOVE: Smoke from the Japanese battleship/carrier *Ise's* anti-aircraft guns smothers the ship as SB2C Helldivers from Air Group 15 press home their attacks. US NAVAL HISTORICAL CENTER

hybrid carriers by removing their aft main gun turrets and constructing short flight decks, three cruisers and eight destroyers. The combined carriers lacked any real offensive power and carried just 116 aircraft, the equivalent of one Essex carrier. Despite its obvious deficiencies, Ozawa's force would play a vital role in Sho-I.

Toyoda's plan centred on a pincer movement that would have his heavy battleships and cruisers attack and destroy the fleet supporting MacArthur's invasion force in the Leyte Gulf. Admiral Shoji Nishimura would lead the Southern Force through the Surigao Strait and attack the defenceless American transports and landing ships. Admiral Kurita's Centre Force, advancing through San Bernadino Strait, would fall on the American fleet from the north.

With no air cover to protect the battleships, Ozawa's carriers would be a decoy – attempting to lure the carriers of TF-38 away from northern Luzon. This would, hopefully, allow the Japanese battleship free transit through the Sibuyan Sea. The plan was complicated, inflexible and had significant weaknesses. After missing the first five major carrier battles of the war, the world's largest battleships would be finally committed to battle.

THE BATTLE JOINED

On the morning of October 17, the Japanese spotted the US invasion fleet heading for Leyte Gulf. On October 18 at 1100 hours Admiral Toyoda ordered the execution of Sho-I. The date set for the destruction of the American landing force was October 25. As the Japanese fleet made steam, American marines landed on Leyte on October 20 against weak opposition. By October 25, 132,400 men were ashore and well supplied with just under 200,000 tons of materiel.

At 0800 hours on October 22, Kurita's Centre Force set course and headed northeast through the Palawan Passage. Nishimura's Southern Force departed at 1500 hours headed through the Balabac Strait into the Sulu Sea. The same day that Kurita departed from Singapore, Ozawa's carriers weighed anchor at Kure. *Zuikaku* was accompanied by the light carriers *Zuiho*, *Chitose* and *Chiyoda*, plus the converted hybrid battleship carriers *Hyuga* and *Ise*, all escorted by three light cruisers and eight destroyers.

Like the Battle of the Philippine Sea, the Japanese were spotted early by two prowling American submarines USS *Dace* and *Darter*. On October 23 at 0116 hours, USS *Darter's* radar picked up Kurita's approaching ships just off the southern entrance of the Palawan Passage. After sending a contact report, the *Darter's* skipper loaded both bow and stern torpedo tubes and attacked.

It was a perfect ambush. First hit was Kurita's flagship, the heavy cruiser *Atago*, followed by the heavy cruiser *Takao*. *Dace* added to the score hitting the heavy cruiser *Maya*. Both attacks were at close range with devastating results. *Atago* and *Maya* were sunk, *Takao* was forced to return to

BELOW: Helldivers from TG-38.3 attack *Musashi*. This was the third raid mounted against the battleship. US NAVAL HISTORICAL CENTER

Brunei. For nothing in return, the Japanese had been hurt and the Americans knew their location.

Admiral Halsey received the contact report on October 24 at 0200 hours but the emergence of the IJN battleship force had caught him flat-footed. TF-38 was not a complete force. TG-38.1 was on its way to replenish at Ulithi. The other three task groups were ordered to close on the Philippine coast and prepare for strikes. At 0810 hours on the 24th, search aircraft from TG-38.2 spotted the IJN fleet off Semirara Island. Minutes later preparations for the first strike were well under way.

At the time of the first report the American carriers were not concentrated. TG-38.2 would be on its own for most of the day. TG-38.3 was too far north to launch immediate strikes and TG-38.4 too far south, but both were closing quickly. And while TG.38.2 was first to attack, it was the weakest of the four task groups with just one fleet carrier – the USS *Intrepid* and light carriers *Cabot* and *Independence*. Its striking power was also hampered by the fact that *Independence* was dedicated to night operations and would play no part in the attacks.

Launching at 0910 hours, TG-38.2's first strike comprised 45 aircraft – 21 Hellcats (VF-18, VF-29), 12 Helldivers (VB-18) and 12 Avengers (VT-18, VT-29). Led by Commander William Ellis, CO of *Intrepid's* Carrier Air Group 18, most of the aviators had never attacked a Japanese warship before, let alone the world's most powerful battleships.

RUNNING THE GAUNTLET

As the first strike approached the sheer size of the Japanese force, including the *Yamato* and the *Musashi*, was unmistakable and intimidating. With no fighter cover, the battleships and cruisers had to rely on their own AA gun defences. In this regard they were heavily armed with hundreds of AA guns. At the time of battle, *Yamato* was armed with a dozen Type 89 5in guns and one hundred and fifty-two 25mm guns – in 50 triple and two single mounts. *Musashi* was armed with a dozen Type 89 5in guns and 130 25mm guns – 35 triple and 25 single mounts.

While the numbers were impressive their effectiveness was very poor when compared to US AA guns and directors. The Type 89 5in guns used barrage fire primarily against level bombers and dive-bombers at medium altitude. The 5in gun also targeted torpedo bombers at a distance of around 7,500 yards.

A well trained crew could generate a high rate of fire, but the fire control system for the Type 89 proved inadequate. The Type 94 High Angle Firing Control Installation was simply too slow to deal with US Navy carrier aircraft and the fire control solutions it generated were inaccurate. This failure forced the Japanese to rely heavily on the smaller and even less effective close-range 25mm AA guns.

The Type 96 triple 25mm mount was crewed by nine men, including six loaders. Rate of fire for the triple mount was 110-120 rounds per minute with an effective range of 1,635 yards. Yet as a short-range AA gun the Type 96 suffered from a number of shortcomings. Frequent changes of the 15-round magazine reduced the rate of fire and the weight of the 25mm shell of just nine ounces caused little damage. Captured wartime documents indicate the 25mm gun crews opened fire at 2,750 yards.

The attack began at 1018 hours and the *Yamato* and *Musashi*, quickly identified, became the primary targets. With no fighter opposition the Hellcats were ordered to strafe the battleships' upper decks – targeting the AA mounts. Armed with 1,000lb armour piercing bombs the 12 Helldivers split up with six each attacking *Yamato* and *Musashi*. Setting their sights of the eastern side of Kurita's formation, eight Avengers from *Intrepid* dove to torpedo height. Two headed towards the heavy cruiser *Myoko* while six turned for *Musashi*. The four Avengers from Cabot were assigned *Yamato*.

Pressing home their attacks, the Americans were met with a visually impressive display of AA fire. The first to score were Helldivers of VB-18, hitting *Musashi's* Turret No 1. The six attacking Avengers landed the first telling blow by hitting *Musashi* with one torpedo, causing a 5.5 degree list. This was reduced to a single degree by counter flooding on the port side.

At second strike from TG-38.2 was launched at 1045 hours. Forty-two aircraft were involved – 19 Hellcats, 12, Helldivers, and 11 Avengers. It was a well-coordinated effort and all aircraft focused on *Musashi*. First in were the Helldivers, hitting the mighty ship twice with 1,000lb bombs and five near misses. The nine Avengers from *Intrepid* came in for another anvil attack and dropped eight torpedoes – scoring with three. One torpedo struck the port side, causing flooding, while the second hit the same side just forward of the armoured citadel. This flooded several large storerooms. The third torpedo found its mark abaft Turret No.2 on the port side.

During the first two attacks the ship's volume of AA fire was impressive but ineffective, forcing just one Avenger to ditch and shooting down two Hellcats. Even after four torpedo hits the enormous *Musashi* was not in danger of sinking, but its speed had been reduced to 22kts and the remainder of the fleet was forced to slow accordingly.

TG-38.3 joined the fight with the third strike of the day. At 1250 hours *Essex* and *Lexington* launched 16 Hellcats (VF-15 and VF-19), 20 Helldivers (VB-15 and VB-19) and 32 Avengers (VT-15 and VT-19). Diving in at 1330 hours the strike targeted both *Yamato* and *Musashi*. Four bombs hit *Musashi*, causing heavy casualties but no serious damage.

Far more damaging were the three torpedo hits – one on either side of the bow forward of the armoured citadel and one hitting the starboard side. These three hits caused extensive flooding that spread across the entire ship on the middle deck.

Musashi endured a terrific pounding, one that would have easily sunk any Allied battleship. Forced to reduce its speed down to just 12 knots, *Musashi* had to finally leave the line

BELOW: USS *Bunker Hill* (CV-17) suffers a near miss by a Japanese bomb, during the air attacks of June 19, 1944. AA fire managed to shoot the tail off the attacking aircraft, seen at the left. US NAVAL HISTORICAL CENTER

SINGLE ENGINE JAP

WHEN SEEN HEAD-ON, JAPANESE SINGLE-ENGINE AIRCRAFT GENERALLY APPEAR TO HAVE ROUND NOSES. WING IS ALMOST ALWAYS SET LOW, WITH EVEN DIHEDRAL FROM THE ROOTS (*i.e.*, NO BREAK IN THE WING)

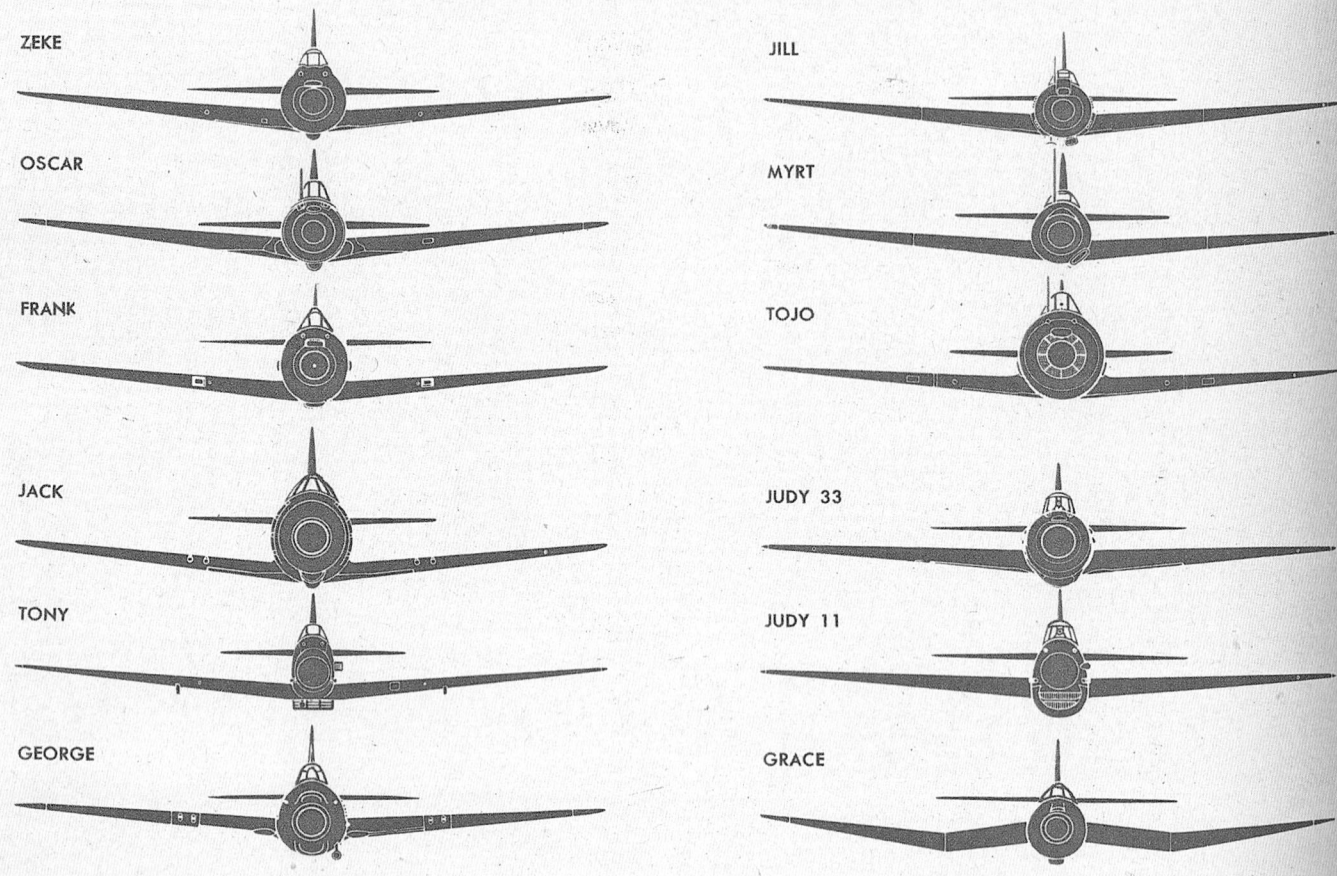

TWIN ENGINE JAP

SINGLE FIN AND RUDDER SET ABOVE A LOW, FLAT TAILPLANE ARE CHARACTERISTIC OF ALL JAPANESE TWIN-ENGINE AIRCRAFT SEEN IN HEAD-ON VIEW. THE WING POSITION USUALLY RANGES BETWEEN MID AND LOW

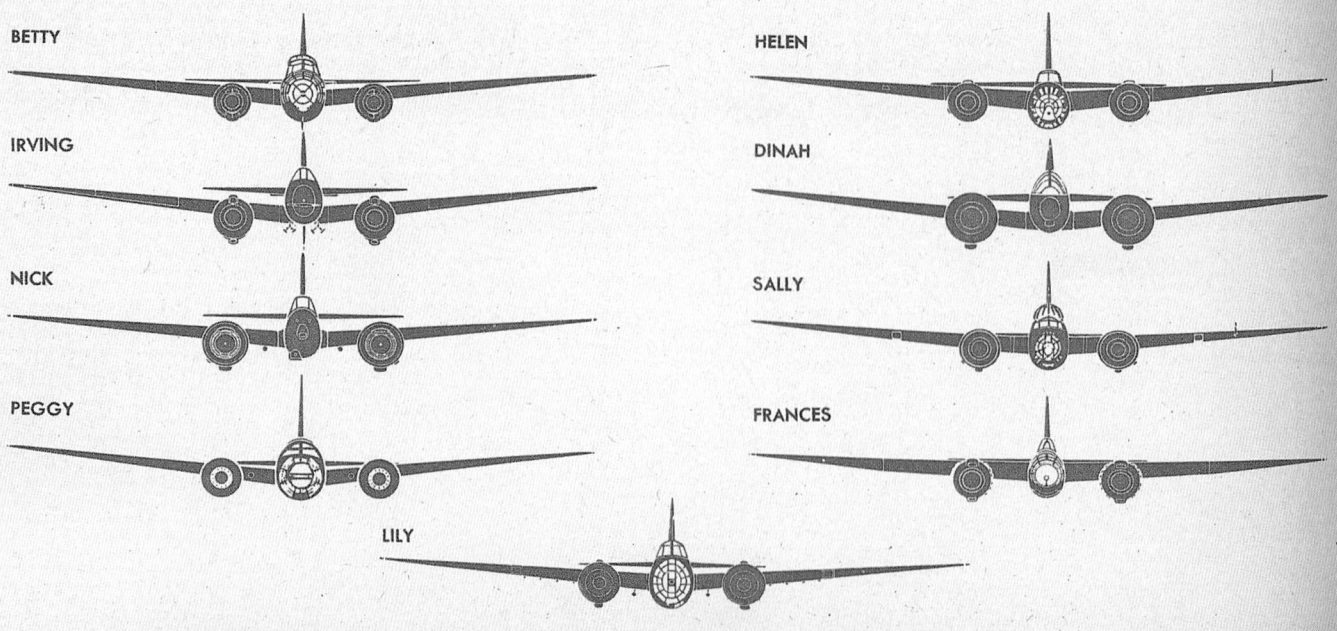

ABOVE: These head on views, as illustrated in the US Army Navy Journal of Recognition, clearly shows how similar Japanese fighters with their radial engines really looked. Japanese fighters claimed by US Navy pilots were almost always described as 'a Zero'. AUTHOR'S COLLECTION

escorted by two destroyers. Remarkably, the *Musashi* still wasn't in any immediate danger of sinking. Damage control parties had stopped any progressive flooding and given the mighty ship a chance of survival.

At 1315 hours the largest raid of the day was launched. *Enterprise* and *Franklin* from TG-38.4 joined the fight with 26 Hellcats (VF-13 and VF-20), 21 Helldivers (VB-13 and VB-20) and 18 Avengers (VT-13 and VT-20).

When the strike force arrived, *Musashi* was on its own and unable to defend itself. Ploughing slowly on and with just a quarter of its AA guns in action, the battleship was essentially a vast floating target. As the strike force split, more than half went after the *Musashi*, the remaining targeted the *Yamato* and its escorts. This time the Hellcats were assigned to strafe the escorting destroyers while the Helldivers and Avengers pummeled the crippled battleship. For the Helldivers it was a near perfect attack with 11 hits and six near misses from 18 aircraft. As damaging as these hits were, it was the torpedo strikes that sealed *Musashi's* fate.

The third strike from *Intrepid* and *Cabot* was the last of the day. It was small, just 16 Hellcats, 12 Helldivers and two Avengers. Beginning at 1550 hours it caused little if any additional damage. *Musashi* was now a dying ship. With just one propeller shaft in operation and uncontrollable flooding, *Musashi* would not answer its helm, circling steadily. The vessel was finally abandoned at 1920 hours, sinking 16 minutes later.

For the loss of just 18 aircraft, TF-38 scored a major victory. In the largest air-sea battle in history up to that point 259 carrier aircraft, in a series of four strikes, sank one of the world's most powerful battleships, hit *Yamato* and *Nagato* with two 1,000lb bombs each and heavily damaged the heavy cruiser *Myoko*.

Even with the loss of *Musashi*, Kurita's remaining battleships and cruisers were a powerful and dangerous force. After such a shocking loss, the Americans expected Kurita to abandon his mission. Indeed, TF-38 scout aircraft reported the Japanese battleships and cruisers retiring westward, convincing Admiral Halsey that the danger had passed. Yet with grim determination Kurita stuck to his orders and reversed course, continuing his journey towards San Bernardino Strait. That night Kurita's four battleships, eight cruisers and 11 destroyers passed through the narrow passage undetected.

ABOVE: Japanese aircraft carrier *Zuiho* still under way after taking several hits from Task Force 38 planes during the battle off Cape Engano, October 25, 1944. Note the elaborate deck camouflage. US NAVAL HISTORICAL CENTER

CARRIER MOVES

As TF-38 continued with their strikes against Kurita's battleship force, both land based IJNAF and IJAAF aircraft launched numerous strikes against the American carriers – three waves of 50-60 aircraft. At the beginning of the battle TF-38 was well equipped to meet the challenge. Nearly 715 Hellcats and 288 FM-2 Wildcats from TF-38 and the escort carriers of Task Force 77 were available for strike and CAP missions.

As TF-38 engaged Kurita's ships in the Sibuyan Sea, Admiral Ozawa's decoy carriers steamed north of Luzon. Ozawa was fully cognisant of his sacrificial role in the coming battle. Too weak to effectively defend Kurita's battleships, his ships were sent to draw TF-38 away from the invasion fleet exposing them to attack from Kurita's main force. At 1145 hours, *Zuiho*, *Chitose* and *Chiyoda* of the First Mobile Force launched 53 aircraft. This strike had little hope of success and was met by the full fury of TF-38's Hellcat CAP.

In one of the most successful intercept missions of the war, leading Hellcat ace Commander David Campbell of VF-15, led seven Hellcats towards the incoming raid. Climbing for altitude, the Hellcats of VF-15 were guided by the FDO from *Essex*. Five Hellcats soon fell behind, leaving just Campbell and his wingman Lt Roy Rushing as the sole defenders of the fleet. Diving into the attack, Campbell and Rushing scored quickly and often. After 90 minutes of combat Campbell shot down nine Zeros with two probables. Rushing flamed six more with the rest of VF-15 scoring a further 10 Zeros and 'Vals'. Campbell had made history, setting the all-time American record for nine victories in one fight.

The Japanese formation had been virtually wiped out with the survivors flying to Clark Field, near Manilla. At 1155 hours *Zuikaku* launched 29 aircraft in what would be the last Japanese carrier strike of the war. The attack was completely ineffective with 14 shot down and all remaining aircraft landing at Clark Field. By the end of October 24, US Navy fighter pilots claimed 270 victories (including both IJNAF and IJAAF aircraft).▶

BELOW: *Gambier Bay* (CVE-73) targeted by Japanese shells while making smoke, during the battle off Samar, October 25, 1944. After these near misses *Gambier Bay* appeared to slow down and fall behind the rest of the task group. Hit twice by Japanese battleship shells, the small flattop capsized to become the only American carrier ever sunk by surface fire. US NAVAL HISTORICAL CENTER

ABOVE: Task Force 38 aircraft attack a Japanese *Chitose* Class CVL October 25, 1944. This ship may be the light carrier *Zuiho*, which was sunk during these air attacks. US NAVAL HISTORICAL CENTER

While the Hellcat CAP put up an impressive score, it wasn't perfect. At 0938 a single 'Judy' dive-bomber streaked out of the clouds and released two 551lb bombs over the light carrier *Princeton*. The bombs crashed through three decks before exploding. Fire soon spread, engulfing the hangar deck where fuel and torpedoes were being prepared for the flight deck. The fight to save the *Princeton* continued into the afternoon but at 1523 hours a massive explosion blew her stern off. At 1600 hours, with no hope of saving the ship, she was ordered abandoned and sunk by five American torpedoes. The *Princeton* was the first US carrier sunk since the *Hornet* (CV-8) had gone down two years before in the Solomons.

At 1640 hours American scout aircraft spotted Ozawa's decoy carriers only 190 miles from the northernmost US carrier groups. Admiral Halsey ordered his three task groups to head them off, sending his battleships to form a battle group up front.

At first light on October 25, search planes were launched followed by strikes involving 180 aircraft (60 Hellcats, 60 Helldivers and 55 Avengers). At 0735 hours the last carrier vs carrier battle began. The small CAP of 25 Zeros was quickly overwhelmed as the Hellcats from VF-15 claimed nine defenders. The first carrier to be hit was *Chitose*. Hit by several bombs, it sank at 0937 hours. *Zuikaku*, the largest carrier, was hit by a torpedo and the *Zuiho* suffered a single 500lb bomb hit. This started several small fires and knocked out the vessel's steering.

At 0835 hours a second strike of 14 Hellcats, six Helldivers and 16 Avengers inflicted severe damage on *Chiyoda* and it had to be taken in tow.

The third strike, starting at 1310 hours, comprised 200 aircraft resulting in seven torpedo and four bomb hits on *Zuikaku*. Unable to survive, the last of the Pearl Harbor attackers slipped under the waves.

The smaller *Zuiho* was also hit by a single Mk 13 torpedo and two bombs. With her engine room fully flooded she was abandoned at 1510 hours and sank at 1526 hours. A fourth strike of 35 aircraft resulted in inaccurate bombing and no real damage. The fifth and final strike of 36 aircraft at 1710 hours caused little damage. For many pilots it was their third strike of the day. The last carrier to sink was *Chiyoda*. Dead in the water and abandoned it was sunk by US cruiser and destroyer gunfire and torpedoes.

The converted battleships *Ise* and *Hyuga* were also targeted. Primarily employed to bolster the AA defences for the carriers, both ships used their 14in guns main guns in the anti-aircraft role – firing the Type 3 San-Shiki shell. These shells were filled with 996 steel tubes measuring

ABOVE: Japanese aircraft carriers *Zuikaku* (left centre) and *Zuiho* (right) under attack by US Navy dive-bombers on October 25, 1945. Both ships appear to be making good speed, indicating that this photo was taken relatively early in the action. Both carriers are emitting heavy smoke. Note heavy concentration of anti-aircraft shell bursts in lower right and a SB2C Helldiver diving in the lower left. US NAVAL HISTORICAL CENTER

25mm x 90mm and containing an incendiary mixture. Great results were expected but despite a reportedly stunning pyrotechnic display they proved totally ineffective in service (both *Yamato* and *Musashi* also used the San-Shiki shell). *Ise* suffered one torpedo hit and 34 near misses by bombs. *Hyuga* suffered splinter damage from a number of near misses.

AMBUSH OFF SAMAR

On the evening of October 24/25 three radar equipped TBM-3Ds from *Independence* scouted San Bernardino Straight and spotted Kurita's force steaming towards Leyte Gulf and the US Seventh Fleet. A warning message was sent to Halsey's Third Fleet Staff, but for reasons that remain unclear it was either blocked, not received or was ignored.

The Battle of Samar has often been described as a 'David and Goliath' affair between ships that should never have been in the same ocean. Against the world's greatest battleship and the most powerful surface fleet deployed by the IJN, the Americans were forced to fight back with 18 escort carriers, and the destroyers and escort destroyers of Task Group 77.4. Organised into three groups, Taffy 1-3, the force's carriers embarked a total of 187 TBF/TBM-1C Avengers plus 292 fighters – a mixture of FM-2 Wildcats and F6F-3 Hellcats.

When Kurita's impressive force (four battleships, including *Yamato*, six heavy cruisers, two light cruisers and 11 destroyers) emerged from the strait in the early morning of the 25th, they expected easy pickings among the transports and landing craft of the Seventh Fleet. As Kurita steamed south along the coast of Samar, he encountered Taffy 3 and began his attack just before 0700 hours.

Outgunned and far slower than the pursuing Japanese, Taffy 3 fought a battle for survival. Turning at its top speed of 18 knots, Taffy 3 tried to escape as its escort of three destroyers and four destroyer escorts laid smoke. *White Plains* and *St Lo* were the first to come under Japanese fire followed by *Kalinin Bay* and *Gambier Bay*. Taffy 2, after flying sorties over Leyte soon came to the aid of Taffy 3. During the battle it was Taffy 2 that contributed the most offensive sorties against the Japanese fleet. Taffy 1's participation was limited due to its attack on the Japanese cruiser force fleeing south from Suriago Strait.

Gambier Bay took the brunt of Japanese shelling. Positioned at the rear of the formation it was struck by one 14in shell and several 8in shells. It was too much for the little flattop – after 26 hits it was abandoned and sank at 0911 hours. *Kalinin Bay* suffered 14 hits and *Fanshaw Bay* was hit by four 8in shells. *Gambier Bay* would be the only CVE sunk during the war by naval gunfire.

While many have believed the Battle of Samar should have been a quick and over whelming victory for the Japanese, a closer look reveals Task Force 77.4 was the more powerful force. In total the three Taffy task groups comprised almost 500 aircraft. While trained for ground support and ASW warfare, the naval aviators showed impressive initiative, pressing home their attacks to such an extent that the Japanese were confused into thinking they were attacking fleet carriers. Armed with .50cal machine guns, bombs, rockets, depth charges and torpedoes the escort carriers mounted 441 sorties against the Japanese surface vessels: 209 by fighters and 232 by Avengers (68 with torpedoes). In comparison to the sorties mounted by the Fast Carrier Task against the same force which sank the *Musashi*, Taffy 2 and 3 flew a greater number ▶

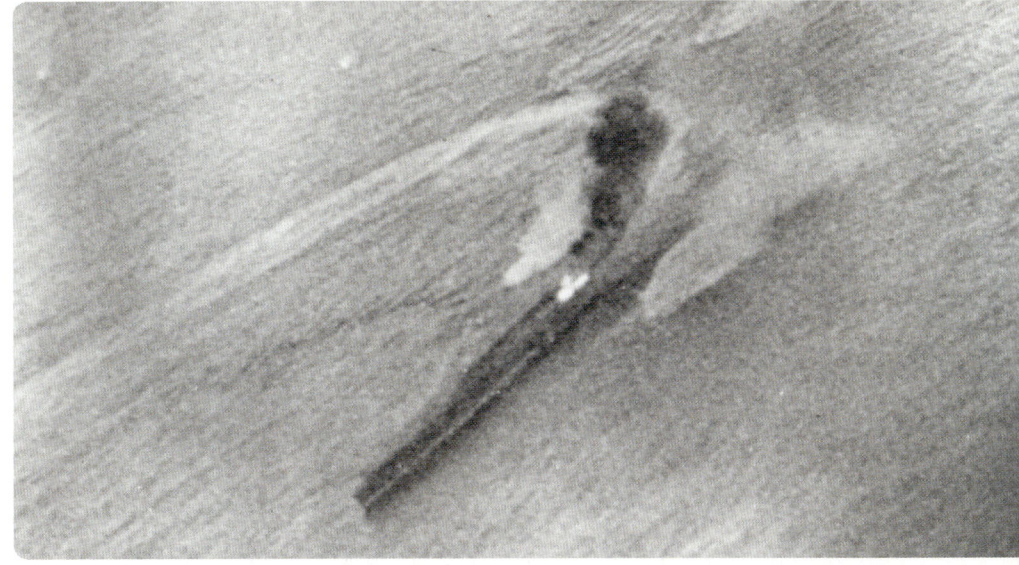

ABOVE: Japanese carrier *Chiyoda* suffers a hit aft and several near misses during air attacks by TF-58 planes, June 20, 1944. US NAVAL HISTORICAL CENTER

TASK GROUP 77.4 VESSELS

★ TAFFY 1
Chenango (CVE 28)
Sangamon (CVE 26)
Suwannee (CVE 27)
Santee (CVE 29)
Petrof Bay (CVE 80)
Saginaw Bay (CVE 82)
(177 aircraft)

★ TAFFY 2
Manila Bay (CVE 61)
Natoma Bay (CVE 62)
Kadashan Bay (CVE 76)
Marcus Island (CVE 77)
Savo Island (CVE 78)
Ommaney Bay (CVE 79)
(147 aircraft)

★ TAFFY 3
St Lo (CVE 63)
White Plains (CVE 66)
Kalinin Bay (CVE 68)
Fanshaw Bay (CVE 70)
Kitkun Bay (CVE 71)
Gambier Bay (CVE 73)
(167 aircraft)

BELOW: *Zuikaku* (centre) and *Chitose* (upper right) shortly before they were sunk on October 25, 1944. *Zuikaku* was the last carrier from the Pearl Harbor attackers to be sunk. AUTHOR'S COLLECTION

ABOVE: Japanese Aichi 'Val' dive-bombers taxi out for a Kamikaze mission from an airfield on the outskirts of Manila, Philippines, in 1944. US NAVAL HISTORICAL CENTER

of attacks. It was the most concentrated USN air attacks on Japanese surface ships of the entire war.

The attacks may have been relentless but they were uncoordinated, with some aircraft carrying weapons unsuited for attacking ships (depth charges). By 0730 hours Taffy 3 had launched 95 aircraft (51 Wildcats and 44 Avengers). Lack of training resulted in piecemeal attacks and when some aircraft ran out of ammunition, they made dummy runs to keep Japanese gunners distracted. Taffy 3 launched its last strike at 1015 hours with two Avengers and two Wildcats.

Taffy 2 added six attacks for the day, the first being 15 Avengers with torpedoes and 20 fighters. The second numbered 16 Avengers with torpedoes and eight fighters. The third strike comprised 12 Avengers (five with torpedoes) and eight fighters. At 1115 hours the fourth and largest strike of the day was launched: 37 Avengers and 19 fighters. The fifth was launched at 1331 hours with 11 Avengers and eight fighters. The last attack of the day was launched at 1500 hours with an impressive 26 Avengers and 24 Wildcats. In total, the carriers of Taffy 2 launched 117 Avengers and 87 Wildcats, which dropped 76 tons of bombs and 49 torpedoes, and fired 276 5in rockets.

At the time of Taffy 2's last strike, Admiral Kurita was a rattled commander who did not have an accurate picture of his enemy and clearly overestimated the force before him.

ABOVE: *Kitkun Bay* (CVE-71) prepares to launch three FM-2 Wildcat fighters during the action on October 25, 1944. Shells from *Yamato* can be seen splashing near *White Plains* (CVE-66). *White Plains* avoided any direct hits but near misses severely damaged its hull. US NAVAL HISTORICAL CENTER

In just 28 hours of intense combat his once powerful flagship *Musashi* had been sunk. Ozawa's decoy carrier force was no more and in fighting the 'baby flattops' he lost three more heavy cruisers: *Chikma*, *Chokai* and *Suzuya*. Convinced he was fighting the fleet carriers of TF-38 and that US battleship reinforcements were on the way, Kurita ordered his remaining ships to reverse course at 0920 hours and head for San Bernardino straight.

The Battle of Leyte Gulf was a devastating loss for the Japanese. In just four days, between October 23 and 26, the Imperial Japanese Navy lost 28 warships, including four carriers, three battleships (two sunk by naval gunfire) and ten cruisers, the vast majority succumbing to carrier airpower. Navy aviators and aircrew claimed 657 enemy aircraft shot down for a loss of 140 of their own lost to all causes. US Navy ship losses included one light carrier, two escort carriers, two destroyers and one destroyer escort.

The Japanese fleet now ceased to exist as an effective fighting force. In a final act of defiance, the Japanese introduced a new and terrifying weapon. An hour after the battle, the Japanese struck back. Approaching at low level, six Zeros with escort approached Taffy 3. Detected by radar, the CAP response was sluggish and unable to intercept. Three Zeros deliberately dove on the USS *Kalinin*, with two hitting the ship, although they caused little damage.

USS *Kitkun Bay* was then hit by a single suicide Zero causing slight damage. The USS *St Lo* was next and would not survive. Battling through heavy AA fire, a single Zero dropped its 551lb bomb before crashing into the flight deck. Penetrating the thin flight deck, the bomb exploded in the hangar deck. In less than 30 minutes the torpedo and bomb magazines exploded – sending her to the bottom.

St Lo was the first victim of Japan's new and desperate method of attack – the kamikaze. For the US Navy, the radical change in Japanese tactics was terrifying and incomprehensible and one they would have to battle until the final day of the war. ■

ABOVE: *Princeton* burning soon after being hit by a 1,100lb bomb from a 'Judy' while operating off the Philippines on October 24, 1944. The bomb hit started a huge fire in the hangar deck where fuel and torpedoes were being prepared for flight operations. US NAVAL HISTORICAL CENTER

RIGHT: After being hit by one of the first kamikaze attacks of the war, the USS *St Lo* suffers an internal explosion, sinking shortly afterwards. October 25, 1944. US NAVAL HISTORICAL CENTER

CHAPTER 7

STEEL RAIN

The kamikaze war,
October 1944–August 1945

"The kamikaze was the only weapon
I truly feared in the war."

Admiral William F. Halsey

The Battles of the Philippine Sea (June 1944) and Leyte Gulf (October 1944) had all but annihilated both the IJNAF and the IJN surface fleet. For the IJNAF there was not enough time to train qualified replacement air crew capable of taking on the US Navy's Fast Carrier Task Force. And even if they had, their remaining carriers and battleships were stuck in harbour due to lack fuel.

The performance of conventional air attacks by both the IJNAF and IJAAF had been remarkably poor. During the Battle of the Philippine Sea just 60 IJNAF aircraft out of a force of 430 aircraft had managed to make bombing attacks and of these only five scored hits. No US ships were sunk and no major damage was caused.

For the Japanese the realisation that their conventional air attacks were completely ineffective had a dramatic effect. US Navy statistics told the story. In the first six months of 1944, of 315 Japanese aircraft that survived the CAP to attack various surface vessels, just 10% scored a hit, causing only minor damage and of those 315 aircraft, 106 were shot down by AA fire.

When attacking the US Fast Carrier Task Force the numbers were even worse. From November 1943 to June 1944 under 5% of daylight attacks hit a target and it was just over 2% for night attacks. Of the 195 aircraft that made daylight attacks 40% were shot down by AA fire.

Japanese losses during the carrier raids of 1943 and the growing power of the Fast Carrier Task Force had already led some in the IJN's leadership to consider suicide tactics. While not adopted as a tactic until late 1944, there were many documented instances of Japanese pilots crashing their aircraft into US ships. Some were examples of damaged aircraft with no hope of survival, deciding to do maximum damage, but on other occasions the act seemed to be deliberate.

On October 26, 1942 during the Battle of Santa Cruz, the carrier *Hornet* (CV-8) was hit twice; once by a D3A1 'Val' dive-bomber and again by a B5N2 'Kate' torpedo bomber. In both cases, minus their ordnance, the aircraft were damaged during the attack with their pilots choosing to sacrifice themselves against the carrier. Another 'Kate' flew into the destroyer USS *Smith* (DD-378) while escorting the carrier *Enterprise* (CV-6).

By August 1944 the cold hard numbers were too grim to ignore. Conventional attacks were no longer viable and a waste of aircrew and aircraft. That summer it was widely accepted that the only way to change the course of the war was to begin suicide operations. The driving force behind the *tokubet su kogeki* – the special attack – was Admiral Takijiro Onishi.

The Japanese never used the term kamikaze during the war, its English translation being 'divine wind'. Yet since the end of the war, kamikaze has become the accepted term and is used in most accounts. Individual units conducting suicide attacks were called *tokubetsu kogeki tai* (or *tokko tai*).

Onishi is generally accepted as the father of the kamikaze. At the beginning of 1944 he was the head of the Aviation Department of the Ministry of Munitions. After the debacle during the Battle of the Philippine Sea he was ordered to take over the First Air Fleet of the IJNAF in preparation for the expected invasion of the Philippines.

Onishi was well aware of the crushing defeats already suffered and the inability of the IJNAF to achieve any success. Before taking on his new post, he informed the Chief of the Naval General Staff and the Navy Minister of his intention to target American ships with 'special attack' units. When Onishi arrived in the Philippines on October 17, his air fleet possessed just 100 aircraft (far fewer were serviceable). The force was so small Onishi knew conventional attacks would be useless so he opted for suicide attacks instead – a decision that would send hundreds of young men to their deaths.

THROUGH THE EYES OF THE KAMIKAZE

Throughout Japan's long history, the samurai class held great influence both politically and culturally and the concept was well established in the new conscript army. Prior to the war Japanese education included military drills and martial arts education. The Emperor and the needs of the state were first and foremost, subjugating the will of the individual to a group consensus.

When IJNAF and JAAF pilots were asked to volunteer for a kamikaze or air-to-air ramming mission, it was virtually impossible for them to say no. For the individual pilot, peer pressure and perceived group approval were his guiding principles. To question or disobey an order was unthinkable.

Japanese pilot training also was incredibly harsh and brutal. Punishment was an integral part of the training process and physical punishment was common. No matter how well a trainee performed, training instructors would punish him regardless. By western standards it was completely incomprehensible. Japanese military training focused on total dedication to the Emperor with a complete disregard for one's self-interest. It also served to instill two main attributes: iron discipline and the offensive fighting spirit.

The average age of the kamikaze pilot was between 20 and 25 and all were volunteers. The first units to form in the Philippines came from established squadrons. Many of the pilots had battle experience and were well aware of the futility of continued conventional attacks against the American carriers. It is not surprising that many made the calculation that dying in a kamikaze attack would be far more effective than

ABOVE and LEFT: These two photos show the approach and hit by a Japanese 'Judy' on *Essex* (CV-9) during a kamikaze attack of Luzon, November 25, 1944. US NAVAL HISTORICAL CENTER

ABOVE: The Japanese used a variety of types for kamikaze attacks including their most modern types like the Yokosuka P1Y 'Frances' twin-engine bomber. Here a P1Y attempts to hit *Ommaney Bay* (CVE-79) in the Sulu Sea, Philippines, December 15, 1944. This plane has flown over the ship and is about to crash. Note the 20mm gun firing at the plane with strikes on the starboard engine. US NAVAL HISTORICAL CENTER

ABOVE: The first line of defence against the kamikaze was the fleet's fighter CAP. This kamikaze Zero is caught and shot down by a FM-2 Wildcat from *Sangamon* (CVE-26) October 25, 1944. US NAVAL HISTORICAL CENTER

perishing in a one-way conventional attack.

Not every pilot was asked to volunteer. Experienced fighter pilots were needed to escort the kamikaze to their targets. Hideo Muraoka, commanding officer of the 20th Sentai JAAF, based in the Philippines remembered: "Initially, *tokkotai* pilots were selected in Japan and then sent out to the Philippines. One of my jobs as CO of the 20th Sentai (flying Nakajima Ki-43 'Oscars') was to select and then escort the chosen kamikaze pilots to their targets."

GATHERING STORM

The kamikaze attacks against Taffy 1 and Taffy 3 on October 25 and 26 were an unqualified success. With just a handful of Zero fighters the Japanese sank one escort carrier and damaged five more, sending several for fleet repair.

The first fleet carrier to be hit by a kamikaze occurred on October 29. By that time the Japanese mustered enough kamikazes to mount the largest attack to date. In comparison to the escort carrier groups, the fleet carrier task group had more fighters and more powerful screening forces. By 1944 *Essex* class carriers and all US ships had been provided with extensive anti-aircraft defences. Standard armament for the *Essex* was 12 5in/38cal guns – eight in twin turrets and for single mounts, 18 quadruple 40mm and 46 20mm guns placed on galleries just below the flight deck.

US fleet defences had proven themselves highly effective, but the kamikaze was a weapon Navy planners had not foreseen. No one had considered using an aircraft as a missile with a human guidance system. The kamikaze was also a double threat. Many Zeros (the most widely used kamikaze aircraft) carried a single bomb and once over the target pilots were trained to release this first to cause as much damage as possible before adding to the carnage by crashing their aircraft into a ship.

For US Navy AA gunners, the introduction of the kamikaze changed the AA equation. AA fire was designed to prevent attacking aircraft from bombing accurately. Shooting an aircraft down was a bonus. Like the German V-1 flying bomb, the kamikaze had to be destroyed outright in order for the AA to be a success.

"The suicide attack represents by far the most difficult antiaircraft problem yet faced by the fleet. The psychological value of AA., which in the past has driven away a large percentage of potential attackers, is inoperative against the suicide plane. If the plane is not shot down or so severely damaged that its control is impaired, it almost inevitably will hit its target. Expert aviation opinion agrees that an unhindered and undamaged plane has virtually a 100% chance of crashing into a ship of any size regardless of her evasive action." Anti-Suicide Action Summary August 1945, COMINCH.

The first line of defence for the fleet was combat air patrols. F6F-5 Hellcats, F4U-1D/FG-1D Corsairs and FM-2 Wildcats were assigned to the task. As the suicide attacks grew in number and intensity the US Navy increased the number of fighters aboard the *Essex*-class fleet carriers from 54 to 73, leaving just 15 SB2C Helldivers and 15 TBF Avengers. The enlarged fighter complement was divided into two units – a fighter squadron (VF) and a fighter-bomber squadron (VBF). This gave the carrier groups more fighters, but more importantly the Americans needed a fighter that was faster and had a better rate of climb than the Hellcat.

Fortunately they had the F4U-1D with a top speed of 425mph at 20,000ft compared to the F6F-5's 386mph at 23,700ft. While previously unsuited for carrier operations, the F4U Corsair was added to the fleet with two Marine squadrons embarking on *Essex* in January 1945. By the time of the Okinawa campaign TF-58 had five US Navy and six Marine Corps Corsair squadrons.

The first requirement for effective fleet air defence was detection. Against the kamikaze this was critical. Unfortunately for the Americans their radar had some serious problems. Against both high and low-flying aircraft the standard SK air-search radar gave an uneven performance.

BELOW: *Ticonderoga* (CV-14) on fire after being hit by a kamikaze off Formosa, January 21, 1945. The carrier was heavily damaged and was out of action until May 1945. US NAVAL HISTORICAL CENTER

ABOVE: *Franklin* (CV-13) dead in the water and burning, after being hit by a Japanese air attack off the coast of Japan, March 19, 1945. USS *Santa Fe* (CL-60) is alongside, helping with fire-fighting. US NAVAL HISTORICAL CENTER

Capable of detecting incoming aircraft well beyond 50 miles, it would lose them as they came closer to the fleet.

If the kamikaze approached below 15,000ft, it could be lost in a null void for a good 25 miles, and remain undetected by radar. The SM radar helped fill the gap, but had limited high altitude range. The Japanese also took advantage of radar 'shadows' cause by nearby islands; they would also latch onto returning US Navy aircraft formations, making it difficult for the radar plotters to identify friend from foe.

To cover both high altitude and low-level kamikaze attacks most CAPs were flown at medium altitudes of 16,400ft.

KAMIKAZE TACTICS

At first glance the idea of crashing an aircraft into a ship was relatively easy, but in fact it was just the opposite. A great deal of pilot skill was required for a successful kamikaze mission.

The first hurdle was the American CAP, once this was evaded intense and accurate AA fire would meet the attacker and would be continuous until he was shot down or crashed into his target. And even if the kamikaze made it through the fighters and AA fire he had to hit a fast and manoeuvring target. By 1945 the majority of the kamikaze pilots were poorly trained – making them easy targets.

Early kamikaze tactics were crude affairs numbering just five or six aircraft, including escort. By December 1944 the number had increased to 10 or 20 aircraft and by the Okinawa campaign that number grew to 50. Larger formations were able to saturate the defences, guaranteeing that some aircraft would get through.

In reaction to the Americans' medium altitude CAP patrols, the Japanese quickly changed their approach by adding both high altitude and low-level attack profiles. For high-altitude attack 19,680-23,000ft was adopted. Once the target was sighted the kamikaze pushed over into a 20 degree descent. This, hopefully, gave him the speed to get through the medium level CAP patrol on the way to his target. When the pilot reached 3,280-6,560ft the attack dive began at an angle of 45-55 degrees.

The second kamikaze method of approach was the most demanding and required a greater degree of flying skill. The low-altitude attack required the pilot to skim the waves at just 30-50ft – well below radar detection. At a range of 3,000ft from the target the kamikaze would perform a 'pop-up' manoeuvre, climbing to 1,300-1,600ft and then diving on his target. The low-altitude approach also negated the effectiveness of American AA fire, forcing them to hold fire to avoid hitting other ships in the formation.

The IJNAF and JAAF used many different types of aircraft as kamikazes including biplane training aircraft. The preferred types were single-engine fighters like the Zero and Ki-43 'Oscar'. Their higher speed and ability to carry a single 551lb bomb, made them the most likely to survive the CAP and cause the most damage. Twin-engined bombers were also employed including the Mitsubishi G4M 'Betty' and more modern Yokosuka P1Y1 'Frances' medium bomber.

ABOVE: The mangled hole in the flight deck of the carrier *Randolph* (CV-15) after being hit by a 'Frances' kamikaze on March 11, 1945. US NAVAL HISTORICAL CENTER

HITTING THE FLEET CARRIERS

The primary target of the kamikaze was the fast carriers of the TF-38/58. The Japanese knew that the only way to slow the US advance was to inflict crippling losses on these carriers. As the IJNAF and JAAF rapidly increased the number of kamikazes, US Navy airmen and gunners braced themselves for a battle that would be terrifying, incomprehensible and seemingly endless.

After the initial success of the October 25/26 attacks on the escort carriers of Taffy 1 and Taffy 3, the Japanese had enough kamikazes available to mount the largest attack to date. On October 29, TG-38.2 mounted several strikes against Japanese airfields in the Manila area. In response 13 kamikazes took off to attack the carriers. The strike was detected early and the CAP shot down all but one of the attackers. The lone 'Val' selected the fleet carrier *Intrepid*, hitting the portside gun gallery. Damage was superficial, but ten sailors were killed and six wounded.

The next carrier to be hit was *Franklin*. On October 30 six kamikazes and five escorts

ABOVE: *Enterprise* (CV-6) is hit by a single Zero kamikaze on May 13, 1945, off Okinawa. This hit would knock the vessel out for the rest of the war. US NAVAL HISTORICAL CENTER

ABOVE: The two kamikaze hits on *Franklin* (CV-17) on May 11, 1945 caused extensive damage to both the flight and hangar decks. NARA

On November 5, TF-38 returned to the Philippines ready to target the kamikaze directly. The battle against the kamikaze was both a defensive and offensive operation. During November 5 and 6, TF-38 mounted a series of strikes against Japanese airfields throughout the Philippines, greatly reducing the number of attacks. On November 5, however, a small formation of four Zeros made it through the CAP to attack the carrier *Lexington*. AA gunners shot down three, but one kamikaze hit the aft end of the island. Damage was light and flight operations continued, but 50 sailors were killed and 132 wounded.

On November 25 the Japanese increased the tempo of attacks, concentrating on the carriers of TF-38. The carrier *Hancock* (CV-19) suffered a near miss, while *Intrepid* was struck a second time by a Zero. With a bomb attached it penetrated the flight deck before exploding and starting a major fire on both the flight and hangar decks. As the blaze spread two more Zeros were spotted, noses pointed toward the ship. The first was hacked from the sky by AA fire, but the second dropped its bomb and slammed into the flight deck amidship. The Zero's bomb penetrated to the hangar deck, starting another major fire.

Two hours later the fire was finally extinguished but the *Intrepid* was left inoperable. Forced from the fleet, *Intrepid* returned to the United States and wouldn't return until March 1945. The light carrier *Cabot* was also hit by a kamikaze Zero, punching small holes in the flight deck, and inflicting heavy casualties in the gun gallery. A second kamikaze barely missed the carrier, but the resulting explosion from the aircraft and its attached bomb damaged the hull, forcing the *Cabot* to retire for repairs.

The kamikazes kept coming. TG-38.3 was next in line when a D4Y3 'Judy' broke through the CAP and hit the carrier *Essex* on the forward flight deck. It appeared to be a devastating hit but the *Essex* emerged lightly damaged and requiring only two weeks of repair.

November 1944 had been a hard month for US Fast Carrier Attack Force. In the weeks following the invasion of the Philippines the USAAF's participation was minimal. The lack of operational airfields left the carrier air groups as the only effective American air force in the area. This forced TF-38 to provide the necessary air support while giving the Japanese juicy targets for their newly formed kamikaze units. As the combat missions mounted – CAPs against the kamikaze, anti-shipping strikes and air cover for the ground troops, the war-weary American pilots and their airplanes began to show the strain. Guns malfunctioned or jammed, engines ran rough and instruments stopped working.

headed for TG-38.4. Skirting the CAP, three of the six suicide attackers headed for the fleet carrier. Three D4Y3 'Judys' dove for the carrier. The first missed, followed by the second hitting the aft flight deck. Penetrating into the hangar deck, the aircraft's bomb exploded causing major damage. The third kamikaze dropped a 551lb bomb missing the *Franklin* by 30ft. The 'Judy' then turned and headed towards the light carrier *Belleau Wood*. The kamikaze found its mark, hitting the carrier by the aft elevator and starting a fire that spread to 11 aircraft on the flight deck. It was a devastating attack for both carriers. Fifty-six men were killed and 60 wounded on *Franklin*, putting here out of action until March 1945 and another 92 were killed and 97 wounded on *Belleau Wood*. The light carrier did not return to action until February 1945. With just two kamikaze strikes TG-38.4 had been cut in half. For the Japanese a carrier put out of action was the next best thing to an outright sinking.

At the beginning of November, TF-38 retired to Ulithi atoll in the Caroline Islands (the main US Navy forward base in the Western Pacific) for much needed rest and replenishment.

For the Japanese the kamikaze was an undeniable success. In just one month the fleet carriers *Intrepid* and *Franklin* and the light carrier *Belleau Wood* had been badly damaged and forced to return to the United States. *Essex* and the light carrier *Cabot* were also damaged retiring to Ulithi for repairs.

While the threat from both the IJN's surface fleet and its carrier force had all but been extinguished, the new threat of the kamikaze was proving to be far deadlier than any conventional attack method. With just a handful of kamikazes, the Japanese had inflicted heavy damage on the US Pacific Fleet, forcing the Americans to fight a battle they had not planned for. New and improved defensive and offensive tactics had to be devised and refined and more resources allocated for the fanatical battle that lay ahead.

STORM OVER THE PHILIPPINES

The end of the Philippine campaign centred on the invasion of Luzon. The Japanese knew the loss of Luzon meant the loss of the Philippines. In response they launched ten days of continuous kamikaze attacks on the invasion fleet.

The first victim was the escort carrier *Ommaney Bay*. As the invasion fleet sailed through the Sulu Sea en route to Luzon, a single IJNAF twin-engined P1Y 'Frances' evaded radar detection, catching the small carrier completely by surprise. Hitting the ship's island it then crashed into the flight deck before smashing into the sea. This caused little damage, but the aircraft's two bombs plunged through to the forward hangar deck and engine room. All power was lost and the resulting fire doomed the carrier. An hour after the hit, *Ommaney Bay* was abandoned and later scuttled.

On January 5 the kamikaze attacks intensified. Three waves headed for the fleet. The first two were defeated by the CAP, but the third of 16 aircraft found a way through. The first to be hit were the heavy cruiser USS *Louisville* (CA-28) along with the Royal Australian Navy destroyer HMAS *Arunta* and cruiser HMAS *Australia*. This was followed by heavy attacks on the escort carriers. Two Zeros targeted *Manila Bay*. One found its mark, hitting the flight deck and penetrating through to the hangar deck. The resulting fire was quickly extinguished. *Savo Island* suffered a near miss as four Zeros headed for the escort carrier *Tulagi*. Intense AA fire brought down three, but the fourth hit the destroyer escort USS *Stafford* (DE-411). Severely damaged, the vessel was forced to return to the US for repairs.

The carnage continued on January 6. Thirteen ships were hit including the battleships USS *California* (BB-44) and USS *New Mexico* (BB40). The damage to the battlewagons was slight due to their heavy armour, but the overall damage to the fleet was unsustainable. It was clear that the escort carriers were incapable of providing adequate CAP patrols. For the Japanese the battle of attrition was working in their favour. Every carrier sunk or heavily damaged and forced to retire meant fewer fighters were available for defence. This opened holes in the CAP giving the kamikazes more opportunities for success.

BELOW: *Bunker Hill* **(CV-17) burning after being hit by kamikaze suicide planes during the Okinawa operation, May 11, 1945.**
US NAVAL HISTORICAL CENTER

ABOVE: Kamikazes armed with bombs were the most destructive. Here a Zero armed with a 551lb bomb dives on *Enterprise* (CV-6) May 13, 1945. This was the kamikaze that knocked *Enterprise* out of the war.
AUTHOR'S COLLECTION

On January 7 the JAAF made an appearance, sending a large group of some 20 aircraft towards the escort carriers. One Ki-43 'Oscar' broke through, striking the *Kadashan Bay* at its waterline. The aircraft's bomb failed to explode, but the resulting large hole forced it out of action until mid-April. Later in the afternoon six kamikazes evaded the CAP. Three were shot down by accurate AA fire, but a single Ki-44 slammed into *Kitkun Bay* at the waterline on the portside. Extensive flooding and loss of power forced it out action for several months.

The final carrier to be hit during the Philippine campaign was recorded on January 13. A single JAAF Ki-84 'Frank' fighter armed with two bombs crashed into the escort carrier *Salamana*. One of the aircraft's bombs detonated in the hangar deck with the second exploding near the waterline after passing through the ship. A major fire developed and although damage control was successful, the ship was forced to retire for repair until April.

The air defence provided by the escort carrier fleet was inadequate. This was due to a number of reasons, some beyond the Americans' control. The land masses and small islands near the ships confused radar and the performance and number of the FM-2 Wildcats available were unsuited to the task of effective CAP defence. The overall American anti-kamikaze tactics suffered from a number of growing pains. Forced to fight a battle against a fanatical foe, the small escort carriers put up a brave fight and would continue to do so until the end of the war.

As the Americans planned and prepared for the invasion of Okinawa on April 1, the leadership of the kamikaze units was given over to Vice Admiral Matome Ugaki on February 10, 1945. Based in southern Japan, Ugaki's Fifth Air Fleet would be responsible for the majority of the IJNAF's kamikaze attacks for the rest of the war.

As the US Pacific Fleet prepared for its next major offensive operations, the Japanese continued to inflict heavy damage on its fleet carriers. On January 21, two small waves of kamikazes were spotted on radar. Nine aircraft headed for TF-38 just off of Formosa. The pattern would once again repeat itself as one Zero penetrated through both fighters and AA fire to hit the carrier *Ticonderoga* (CV-14). At the time the deck was packed with a fully armed and fuelled air group. Hitting aft of the forward elevator, the Zero's bomb exploded causing a major fire among the parked aircraft. A second kamikaze slammed into the island with slight damage. The carrier survived the inferno, but not before 143 sailors were killed or listed missing with another 202 wounded. Severely damaged, *Ticonderoga* was out of the war until May.

US Marines stormed the beaches of Iwo Jima on February 19, 1945. Air support was provided by the fleet and escort carriers of TF-38. Operating close the island, the carriers provided the Japanese with targets that were easy to find, if not hit. On February 21 a mixed formation of 32 aircraft – 12 support aircraft and 20 kamikazes – approached the fleet. For this strike the Japanese introduced a new tactic.

Several aircraft began dropping chaff (metallic strips) to confuse American radar. Breaking out of low cloud six kamikazes targeted the combat veteran, *Saratoga*. Incredibly after six hits or near misses the ship was damaged but was never in danger of sinking. Many fires were started, but damage control teams brought them under control. Like all the carriers previously struck, *Saratoga* was forced from the field of battle with 123 dead and 192 wounded.

That evening radar performance was spotty, allowing a group of kamikazes to sneak through. Coming in low, a G4M 'Betty' bomber made straight for the escort carrier *Bismarck Sea*.

BELOW: *Franklin* (CV-13), at right, and *Belleau Wood* (CVL-24) on fire after being hit by kamikaze suicide planes, while operating off the Philippines on October 30, 1944. US NAVAL HISTORICAL CENTER

ABOVE: *Intrepid* (CV-11) afire, after a kamikaze strike off Okinawa on April 16, 1945. A *Fletcher* class destroyer provides AA assistance with its 5in guns trained toward the sky. US NAVAL HISTORICAL CENTER

Flying through a barrage of accurate AA fire, the 'Betty' crashed into the carrier abeam of the aft aircraft elevator. Fire spread through the parked aircraft in the hangar bay. A second kamikaze struck causing another large explosion and making fire-fighting efforts all but impossible. *Bismarck Sea* succumbed to her wounds, sinking with 318 sailors lost. There were 605 survivors.

In what might have been the most spectacular kamikaze attacks of the war, the Japanese launched a surprise mission that could have crippled the US carriers. On March 9, Japanese long-range aircraft from Truk Lagoon spotted the Fast Carrier Task force at anchor in Ulithi Atoll, the US Navy's operating base in the Western Pacific. Located 800 nautical miles from the Japanese home islands, the Americans considered it a relatively safe area from attack. But the Japanese knew their P1Y1 'Frances' aircraft could reach the target armed with bombs (the P1Y1 had impressive performance with a top speed of 340mph with a 2,200lb bomb load) – albeit only on a one-way trip.

Twenty-four 'Frances' bombers took off at dusk on March 11, although 11 of them had to return due to mechanical issues. The remaining 13 pressed on but poor weather and inaccurate navigation caused 11 to miss Ulithi completely – leaving just two for the attack.

Surprise was complete. The anchorage was entirely lit, giving the Japanese bombers more than enough light to select their targets. For some reason one of the bombers crashed into a lighted baseball field on a nearby island. The second, however, found the new fleet carrier USS *Randolph* (CV-15). Crashing into its fantail, the aircraft's bombload exploded, carving out a big hole in the flight deck. The repairs would keep *Randolph* out of action for a full month. The Americans had dodged a bullet. With better trained aircrew and more reliable aircraft, the Japanese could have landed a devastating blow.

A MOST DEVASTATING ATTACK

This raid forced the Americans to react by attacking the main kamikaze air bases. On March 18, TF-58 sortied from Ulithi headed for southern Japan. Steaming just 50 miles off the coast of Kyushu, TG-58.2 with the carrier *Franklin* launched a fighter sweep on the morning of the 19th. Their mission was to hit kamikaze bases on Kyushu island in preparation for the planned April 1 invasion of Okinawa.

The Americans had come to the realisation that the best countermeasure to the kamikazes was to destroy them on the ground before they could be used. In response, Ugaki mounted both conventional and kamikaze attacks. The first to be hit was *Franklin*. In a surprise attack a single D4Y 'Judy' dive-bomber popped out of the clouds directly over the carrier. Making a low level run, the D4Y dropped two 551lb bombs. The first hit the centre-line of the flight deck and exploded after penetrating to the hangar deck. Below were 16 aircraft, some fully fuelled.

Fire quickly engulfed the aircraft setting them off like bombs. The second bomb hit aft, slicing through two decks and exploding. This second explosion set off ammunition, bombs and rockets. Within minutes power and communication was lost throughout the ship. Drifty helplessly, *Franklin* took on a 13-degree list. By late afternoon however the fires aboard *Franklin* had been brought under control. Power was restored, and the ship managed 15 knots. *Franklin* was one of the few carriers to be severely damaged by a conventional attack and not by a kamikaze. But the destruction was just as devastating – 807 dead and 487 wounded out of 2600 crew making it the greatest loss of life on any Navy ship during the war after the *Arizona* at Pearl Harbor.

Two other kamikaze attacks followed, damaging the carrier *Intrepid* with a near miss and *Wasp* with a single bomb, dropped from a kamikaze. The hit on the *Wasp* penetrated the flight deck and caused a significant fire, killing 101 sailors. Neither ship was forced from the line though and both remained operational.

INTO THE FIRE

After five months of kamikaze attacks, the US Navy's ability to defeat Japanese suicide attackers using fighters and anti-aircraft guns had revealed some weaknesses. The Japanese tactics of using both high and low-level attacks and the gaps in US radar coverage meant too many were getting through. And the numbers added up. Scoring a single bomb or torpedo hit

ABOVE: A 'Judy' Kamikaze attempts to hit *Essex* (CV-9) off Japan, on March 19, 1945. In order for the fighter and AA defences to be effective against the kamikaze the aircraft had to be destroyed outright. Even with half of its wing blown off this kamikaze continued the attack but missed. US NAVAL HISTORICAL CENTER

ABOVE: *Ommaney Bay* CVE 79 on fire after being hit by a lone 'Frances' on January 4, 1945. The aircraft hit caused little damage, but its two bombs penetrated through to the forward hangar deck and engine room, before exploding. After just one hour the ship was abandoned and later scuttled. US NAVAL HISTORICAL CENTER

ABOVE: With 5in guns blazing *Essex* (CV-9) suffers a near miss by a kamikaze on April 15, 1945. NARA

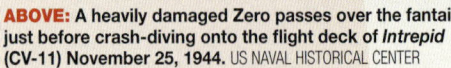

ABOVE: A heavily damaged Zero passes over the fantail just before crash-diving onto the flight deck of *Intrepid* (CV-11) November 25, 1944. US NAVAL HISTORICAL CENTER

using conventional methods required 37 aircraft, the majority of which would be shot down. For a kamikaze attack it was just 3.6 aircraft. The damage inflicted was, in many cases, also far greater.

The 20mm Oerlikon and 40mm Bofors guns had proven excellent guns in repelling conventional air attacks, but against the kamikazes they were not powerful enough and were found to be alarmingly ineffective. Even when they caused major damage by knocking off a wing or tail plane surface, the kinetic energy of the aircraft kept it on line to the target, causing a near miss or direct hit.

The most effective anti-aircraft guns, capable of destroying a suicide attacker far enough away, were the proven 5in/38 dual purpose and older 5in/25. Both weapons with their fire control systems could effectively engage a target beyond 15,000 yards (a four-gun 5in/38 battery under director control was effective up to 10,000 yards). The speed and unpredictable manoeuvres of the kamikaze, however, negated the power and accuracy of these weapons.

The Mk 32 proximity-fuse (VT variable timing) shell helped redress the balance though, giving the 5in gun a greatly increased effectiveness. Four times more effective than a conventional AA shell, the VT fuse was effective at both short and long ranges. Always in short supply the VT round was used sparingly against the kamikaze. That left the medium and close defence to the reliable 20mm and 40mm guns.

In preparation for Operation Iceberg – the invasion of Okinawa – the US Navy introduced the picket destroyer. Fifteen stations were set up between 15 and 100 miles from the island. Each station was manned by a destroyer and some smaller supporting craft. Their job was to provide early radar warning for the fleet. The Japanese quickly realised their importance and struck at these vulnerable targets with heavy losses.

Fighter cover was also improved. For the Okinawa campaign the carriers of TF-58 were reinforced with five US Navy and six Marine Corps Corsair Squadrons. For the coming battle TF-58 would muster approximately 1,111 F6F-3, F4U-1D and FM-2s. A total of 192 F4U-1Ds and 30 F6F-5s would join the fight once airfields were established on Okinawa (this fighter force was augmented by the 170 F4U, F6F and Supermarine Seafire Mk IIIs of the British Pacific Fleet).

The US Navy also devised 'Jack' patrols. To provide a last-ditch counter to kamikazes which approached at sea-level or had evaded the outer patrols, a fighter CAP was mounted at less than 3,000ft within 10 miles of the destroyer screen. These low-level CAPs were controlled by visual fighter directors using a common local air defence R/T frequency. The Hellcat was the most numerous fighter in the fleet and during the 83 day battle the carrier based F6Fs shot down an average of ten enemy aircraft a day.

For the coming battle the carrier task groups continued with the circular formation as the standard anti-aircraft defensive tactic. It provided defence in depth while allowing the task group to change direction easily.

REVISED KAMIKAZE TACTICS

For the coming battle the Japanese had revised their suicide tactics. In what would be the most

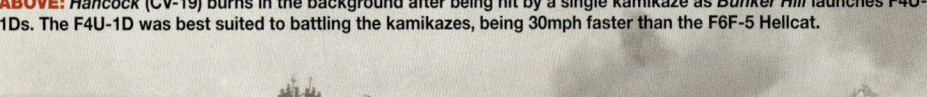

ABOVE: *Hancock* (CV-19) burns in the background after being hit by a single kamikaze as *Bunker Hill* launches F4U-1Ds. The F4U-1D was best suited to battling the kamikazes, being 30mph faster than the F6F-5 Hellcat.

BELOW: This photo gives a sense of the horror felt when a kamikaze got through the defences and found its mark. Here an 'Oscar' streaks through AA tracer fire and exploding 5in shells towards *Kadashan* CVE-76 on January 8, 1945. The kamikaze hit at the waterline, creating a large hole and knocking out the carrier until April 1945. US NAVAL HISTORICAL CENTER

TASK FORCES 58 AND 57

★ TG-58.1	★ TG-58.2	★ TG-58.3	★ TG-58.4	★ TG-57
Hornet	Enterprise	Essex	Yorktown	HMS Indomitable
Wasp	Franklin	Bunker Hill	Intrepid	HMS Victorious
Bennington	Randolph	Hancock	Langley	HMS Illustrious
Belleau Wood		Cabot	Independence	HMS Indefatigable
San Jacinto		Bataan		HMS Formidable

intense and prolonged air-sea battle in naval history, the Japanese used large formations of kamikaze for the first time. But while the attacking formations were substantial, the suicide attackers did not concentrate their mass. Instead they broke up their formations to attack singly or in small groups from different directions. The commanders of TF-58 considered that the Japanese were showing clever execution and enormous determination. As they approached the US ships they made radical course changes and varied their altitude. And when intercepted they would disperse and use cloud cover to hide and then strike with great effect. Decoys were used to draw CAP fighters, chaff was released to blind US radar and many kamikazes tried to follow US strike aircraft on their return to avoid detection.

Both the JAAF and IJNAF used their more experienced pilots and aircraft as escorts (IJNAF Kawanishi N1K2 Shiden Kai 'George' and JAAF Nakajima Ki-84 Hayate 'Frank' fighters). The IJNAF could muster nearly 4,000 Special Attack aircraft with the JAAF adding another 1,600. While the JAAF targeted mostly transport and support vessels, the IJNAF went after the US Navy's fleet units. Fortunately for the Americans, the Japanese pilots at this stage were poorly trained – making them easier to shoot down and less capable of hitting their target.

On the eve of battle, TF-58 was a formidable force with 11 fleet carriers, six light and 22 escort carriers. This would be supported by the five Royal Navy Fleet carriers of Task Force 57.

During 1945 the Fast Carrier Task Force used two fleet commanders. The fleet's designation changed when the commander changed. So when Admiral Spruance took command prior to Operation Iceberg his ships were designated the 5th Fleet and the carriers became Task Force 58. When Admiral Halsey relieved Spruance, the carries became part of 3rd Fleet and were designated Task Force 38.

The invasion of Okinawa did result in an immediate massed kamikaze attack – which had been anticipated by the Americans. Limited attacks on April 1 resulted in damage to two transports, a destroyer minelayer and the battleship USS *West Virginia* (BB-48).

On April 6, Ugaki unleashed the first of several massed strikes. Each of strike was named Kikusui (Floating Chrysanthemum). Some 200 kamikazes, plus their escorts, soon flooded the US radar screens. At 1500 hours Kikusui No 1 began. This was the biggest single kamikaze attack of the war to date. After two days of intense combat the carriers of TF-58 escaped, but not before nine ships were sunk, 11 more damaged with 370 dead and 475 wounded.

The Radar Picket (RP) stations quickly became favourite targets for the kamikazes. The Japanese knew the RP destroyers were an integral part of the US fleet's air defence. On April 6 the destroyer USS *Bush* (DD-529) was hit twice by kamikazes and the USS *Colhoun* (DD-801) was hit four times and scuttled. The next day the kamikazes scored a hit on the carrier *Hancock*. Damage was light, but 62 sailors were killed and 71 wounded.

The first carrier knocked out of the fleet was *Enterprise*. On April 11, TF-58 came under attack ▶

BELOW: A captured Yokosuka MXY7 Ohka piloted flying bomb on Okinawa. The small size of the Ohka would have made it a difficult target to shoot down either by fighters or AA fire. US NAVAL HISTORICAL CENTER

ABOVE: This gun camera sequence records the final moments of a Japanese Mitsubishi G4M2E carrying an Ohka rocket powered glide bomb. This was one of 18 'Bettys' launched on March 21, 1945, during the first Jinrai (Divine Thunder) sortie armed with the Ohka. All 18 'Bettys' were shot down. NARA

once again. Two 'Judys' hit *Enterprise*, causing enough damage to require three weeks of repair.

The second massed Kikusui was mounted on April 12-13 and numbered some 183 suicide aircraft. Once again the RP destroyers came under heavy attack. This battle also saw the introduction of the highly destructive Yokosuka MXY7 Ohka (Cherry Blossom) piloted rocket bomb. Air launched from a G4M2E 'Betty' bomber, the Ohka was armed with a 2,646lb Tekkou armour-piercing warhead. With a top speed of 576mph, it could not be intercepted and had the potential to sink a fleet carrier with a single hit. The first and only ship sunk by an *Ohka* was hit on April 12 after nine 'Bettys' attacked the US Fleet off Okinawa. After first being struck by a Zero, the destroyer USS *Mannert L. Abde* (DD-733) was crashed into by a single *Ohka*. It took just four minutes for the Summer class destroyer to sink.

On April 16-17 Kikusui No.3 was launched, with 165 IJNAF and JAAF aircraft. Only a small number were able to penetrate the CAP and find the carriers of TF-58. *Intrepid* would be the unfortunate victim – being hit for a fourth time by a kamikaze. The suicide aircraft scored a direct hit near the aft elevator, slashing through to the hangar deck and causing a large fire. Excellent damage control saved the ship, but the carrier was forced to return to the United States and was out for the rest of the war.

On May 3-4 the Japanese launched numerous further attacks. The fleet carriers were spared but the escort carrier *Sangamon* was hit by a single bomb armed Ki-45 'Nick'. The resulting fire caused extensive damage and forced the escort carrier from the fleet for the rest of the war.

A FAILING WIND

Before the savage battle of attrition came to an end on Okinawa, Ugaki ordered five more massed suicide attacks. Knowing Okinawa was a lost battle, the Japanese began to hold back on the number of suicide aircraft sent for attack, saving them for the expected invasion of Japan.

ABOVE: The Yokosuka P1Y1 Ginga 'Frances' was fast and hard to intercept, making it one of the most effective kamikaze aircraft. Fortunately for the Allies it was built in relatively small numbers (just over 1,000 were built) and there were too few trained pilots to make it a real threat. NARA

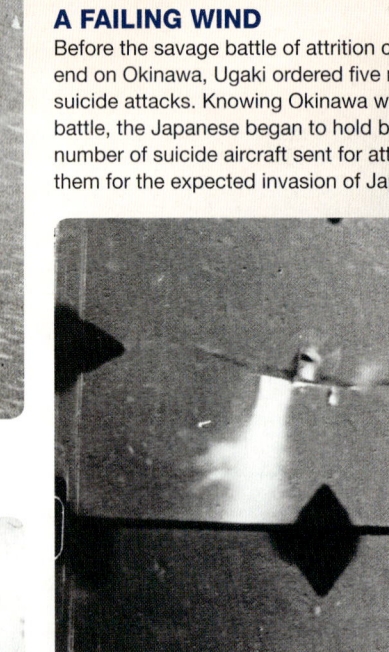

ABOVE: A Mitsubishi Ki-51 'Sonia' light bomber is shot down by a Hellcat pilot near Okinawa on April 3, 1945. Obsolete by 1945, the 'Sonia' was used extensively as a kamikaze. NARA

LEFT: Gun camera image from an F6F Hellcat shows a Yokosuka D4Y2 'Judy' just before the aircraft is shot down off Okinawa. The bombload capacity of the 'Judy' made it one the more feared kamikazes. NARA

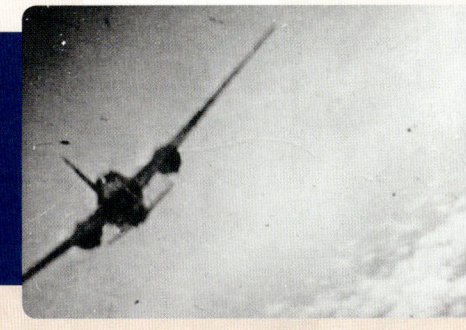  

In the early morning hours of May 11, the kamikazes launched one of the most successful missions of the entire war. Four bomb-equipped Zeros avoided radar and approached TF-58 unseen and undetected. Masked by low cloud, the pilots achieved complete surprise and dived on the carrier *Bunker Hill*. In a thirty second span two Zeros slammed into the ship, creating a huge fire on the flight and hangar decks. It was a major hit and the fires took hours to bring under control, but not before 346 sailors were killed, 43 listed as missing and 264 wounded.

Bunker Hill returned to the United States and was still in the Bremerton Naval Shipyard when the war came to an end. On the 13th TF-58 lost another fleet carrier. After returning from repairs from an earlier kamikaze attack the combat veteran *Enterprise* was knocked out of the war for the last time. A single Zero hit just aft of the forward elevator, killing 14 and wounding 34.

The final large formation suicide attack was Kikusui No. 10 between June 21-22. Just 45 aircraft were involved, resulting in one landing craft and the already damaged fast transport *Barry* being sunk.

The largest and most savage air-sea-land campaign was over. Despite the intense onslaught and some success against the carriers, TF-58 operated continuously for more than 70 days – all while within easy reach of Japanese airfields on Kyushu. The kamikaze was a formidable weapon, but in most cases its terminal velocity was insufficient to penetrate deeply into a ship. Most of the crippling damage was caused the aircraft's bomb and not the impact of the aircraft itself.

Armoured cruisers and battleships were able to absorb the attacks and were never in danger of sinking. Carriers, however, were extremely vulnerable. Essentially a floating box filled with aviation fuel, ordnance and aircraft, a single bomb armed kamikaze was enough to heavily damage a carrier. However, for all their ferocity the kamikazes were unable to sink a single *Essex* class carrier. The escort carriers suffered the most. Due to their light construction and smaller damage control crews a single kamikaze would cause extensive damage.

Between late 1944 and 1945 the kamikazes hit *Essex*-class fleet carriers 16 times, with only one coming close to sinking, two light carriers were damaged, 16 escort carriers were damaged and three sunk.

By the time of the Okinawa campaign the overall effectiveness of the kamikaze was in sharp decline. There were three main reasons: the attacks were being flown by novice pilots, target recognition was poor or non-existent with most pilots choosing the closest target, and US Fleet air defence and anti-aircraft gunners were improving their tactics with startling results. From February to May 1945 the Japanese launched an estimated 1,100 kamikaze sorties. Of these the fighter CAP shot down roughly 500 with anti-aircraft fire taking another 420. Just 180 kamikazes hit their target. By 1945, 84% of kamikazes were missing their target. ∎

ABOVE: As the kamikaze campaign continued, pilot skill deteriorated. Here a Ki-61 'Tony' dives on the *Sangamon* (CVE-26), missing the carrier by just 25ft on May 4, 1945. US NAVAL HISTORICAL CENTER

CHAPTER 8

THE FORGOTTEN FLEET

★

British Carrier Strikes in the Pacific 1944-45

The British Pacific Fleet (BPF), formed in November 1944, and was assigned to fight alongside the Americans in the Central Pacific. It was a formidable force centred on three fleet carriers – HMS *Illustrious*, *Victorious* and *Indomitable* and was joined by the *Formidable*, *Indefatigable* and *Implacable* and the light carriers *Colossus*, *Glory*, *Venerable* and *Vengeance* in 1945. This would be the largest deployment of Royal Navy Fleet carriers and aircraft during the war.

The 1st Aircraft Carrier Squadron (ACS) was formed and would grow to 364 aircraft in five fleet carriers. The fighter component consisted of 88 Mk LIII Seafires, along with 24 Mk I Fireflies, 39 F6F-3 Hellcats 108 F4U-1 Corsairs and 105 TBM-1 Avengers – the Seafires representing 27% of the total Royal Navy fighter strength in the Pacific. The bulk of the fleet's fighter defence would be conducted by the Seafire, leaving escort and sweeps to the Hellcats and Corsairs. The carriers were organised to operate for two days of strikes followed by two days of replenishment.

Long before the formation of the BPF, British carriers had already served in both the Pacific and Indian Ocean. After the carrier battles of 1942 the US Navy had just one carrier operational, *Saratoga*. It was a critical situation and to help reinforce the US fleet HMS *Victorious* was dispatched. After several months of training and modifications beginning in December 1942, *Victorious* was well versed in US Navy operational procedures. By February 1943, *Victorious* was fully equipped with three squadrons of 36 Martlet Mk IVs

(F4F-4 Wildcat) and one squadron with 16 TBF-1 Avengers.

Frontline operations began on May 7, 1943 and in June *Victorious* (*Victorious* was given the US name USS *Robin* for operations in the Pacific) joined *Saratoga* to cover the US landings on New Georgia, in the Solomon Islands. *Victorious* then spent a short period operating in the Coral Sea and after just six months of operations in the Pacific it was released back to the British Home Fleet.

By July 1943 the war in Europe had changed dramatically. In September 1943 the Italians signed an armistice, freeing the Royal Navy of its duties in the Mediterranean. With the Kriegsmarine's surface units firmly bottled up in their Baltic and Norwegian Ports. The Royal Navy could now focus more resources on its third front in Southern Asia. In the first sign of what was to come was the arrival of HMS *Illustrious* in Ceylon on January 27, 1944. On board were the first two fully operational Corsairs squadrons with 14 each and 24 Fairey Barracudas.

In early April 1944 US Admiral King asked the British Eastern Fleet (EF) to mount a diversionary raid on the IJN base at Sabang near the northern tip of Sumatra to help divert Japanese units away from the Allied landings at Hollandia in Dutch New Guinea. On April 13 the second operation to feature both a British and American carrier began. Code named Operation Cockpit, it was led by *Illustrious* in company with USS *Saratoga* with Air Group 12: 36 F6F-3 Hellcats, 24 SBD-5 Dauntlesses and 18 TBF-1 Avengers.

On April 19 *Illustrious* launched 17 Barracudas, each armed with two 500lb and two 250lb bombs. They were escorted by 13 Corsairs. Saratoga contributed 11 TBF-1s, four with 2,000lb bombs and the remainder with four 500lbs bombs, and 18 SBD-5s armed with a single 1,000lb bomb each. Escort was provided by 16 Hellcats. The raid was a moderate success with extensive damage to harbour and airfield installations. One small merchant ship was sunk and three enemy aircraft were shot down. Another 21 were destroyed on the ground at Sabang airfield. Three Japanese B5N1 'Kates' approached the fleet, but were quickly shot down by fighters.

The second combined strike was code named Operation Transom. This time the target was the IJN base at Surabaya in Java and the Wonokromo oil refinery. At 0430 hours on May 17, 1944 the carriers turned into the wind. Two strike forces were launched, A and B. Force A comprised nine Avengers from *Illustrious* armed with four 500lb bombs each and 12 SBDs from *Saratoga*. Escorted was provide by eight Corsairs from *Illustrious*. Force B comprised 18 Avengers armed with four 500lb bombs and six SBDs with 1,000lb bombs, escorted by eight Corsairs and 12 Hellcats.

The attack was well synchronised with both forces attacking from different directions at the same time. Just one Avenger from *Saratoga* was shot down by AA fire. Considerable damage was inflicted with the Wonokromo oil refinery set on fire. After the strike, *Saratoga* and its escorts returned to the United States for a refit and modernisation.

On July 5, 1944 the fleet carriers *Victorious* and *Indomitable* joined the Eastern Fleet in the Indian Ocean. Both participated in Operation Crimson – a battleship bombardment of Sabang with the fleet carriers providing air cover, naval gunfire spotting, ground attack and reconnaissance. At dawn on July 21, 24 Corsairs were launched. Their targets were the airfields at Sabang, Lho Nga and Kotaraja.

> "The British force will greatly increase our striking power and demonstrate our unity of purpose against Japan. The United States Pacific Fleet welcomes you."
> — Admiral Nimitz

ABOVE: HMS *Indefatigable* heading through the Panama Canal on the way to the Pacific in late 1944. AUTHOR'S COLLECTION

ABOVE: Fleet Air Arm Avenger 4H-Q of No. 854 NAS ends up on its nose after missing the wires in early January 1945. AUTHOR'S COLLECTION

THE BRITISH PACIFIC FLEET

★ TF-118 – THE STRIKE FLEET
Indomitable, Illustrious, Victorious, Indefatigable

The aircraft units embarked on these vessels formed the 1st Aircraft Carrier Squadron (ACS) which consisted of 215 aircraft – 40 Supermarine Seafire FIII and LIIIs, 73 F4U-1A Corsairs (Mk IIs in British service), 38 F3F-3 Hellcats (Mk I), 12 Fairey Firefly Mk Is and 52 TBF-1 Avengers.

In support were two battleships, five heavy cruisers, and 16 destroyers.

When the Corsairs arrived over the airfields it was still too dark to identify individual aircraft, resulting in inaccurate strafing runs. The attack was unsuccessful and one Corsair was shot down.

In the middle of August the two carriers joined forces again for Operation Banquet. The targets were the airfield at Padang, Emmahaven harbour and the Idaroeng Cement Works on Sumatra. On August 24 at 0550 hours the first strike of ten Barracudas and 19 Corsairs from *Victorious* was launched. The second strike of nine Barracudas from *Indomitable*, three from *Victorious* and 12 Corsairs from *Victorious* was launched at 0710 hours. Poor intelligence meant that the targets hit were of little value, however. Bombing was accurate but one Corsair was shot down by AA fire.

The last strike mounted by the BEF was Operation Millet which again included *Indomitable* and *Victorious*. This was the final 'work-up strike' and was intended to draw Japanese attention away from the American landings in the Philippines. It was also the last operation for the Barracuda, which was found to be poorly suited to conditions in the Pacific. On October 17 *Indomitable* launched eight Barracudas with 500lb bombs, escorted by Hellcats. *Victorious* added eight Corsairs as top cover and 19 more for strafing attacks. Their target was the airfields and harbour on the Nicobar Islands. Surprise was complete and the bombing was accurate with the steamer *Ishikari Maru* sunk by a single bomb hit. One Barracuda and two Corsairs crashed and one Hellcat was lost on landing.

From March to the end of October 1944 the British Eastern Fleet and her fleet carriers launched a total of eight strikes. The British Pacific Fleet formed officially on November 22, 1944 under the command of Admiral Sir Bruce Fraser. The experience gained with the limited strikes in 1944 had proven valuable, but these were against lightly defended targets. Fraser was eager to demonstrate the BEF's ability to strike a decisive blow against strategic targets of importance.

ABOVE: No. 854 NAS Avengers outbound on the second Sumatran strike on January 29, 1945. This angle shows the Avenger's large bomb-bay capable of carrying up to 2,000lb of bombs. AUTHOR'S COLLECTION

THE SUMATRAN OILFIELDS

At the request of US Admiral Nimitz, the first targets for the newly formed BPF were the Japanese oil refineries in Sumatra. These facilities produced the largest quantity of aviation fuel available to the Japanese and were considered to be of major strategic importance.

On January 1, Task Force 65 – *Indomitable*, *Victorious* and *Indefatigable* – set sail for Operation Lentil. On board was a mixed force of Corsairs, Hellcats, Avengers, Seafires and Fireflies. At 0600 hours on January 4 the carriers turned into the wind 130 nautical miles from the Pangkalan Brandan refineries. Prior to the main strike would be a sweep of 16 Corsairs and Hellcats. These took off before sunrise and headed to the airfields at Bindjai, Medan, Tandjonporea and Treomon. At 0740 hours the main strike force of 12 Fireflies, 32 Avengers and 32 Hellcats and Corsairs was launched.

First in were the Fireflies, each armed with eight 60lb air-to-ground rockets. Next came the Avengers. Armed with four 500lb bombs each, the Avengers began their shallow dives at 0831 hours. Their bombing was accurate, setting the main Pangkalan Brandan refinery on fire and damaging the nearby Edeleanu Plant. By this time enemy fighters including Nakajima Ki-44s had intercepted the strike force, damaging one Avenger. Seven enemy fighters were shot down by the escort.

ABOVE: Smoke from the second Sumatran oil field strike confirms another success on January 29, 1945. As the Avengers head to their rendezvous point, two Japanese Ki-44s can be seen in the upper left diving into the attack. Avenger gunners claimed two Ki-44s shot down during the encounter. AUTHOR'S COLLECTION

Post-strike photos showed both the strike and fighter sweep had been effective. Thirty Avengers reached the target and dropped 101 of their 120 bombs with sufficient accuracy to reduce production by a full third. Seven aircraft were destroyed on the ground, two more shot down while caught in the airfield circuit pattern. Just one Firefly was lost, forced to ditch while in the landing circuit. The crew were rescued by a destroyer.

OPERATION MERIDIAN I

The next targets for the BPF were the refineries at Palembang on Sumatra. It would be the

LEFT: A Fleet Air Arm Corsair pours on the power for a go-around and torque stalls, slamming into the crash barrier aboard HMS *Illustrious*. AUTHOR'S COLLECTION

BELOW: When the British Pacific Fleet began operations, it was equipped with 38 Grumman F6F-3 Hellcats. Hellcat 5A/JX758 of No. 1839 NAS misses the wires and goes over the side of *Indomitable*. In total the FAA would receive 1263 F6F-3 and -5s during the war. AUTHOR'S COLLECTION.

largest fleet carrier attack against an individual target mounted by the Royal Navy in the Second World War. The BPF's four carriers – *Illustrious, Indomitable, Victorious* and *Indefatigable* formed Task Force 63 with 238 aircraft.

Palembang was an important centre for river, road and rail transportation, it was also the Japanese headquarters for all of Sumatra. The main targets were the two refineries five miles south of Palembang. The Pladjoe and Songei Gerong refineries was capable of producing three million tons of crude oil a year and supplied 75% of the aviation fuel for the IJNAF and JAAF.

Intelligence estimated Japanese fighter resistance to include 50 Ki-44 'Tojos' and 30 Ki-43 'Oscars', along with a good number of both heavy and light AA guns. Forty-eight Avengers – 12 from each carrier – provided the heavy ordnance for the raid. Each was armed with four 500lb medium capacity (MC) bombs with TD 025 fuses. Five percent were fitted with time delay fuses to cause maximum disruption after the raid. The escort would be led by 32 Corsairs and 16 Hellcats.

The 12 Fireflies from *Indefatigable* were assigned two tasks – attack specific targets with cannon fire and provide an escort between the target and rendezvous point. The first to arrive would be the 24 Corsairs flying a 'Ramrod' ahead of the strike. Their assignment was flak suppression and airfield strafing. This would be supported by a strike force of four Avengers and four Hellcats to help neutralise the Japanese fighter response from Mana airfield. All fighters including the Fireflies were equipped with drop tanks to stretch their radius of action.

The first launch began at 0615 hours and by 0704 hours the strike force set course for their target. Flying a separate route to its target, the 'Ramrod' fighters overtook the main strike on its outward journey. The Japanese airfield at Lembak was caught by surprise with several fighters destroyed on the ground.

The 'Ramrod' flew on to Palembang and then Telengbetoetoe, but was met with fully alerted Japanese defences. Three Corsairs were lost to AA fire and collision. At 0804 approximately 24 Ki-44 'Tojos' engaged the top cover, setting off a fierce dogfight. At the same time the Japanese also began to release barrage balloons above the refinery.

At 0814 hours the Avengers began their bomb runs from 10,000ft. Flying through heavy AA fire and dodging the unexpected barrage balloons they dropped their bombs from between 3,500ft and 2,500ft. By 0820 hours the attack was over. A giant column of oily black smoke from the refinery rose to over 10,000ft, marking the Avengers' exit as they made their way to the rendezvous point.

As the Avengers formed up for mutual support, Japanese fighters continued their attacks. By 0826 hours they had broken off, leaving the strike force free to join their carriers. Post-strike photos revealed extensive damage. One hundred and fifty-three bombs were dropped and subsequent intelligence revealed oil production from the Pladjoe refinery had been cut in half. Losses amounted to six Corsairs, two Avengers and one Hellcat shot down during the attacks. For the fighter pilots of the Fleet Air Arm it was an impressive day with 34 Japanese aircraft destroyed on the ground and in the air.

OPERATION MERIDIAN II

The carriers of TF-63 refuelled at sea on January 26-27. The refuelling was so tortuously slow and the large amounts of fuel oil and aviation gas transferred meant the planned second and third strikes against Palembang were scaled back to just one attack. The next target was the untouched refinery at Songei Gerong. The planning staff knew the Japanese would expect an attack there in the near future. With Japanese fighter assets and strike aircraft capable of attacking the fleet during launch operations, British planners were forced to reduce the strike's escort. Backing up the Seafire CAP would be four fighters from each carrier.

Lessons learned from the first Meridian strike were quickly incorporated into the new attack plan. 'Ramrod' tactics were changed and the withdrawal route for the Avengers from the target to the rendezvous point was compressed.

Japanese fighter reaction clearly showed the first mission's 'Ramrod' had too many targets and had taken too long. For Meridian II, two independent 'Ramrods' with 12 and 13 Corsairs each was mounted. These 'Ramrods' were timed to arrive over the enemy's two main fighter fields simultaneously. After their strafing runs they would then CAP over the airfields and intercept any aircraft trying to take off.

In total 127 aircraft were earmarked for the strike – 48 Avengers, 24 Corsairs, 16 Hellcats and ten Fireflies for escort. Two 'Ramrods' of 12 Corsairs each and two F3F-5Ps Hellcat rounded out the force.

At 0640 hours on January 29 the first Avengers began to lift off. They were followed by the Fireflies and PR Hellcats. Last off was the 'Ramrod' Corsairs which overtook the strike force and arrived over their assigned airfields 15 minutes before the Avengers.

Unfortunately the 'Ramrods' were too late to catch Japanese fighters on the ground. Both airfields were nearly empty, but the light and medium AA fire was intense.

At 0845 hours the Avengers began their glide bombing attacks on the Songei Gerong refinery. Once again the Japanese launched barrage

BELOW: A rare colour photograph of a British Supermarine Seafire Mk III in the Pacific. Seen here at Clark Field in the Philippines in 1945, it is either a fleet replacement aircraft or was used by the Technical Air Intelligence Unit for flight testing against Japanese fighters. AUTHOR'S COLLECTION

balloons over the target. The first bombs soon found their marks – causing fires and billowing black smoke and making it more difficult for the follow-on squadrons to bomb accurately. AA fire was inaccurate at first but quickly improved as the attack developed. Two Avengers hit balloon cables, with one crashing into the burning refinery and the other crashing at an unknown location.

As the Avengers climbed away from their targets and toward their rendezvous point, Japanese fighters began their attack. It was a mix of Ki-43 'Oscars' and Ki-44 'Tojos' of the 47th Sentai. Seven Avengers were attacked by 'Oscars' as they made their way to the rendezvous. Fortunately the Japanese attacks were not pressed home and their aim was generally poor, but several Avengers were damaged. The fighter escort was once again heavily engaged, and those fighters that were able to come to the bombers' aid had a hard time finding their charges due to the clouds of oily smoke. Total losses over the target amounted to four Avengers, a Firefly and one Corsair.

By 0900 hours the ragged strike force had re-formed and set course for the fleet. As the second strike recovered, the Japanese made an appearance heading towards the fleet. The first to be shot down was a Mitsubishi Ki-46 'Dinah', mostly likely on a reconnaissance mission. This was followed by an attack involving seven Ki-21 'Sally' and Ki-84 'Lily' bombers. All seven were shot down. Six by the Seafire and Hellcat CAP and one by the fleet's gunfire.

The two Meridian strikes cost the BPF 16 Avengers, 15 Corsairs, five Seafires, four Hellcats and a Firefly to all causes; a total of 41. Of that total six Avengers, eight Corsairs, one Hellcat and one Firefly were shot down by fighters and AA fire.

Meridian I and II were not perfect, but they were effective and gave the pilots of the BPF the chance to hone their skills and measure their abilities against a determined enemy. They now had the confidence to move forward and join their American carrier cousins in the coming battles ahead.

OPERATION ICEBERG

On March 7, 1945 the British Pacific Fleet arrived at its forward base at Manus. There waiting for them were 27 support ships including the replenishment carriers *Striker* and *Slinger*.

As the BPF waited for their next assignment, training exercises were mounted and the short-range of the Seafire was addressed. While at Manus, No 38 Naval Fighter wing traded two crates of whiskey for 60 American P-40 drop tanks. These 89-gallon tanks doubled the Seafire's range, giving it the ability to provide escort for strike missions.

ABOVE: A near kamikaze miss on HMS *Victorious* on April 1, 1945. The resulting bomb explosion threw tons of water, petrol, and aircraft fragments onto the flight deck. A Corsair can be seen directly above the carrier. AUTHOR'S COLLECTION

ABOVE: Like the Seafire Mk III, the Fairey Firefly Mk I's wings had to be folded and unfolded with the use of manpower. Here a No. 1770 NAS Squadron Firefly is prepared for the Sumatra strike on January 24, 1945. AUTHOR'S COLLECTION

ABOVE: "Not difficult to fly, but it was easy to mishandle." The Fairey Barracuda, like most British carrier aircraft, was designed as a multirole combat aircraft. In the dive/torpedo bomber role the Barracuda never distinguished itself in combat. AUTHOR'S COLLECTION

The final decision to use the BPF for operations in the Pacific, alongside the US Fifth Fleet was made shortly after its arrival at Manus. Despite late opposition, Admiral Nimitz had lobbied hard for the BPF to be part of his Central Pacific Command. The recent kamikaze damage to the US carriers *Intrepid*, *Wasp* and *Franklin* all but confirmed the BPF's participation for the up-coming invasion of Okinawa – Operation Iceberg.

Designated Task Force 57, the British were given the task of preventing the Japanese from staging aircraft from Formosa to the combat area through the airfields on the islands of Miyako, Ishigaki and Mihara in the Sakishima Gunto.

Under the command of Vice Admiral Sir Bernard Rawlings, Task Force 57 now comprised five fleet carriers: *Indomitable*, *Victorious*, *Illustrious*, *Indefatigable* and *Formidable* (en route). In support were two battleships, five cruisers and 11 destroyers. The four British carriers embarked about 220 aircraft compared with about 320 in the average USN Task Group. This was due to the fact that British carriers were built with armoured flight decks, resulting in less hangar space. British carriers were also not designed for hot climates – resulting in sweltering conditions below decks.

All the aircraft had the new 'Pacific' roundels applied based on the USN system. The red circle used at the centre of British markings could be mistaken for the Japanese 'rising-sun' marking so the new roundels were sized to be as large as possible and comprised a white, round centre with a blue circle around it and thin white edge outside of that – white bars with blue edges on each side completed the roundel.

On March 23, US TF-58 began direct strikes against targets on Okinawa. TF-57 joined the fight on the 26th assigned to neutralise six airfields on the islands of the Sakishima Gunto. Photo reconnaissance revealed the most heavily defended airfields were Ishigaki Main with 26 heavy and 66 light anti-aircraft guns and Hirara with 12 heavy and 44 light anti-aircraft guns.

The tactic chosen to neutralise the airfields was straightforward: bomb the airfields, crater the runways and disrupt repairs as often as possible; destroy any aircraft on the ground and provide a CAP over the airfields to destroy any airborne aircraft in daylight. When it was time to withdraw and replenish, TF-57 would be temporarily replaced by a fast American carrier task group from TF-58 or escort carriers from TG- 52.1.

Fighters would play a major role in the coming

ABOVE: A mix of Barracudas and Corsairs on the bow of HMS *Illustrious*, January 1945. The Barracuda's performance in the humid conditions of the Pacific was disappointing. It was replaced by the proven Grumman Avenger. AUTHOR'S COLLECTION

ABOVE: On May 5, 1945 a single bomb armed Zero kamikaze hit HMS *Formidable*. The explosion was devastating, with 11 aircraft destroyed, eight sailors killed and 51 wounded. Because of its armoured deck, *Formidable* was out of action for just five hours. AUTHOR'S COLLECTION

operation, providing CAP stations over the fleet and target islands, fighter sweeps, strike escort and 'Jack' patrols. These were usually flown by Seafire LIIIs flying at 3,000ft. The Corsair, with its better high altitude performance, flew high CAP; Seafire FIIIs flew the medium and Seafire LIIIs low level.

OPENING SALVO

At dawn on March 26 TF-57 arrived at its first operating area about 100 miles south of Miyako Island. The opening attacks began with a 48 aircraft fighter sweep on all the airfields, followed by two escorted Avenger strikes and then a Hellcat fighter/bomber strike. The results were limited with 23 enemy aircraft destroyed of which 11 were assessed as dummies. Four aircraft were lost in combat, with three pilots missing.

At sunrise on the 27th a fighter sweep of 24 Hellcats and Corsairs was launched. This was followed by two Avenger strikes of 24 aircraft each and four Fireflies armed with 60lb rockets. Runways, airfields, barracks and aircraft dispersal areas were targeted. No enemy fighters were encountered but two British aircraft were shot down by AA fire. After the strikes, TF-57 withdrew for replenishment in preparation for the invasion of Okinawa.

At 0630 hours on March 31 the BPF began its second series of strikes. Fighters once again flew their sweeps followed by two Avenger strikes of 11 aircraft each armed with four 500lb bombs. A continuous CAP was flown over the islands during daylight, with the Seafires providing CAP over the fleet.

April 1 was 'L-Day' and the invasion of Okinawa began. In support, TF-57 began launching its first fighter sweeps at 0640 hours. Ten minutes later 'bogies' were detected on radar 75 miles from the fleet at 8,000ft and closing fast. More fighters were launched and those on the sweep were vectored toward the intruders. Forty miles from the fleet eight to ten Zeros were intercepted. Four were quickly shot down, sending the survivors diving away. At 0730 hours a Zero broke through the CAP, strafing *Indomitable's* flight deck. It then strafed *King George V* before crashing into the base of *Indefatigable's* island. It was the first successful kamikaze attack on the BPF. Four officers and ten ratings were killed and 15 others were wounded. *Indefatigable's* deck was dented about 3in, but rapid damage control and repairs had the carrier operational after just 40 minutes. On April 3, TF-57 retired for refuelling and aircraft replacement.

Strike operations resumed on April 6. At 1700 hours four kamikazes broke through low cloud aimed at *Illustrious*. Radical evasive manoeuvres saved the ship with just one Zero crashing into the water for a near miss, its bomb exploding on impact.

Two days of strikes had been planned for the Sakishima Gunto staring on April 10, followed by a withdrawal to Leyte Gulf for a week of major replenishment. That quickly changed when TF-57 received a request from Admiral Spruance to attack airfields on northern Formosa. The request was accepted with much enthusiasm and a new course was set.

Bombing and fighter missions carried out between April 11 and 13 proved to be the BPF's most successful to date. Damage to the airfields and road and rail targets on Formosa was heavy with 16 enemy aircraft shot down for the loss of just three BPF aircraft.

However, by the middle of the month post-strike photos revealed the destruction of Japanese airfields was not as great as hoped. The runways were made of crushed coral, which the Japanese had in abundant supply. At night the bomb craters were filled, rolled flat and made ready for operation. Dropping more 500lbs wouldn't make much difference.

On April 21, after 32 days of constant operations, TF-57 finally sailed for San Pedro Bay in Leyte Gulf for much needed rest and replenishment. For the BPF the numbers were impressive. 2,444 sorties flown – 1,961 by fighters, 483 by Avengers. 412 tons of bombs dropped and 315 rockets fired against a variety of targets. One hundreds and twenty-four enemy aircraft were destroyed for the loss of 68 BPF aircraft to all causes.

ARMOUR VS KAMIKAZE

On May 4, TF-57 resumed operations off Sakishima Gunto. The same cycle of airfield suppression was followed with two airfields put out of action. It was here the kamikazes also made their most destructive attacks.

At 1131 hours a handful of Zeros approached the fleet. Using cumulus clouds as cover, they were able to surprise the carrier *Formidable*. Diving from 3,000ft a single Zeke made a strafing ▶

run on the carrier before returning to drop its 500lb bomb and crashing into the flight deck. A two foot square hole was blown in the flight deck, followed by a large fire in the hangar deck. Water and foam was poured into the hole. After the fire was brought under control the hole was patched with wood, concrete and thin steel plate. After a day of repairs the *Formidable* was made fully operational.

The next carrier to be hit was *Victorious*. On May 8 at 1645 hours bogies were detected very low, only 20 miles from the fleet. Seafires intercepted but one Zero broke through, diving onto *Victorious*. Hit repeatedly by automatic AA fire the Zero continued its path – hitting the flight deck where its bomb exploded and caused the aircraft to disintegrate. A fire broke out and damage was significant. Minutes later a second kamikaze hit *Victorious*. Again the aircraft was hit by a barrage of AA fire but managed to hit the afterdeck park anyway, bouncing off the armoured flight deck and into the sea about 200 yards off the port beam.

At 1705 hours a fourth kamikaze headed for *Formidable* and *Indomitable*. Both ships opened fire and made hard turns, but the aircraft found its mark, hitting *Formidable*. The result was an explosion and a large fire. Eighteen aircraft were destroyed and although the vessel was able to operate aircraft again after just 50 minutes only four Avengers and 11 Corsairs survived the attack. *Victorious* had just 28 Corsairs serviceable and was limited in her ability to operate aircraft.

While the damage to the ships was not crippling, Admiral Rawlings was forced to

LEFT: On April 13, 1945, Avengers from HMS *Victorious* attacked Shinchiku Airfield on Taiwan. The bomb damage was extensive, but the Japanese ability to quickly repair their airfields required repeated attacks. AUTHOR'S COLLECTION

BELOW: In early March 1945 the British Pacific Fleet was designated as Task Force 57 for the upcoming invasion of Okinawa. With four carriers it was given the task of neutralising airfields in the Sakishima Gunto archipelago. Here Avengers attack Hirara Airfield on Miyako in early April 1945. AUTHOR'S COLLECTION

FLEET AIR ARM AIRCRAFT

FAIREY BARRACUDA MK II
Intended as a replacement for the Fairey Swordfish and Albacore, the Barracuda resulted from Air Ministry Specification S.24/37 for a new monoplane torpedo/dive bomber. Entering service at the same time as the Grumman Avenger, the Mk II could carry roughly the same bombload, but for shorter ranges. Powered by the Rolls-Royce Merlin 32 engine with 1,640hp, the Barracuda had a top speed of 240mph without a torpedo. Stressed for both dive-bombing and low-level torpedo attack, the Barracuda was overweight and under-powered. In the hot, humid conditions of the Far East its radius of action with a full bomb-load (1,600lb) was just 100 nautical miles. The Avenger's superior performance forced the British to replace all their home-grown Barracudas with the reliable Grumman.

FAIREY FIREFLY MK I
The Fairey Firefly was ordered as a two-seat reconnaissance fighter. The Firefly prototype flew on December 22, 1941 and the following year 200 Mk 1s were ordered.
Between 1943 and 1946 850 Mk Is were delivered to the FAA. Powered by a 1,730hp Rolls-Royce Griffon II engine, the Firefly Mk I had a top speed of 316mph at 14,000ft.
Armament consisted for four 20mm Hispano cannon, plus provision for eight 60lb rocket projectiles or two 500lb or 1,000lb bombs.
Slower than single-seat fighters, it was used mainly as a 'flak suppressor'. The Firefly was arguably the best British built naval aircraft to enter service during the war.

SUPERMARINE SEAFIRE FIII AND LIII
The Seafire was a fighter born out of desperation. It emerged from an urgent requirement by the Fleet Air Arm for a fast single-engined fighter capable of meeting land-based opponents on better or equal terms. After it proved itself during the Battle of Britain, the British Admiralty demanded a navalised version of the Spitfire. Adopting a land-based aircraft for naval operations was problematic. But the urgency of war pushed those worries aside – resulting in the Seafire. Powered by a 1,585hp Rolls-Royce Merlin engine, the Seafire L III had a top speed of 358mph at 6,000ft. Armament consisted of two 20mm Hispano cannon and four .303in Browning machine guns.

withdraw for quick repairs. The armoured decks had proven their worth. Similar hits on American carriers usually caused severe damage putting them out of service for weeks and sometimes months.

These attacks would be the last of their kind aimed at BPF carriers and on May 25, with Okinawa largely in American hands, the fleet flew its final strikes. Shortly thereafter TF-57 dispersed to various Australian ports for much needed, refits, repairs and rest.

For the Royal Navy, Operation Iceberg had been an impressive display of British carrier air power. Between March 26 and May 25 the four carriers of TF-57 launched 4,893 sorties of which 2,073 were strikes, plus 2,820 CAP and fighter sweeps. Bombs dropped amounted to 958 tons and 950 rockets had been fired. British aircraft losses amounted to 160 from all causes. Of that number 26 were shot down or lost in combat; 72 lost in operating accidents and 61 destroyed by kamikaze hits.

American commanders were also impressed. On May 27 Admiral Spruance sent this message to Admiral Rawlings: "On completion of your two months' operation as a Task Force of the Fifth Fleet in support of the capture of Okinawa, I wish to express to you and to the officers and men under your command, my appreciation of the fine work you have done and the splendid spirit of co-operation with which you have done it. To the American portion of the Fifth Fleet, Task Force 57 has typified the great traditions of the Royal Navy."

FLEET AIR ARM – IN SEARCH OF AN AIRCRAFT
Had the British Pacific Fleet entered the war in the Pacific with British-built naval aircraft, its ability to mount any significant strike operations would have been restricted. Without access to the American F4U Corsair, F6F Hellcat and TBF Avenger, the BPF would have entered the Pacific theatre with the Supermarine Seafire Mk III, Fairey Barracuda Mk II and Fairey Firefly Mk I. With these three aircraft the BPF would have been unable to mount any long-range carrier strikes.

The Seafire was an excellent fighter, but its short range limited its role to fleet defence. The Barracuda suffered from short range and only the Firefly had sufficient combat radius and bombload capability to be of any use in the strike role, and at the time of its formation, the BPF had only one operational squadron.

One of the main reasons the F4U Corsair was first cleared by the British for carrier operations was its availability. Unable to procure the F6F Hellcat – the US Navy had priority on all deliveries – the Royal Navy was offered the F4U-1 instead. Desperate for a good carrier fighter the Fleet Air Arm (FAA) quickly developed the curved landing technique to overcome the Corsair's difficult handling characteristics around a carrier deck. By early 1944, eight squadrons would be equipped with the Corsair. And by the summer of 1943 production of the F6F reached sufficient levels for the FAA to began to receive the first of 1,263 aircraft.

LOW-LEVEL KAMIKAZE KILLER
Developed from the famous Supermarine Spitfire, the Seafire was the only land-based fighter modified for carrier operations to see large-scale naval service.

When Reginald Mitchell first designed the Spitfire, he never expected it to be used as a Fleet Air Arm fighter. Even a cursory look at the Spitfire reveals why: its narrow-track landing gear was short and weak in comparison to most purpose-built shipboard fighters, the view forward from the cockpit was extremely poor, and its small size did not allow for an increase in internal fuel to extend range.

ABOVE: The folding wings on the Seafire were not hydraulically powered and required lots of manpower – slowing deck operations. This Seafire of No 38 Naval Fighter wing is being made ready for another sortie in June 1945.
AUTHOR'S COLLECTION

Consequently, much of what the new Seafire was expected to do was beyond its capabilities, especially at the outset. But later, in the hands of a cadre of well-trained pilots, it outshone other carrier fighters in an interceptor role more suited to its design.

How did the Supermarine Seafire stack up against its carrier-borne contemporaries? During the Second World War, naval fighters had to perform a variety of tasks. Interception was their primary roll, but other tasks included long-range escort, ground-attack, reconnaissance, fighter sweeps, dive-bombing and spotting for bombardment by surface ships.

To fulfill these many rolls, the carrier-borne fighter must possess three attributes: first power, performance and armament equal to or better than land-based interceptors and other naval fighters; second the ability to escort strike aircraft or remain on patrol for extended periods of time; and third a rugged structure, good deck landing characteristics and safe deck handling under all conditions. Only two wartime naval fighters possessed all three virtues at the time of their introduction: the Mitsubishi A6M2 Zero and Grumman F6F-3 Hellcat.

From October 1942 until August 1943, the Seafire held the crown as the fastest carrier fighter afloat, eclipsed only by the introduction of the A6M5 and F6F-3. While its low- to medium-level speed performance was respectable, its rate of climb and acceleration were remarkable. The L.IIC climbed at nearly 3,500ft per minute up to 10,000ft—some 1,500ft per minute better than the Hellcat or F4U-1 Corsair, and 1,000ft per minute better than the A6M5. For sheer acceleration the Seafire had no peer. In 1945 it was still the fastest and steepest climbing Allied naval interceptor. That turned out to be of great tactical value because once targets had been identified on radar, the Seafire required less distance and time to reach any given altitude.

Fleet Air Arm (FAA) veteran Gerry Murphy of 887 NAS Squadron, aboard the carrier HMS *Indefatigable*, was involved in the very last carrier strike of the war and scored the last two air-to-air victories. The often-maligned naval variant of the Spitfire never let Gerry down. Here are his thoughts on the Seafire III: "When I first flew the Seafire it was pure exhilaration. Having flown the standard training aircraft, which didn't have anything approaching the speed and response, it was great in a climb and turning and you felt really in control. Extremely responsive. I also flew the Hellcat, which was a very robust aircraft, but it was like flying a steamroller compared to the Seafire.

"It was big and heavy, but a great war horse and it could take an awful lot of punishment. Compared to the Hellcat the Seafire was rather delicate. The Hellcat didn't have the response of the Seafire. It was the difference between a racehorse and a carthorse. The Seafire III was about 16 knots faster than the Hellcat and Corsair at low and medium altitudes'.

The Seafire's armament of two 20mm Hispano cannon and four .303in Browning machine guns remain unchanged throughout the war. This configuration proved more than adequate against lightly built Japanese aircraft.

The deck landing and handling qualities of the Seafire were, to put it kindly, not good. As a land-based interceptor, its landing technique called for long runways and a fairly fast approach speed down a two-degree glide path, followed by a last-second flare. Carrier deck landings required a totally different technique, one that was foreign to the finely balanced Seafire.

While the faults of the Seafire as a carrier aircraft were many, its performance as a low to medium level interceptor was superb. In the Pacific, the Seafire would encounter a new and formidable foe – the kamikaze. To meet this threat the Seafire was fortuitously equipped.

When the British Pacific Fleet first encountered the kamikaze in 1945 the Japanese

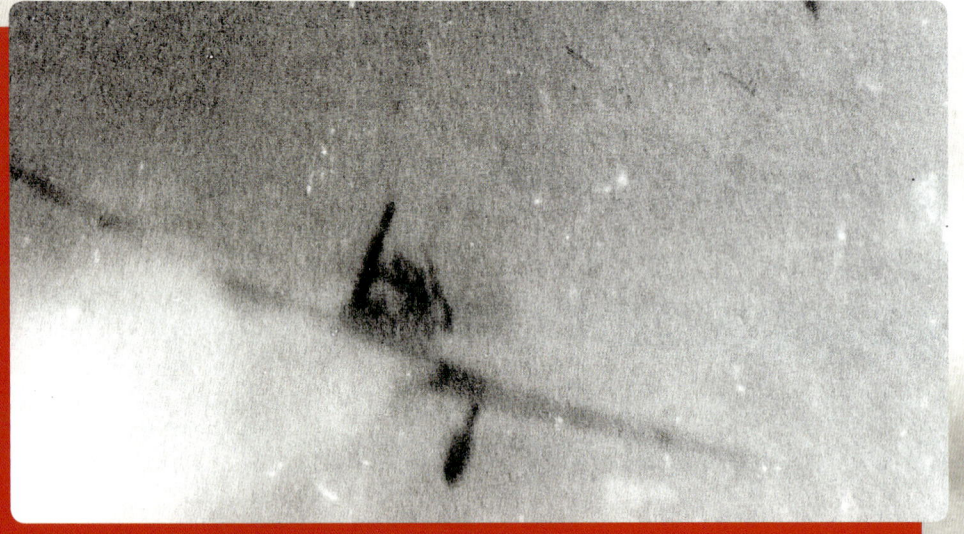

ABOVE: A Japanese Ki-51 is shot down by a Firefly Mk 1 from No 1770 NAS on April 12, 1945. AUTHOR'S COLLECTION

BELOW: Carrier operations were inherently dangerous. Many aircraft and well-trained pilots were lost while trying to land their high-performance aircraft on a pitching deck. While one Corsair tries to catch a wire, a second is forced to ditch in the ship's wake. AUTHOR'S COLLECTION

ABOVE: When the BPF moved into the Pacific new roundels were adopted to avoid any confusion with Japanese markings. This Corsair from No 1834 NAS clearly shows the new white bars and white circle roundels, designed to be similar to US Navy markings. AUTHOR'S COLLECTION

LEFT: A rocket armed Firefly Mk I of No 1771 NAS from HMS *Formidable* heads for a target in Japan in July 1944. AUTTHOR'S COLLECTION

had developed their tactics with the 'zero feet' approach with a twist. The vast majority of kamikaze pilots were inexperienced, requiring an escort to guide them to their targets. When approximately 20 miles from the Allied fleet, the more experienced escort pilots would quickly pull up, exposing themselves to radar. It was hoped that this tactic would bait the high-flying Hellcats and Corsairs and leave the low-level intruders unmolested.

To counter this tactic the British adopted the American 'Jack' patrols. It was a last-ditch method designed to catch kamikazes coming in at sea level and the best aircraft for this role turned out to be the Seafire LIII. Each 'Jack' CAP would consist of eight Seafires, equipped with 90-gallon slipper tanks. Held at less than 3,000 feet and within ten miles of the destroyer screen, this would be the last interceptor barrier before the fleet anti-aircraft guns would be called into action. Even with this well coordinated defensive system, British carriers were hit several times, but never put out of action.

The first two kamikaze Zeros shot down went to Sub-Lieutenant Richard H. Reynolds on April 1, 1945 during Operation Iceberg, the invasion of Okinawa. In total Seafire pilots accounted for eight A6M Zero kamikazes shot down and one damaged. They also shot down one D3A 'Val' and one Ki-61 'Tony' possibly damaged. While the numbers may seem small when compared to US Navy claims, it's clear that without the Seafire the damage would have been far worse.

Lieutenant Commander R. 'Mike' Crosely of 880 NAS Squadron had these thoughts regarding the kamikaze threat: "The kamikaze was a weird form of terrorism which seemed to us to deserve nothing but a painful death and eternal damnation. With their clever, decoy-led, low-level approach below the radar of the carrier air defence, it was worrying to think that 100% kills would be necessary before a sure defence could be provided.

"Each one of these part-trained, one-way aviators could park a 500lb bomb within a few feet of his aiming point if he was allowed to get within a few miles of the fleet. However, we felt that the Seafire of all aircraft, would be the best possible defence in such circumstances, and we were not too frightened provided we could see them coming."

It took a while, but in the closing weeks of the war the Seafire proved itself a capable carrier plane. From any perspective, it was not an ideal naval aircraft, but when properly equipped and operated by well-trained pilots and maintenance personnel, it finally gained a respectability undreamed of when it first appeared on a carrier deck.

Despite its many shortcomings, the Seafire achieved a respectable degree of success. At war's end 12 Seafire squadrons were in frontline carrier service. During air combat operations they destroyed 37 enemy aircraft (15 being A6M Zeros), probably destroyed another two and damaged 25, for the loss of eight Seafires in air-to-air combat.

In the last operations of the war, the success of the two Seafire wings (88 aircraft) aboard the carriers *Indefatigable* and *Implacable* came as a surprise to all but the pilots themselves. Striking targets on the Japanese Home Islands between July 17 and August 15, 1945, Seafires of Nos. 801, 880, 887 and 894 squadrons amassed an impressive record: 1,186 sorties flown, comprising 705 combat air patrol, 324 fighter sweep and 157 anti-shipping missions. In all, those operations expended 43,600 rounds of 20mm and 169,270 rounds of .303in ammunition. A total of 87 enemy aircraft were damaged or destroyed on the ground, and 11 in the air. The toll on enemy shipping was extensive: 3,700 tons sunk, 1,615 tons probably sunk, with 24,700 tons damaged. ∎

CHAPTER 9

"I wasn't score happy, and I knew that one more kill wasn't going to end the war any sooner."

Hellcat pilot

BELOW: Two Helldivers from VB-9, *Lexington* head towards Japan on February 16, 1945. Along with their internal load of bombs each is armed with wing mounted 250lb bombs. NARA

TOKYO BOUND

Japan carrier strikes 1945

By January 1945, Japan's strategic military and economic situation had reached intolerable levels. Pummeled and strangled from the air and sea, Japan would be subject to unprecedented levels of destruction. From the air B-29 strategic bombers laid waste to its cities and sowed Japanese harbours with mines. US submarines decimated the Japanese merchant fleet, leaving the nation critically short of food and fuel. Starting in February 1945, and lasting until the end of the war, the US Navy's Fast Carrier Task Force (supported by the British Pacific Fleet) would add to the destruction by attacking Japan directly. Airfields, shipping facilities, factories and transportation infrastructure were the main targets while at the same time wearing down the IJNAF and JAAF air strength through attrition.

For the coming strikes the Fast Carrier Task force had grown to 12 Essex carriers and six light Independence carriers. On board a staggering 1,365 aircraft were available, nearly three quarters of them fighters. Each large carrier air group now averaged 102 aircraft, with the light carriers numbering 27 aircraft. Hellcats still represented over 80% of the total fighter force, the majority being F6F-5s. In total there were 820 Hellcats along with 174 F4U-1D Corsairs.

The fighters of the fleet were now also equipped with the new Mark 21 gyro-stabilised, lead computing gunsight. It was a brilliant piece of equipment and gave the average pilot a vastly improved chance of hitting his target. First available in the autumn of 1944, it began to appear in the fleet in early 1945. Deflection shooting or leading the target was a difficult skill to master for most fighter pilots, but the Mark 21 sight automatically showed the pilot the correct deflection when tracking a hostile fighter. The sight required more training to master and with little time to practice before entering combat most squadrons opted to keep the lead-computing sight locked in and used it like the standard reflector sight they had trained on.

At the beginning of the war the Japanese were well aware that air attacks on their home islands were a real possibility. The reality of the B-29 attacks and the coming carrier strikes forced the IJNAF and JAAF to allocate more resources to air defence. Japan's only hope of saving itself from aerial destruction was to inflict unacceptable losses upon both the B-29 and US carrier strike aircraft. To do that the JAAF and IJNAF needed new fighters and more well-trained pilots.

By late 1944 the aerial battles over the Philippines and the two years of attrition in the southwest Pacific, Burma and China had virtually destroyed both air forces. Lack of fuel curtailed training and the novice pilots that were trained were doing little more than filling a seat. Surprisingly, no more than 26% of the total Japanese fighter force was assigned to the defence of Japan. By January 1945 Japanese home defence squadrons were equipped with just 400-500 single-seat and twin-engine fighters. It was a mixed bag with the vast majority being the latest models of the A6M5 Zero, followed by smaller numbers of the J2M3 Raiden 'Jack', N1K2-J Shiden Kai 'George', Ki-43-II 'Oscar', Ki-44-II 'Tojo', Ki-84 'Frank', Ki-61 'Tony' and Ki-100.

For US Navy and FAA aircrew the biggest threats would be the weather and the thousands of AA guns that surrounded Japan's most vital

ABOVE: February 16, 1945, F6F-5 Hellcats aboard *Essex* warm up for the first carrier strike against Tokyo. The Hellcats are equipped with a 150 gallon centreline drop tank, giving the aircraft a total of 385 gallons. NARA

ABOVE: F4U-1D Corsairs aboard *Essex* prepare for another airfield strike on the Island of Formosa in January 1945. The F4U-1D did away with outboard internal wing fuel tanks, relying instead on the belly mounted 160 gallon drop tank for a range of 1,051 miles. NARA

airfields, harbours and factories. Carrier aircraft had to bomb and strafe below 3,000ft. This was where light anti-aircraft gunfire was the thickest and most accurate.

THE LAST SAMURAI

As the end approached, Japan was producing some of the best fighters of the war. In terms of performance they were equal to and in some cases better than the F6F Hellcat and F4U Corsair. But low production numbers, poor serviceability and a shortage of pilots meant these new fighters were in short supply. When encountered in the hands of veteran pilots, however, they were often deadly and could cause heavy losses.

The defence of the Japanese Home Islands was shared by both the IJNAF and JAAF so the US Navy and FAA pilots would encounter a number of different fighters. Some would be new but for the majority would be the ubiquitous A6M5 Zero.

KAWANISHI N1K2-J SHIDEN-KAI 'GEORGE'

In October 1944, US Navy Hellcat pilots encountered a new radial-engine fighter over Formosa and the Philippines. The combats were fleeting, but Hellcat losses were unusually high and concerning. What they had encountered was the N1K1-J Shiden (code named 'George') a land-based fighter derived from the Kawanishi K1K1 Kyofu floatplane fighter. First flown in May 1942 the N1K1 proved to be extremely pleasant to fly and with its combat flaps was extremely manoeuvrable. By December 1943 production of the N1K1 was just 15 per month with the last of 97 Kyofus delivered in March 1944. Production was halted in favour of a land-based version: the N1K1-J Shiden.

Work on the Shiden began while work on the N1K1 Kyofu was still in progress. The Kawanishi design team knew the land-based version would have better performance and although no official

ABOVE: A reconnaissance photo taken by a F6F-5P from VF-31 clearly shows a well camouflaged Japanese airfield near Central Honsho in August 1945. NARA

ABOVE: With the arrival of US Navy fighters over the homeland the Japanese were forced into hiding. Desperate to protect their remaining air assets the Japanese used extensive methods of camouflage. Here a Zero is covered in pine branches. NARA

specification was issued for the new fighter, the IJNAF was impressed enough to give Kawanishi the green light.

Few modifications were made in the construction of the N1K1-J Shiden Model 11. The biggest was the replacement of ventral and outrigger floats with fully retractable landing gear. Powered by the new 18-cylinder Nakajima 1,990hp NK9H Homare (Honor) model 21 radial engine, the fighter was armed with four 20mm Type 99 cannon and two 7.7mm Type 97 machine guns. The NIK1-J made its combat debut over Formosa and the Philippines but only in small numbers. Performance-wise the Shiden was only 13mph slow than the F6F-3 Hellcat and 23mph slower than the F6F-5 and its armament and protection were substantially better.

The NIK1-J was followed by the NIK2-J Shiden Kai Model 21. Externally the Model 21 differed appreciably from the Shiden Model 11. A low wing supplanted the mid-wing and the fuselage was lengthened substantially. The engine cowlings were improved. From a performance standpoint the Shiden Kai was only 6mph faster with a top speed of 369mph at 18,000ft.

US Navy fighters encountered the N1K1-J for the first time on October 12, 1944 when Hellcats from TF-38 attacked targets on Formosa. Between December 1943 and August 1945 just 428 Shiden Kais were built.

NAKAJIMA KI-84 HAYATE 'FRANK'

In the summer of 1944 the JAAF introduced a formidable new fighter. The Ki-84-Ia was regarded as the most potent fighter fielded by the Japanese from that time until the end of the war. Design work on the Hayate began in April 1942 as a replacement for the lightweight Ki-43 'Oscar'. To combat the advance of Allied fighters then under development, the JAAF needed a fighter with greater performance and survivability than the 'Oscar'.

After just 11 months of design and construction, Nakajima produced the first prototype. Powered by a Nakajima NK9A Homare Model 11 engine rated at 1,900hp, flight trials began. With armour protection, self-sealing fuel tanks and an armament of two 12.7mm machine guns in the nose and two 20mm Type 1 Ho-5 cannon in the wings, the Ki-84 had excellent performance and was considered equal to any Allied fighter. When using hit and run tactics the Ki-84 was able to dive on American fighter formations, fire a quick, deadly burst and then climb back to altitude with a rate-of-climb superior to the F4U Corsair and F6F Hellcat.

Nakajima sent the prototype to the JAAF for evaluation and testing. Maximum speed was determined to be 387mph – a first for a JAAF fighter. While the Ki-84 failed to meet its rate-of-climb numbers, its overall performance and handling were impressive.

Like all new fighters the Ki-84 had its share of problems. The Ha 45 engine was a constant source of problems and required regular highly skilled maintenance. The hydraulic system was poorly designed and unreliable, and the undercarriage legs were considered fragile and unable to stand up to rough field operations. Even with these problems the JAAF was anxious to get the new fighter into production as quickly as possible and in April 1944 the Ki-84 was accepted into service.

Now for the first time the JAAF had a fighter that could match the performance of its Allied counterparts. Fortunately for the Allies, Japanese mass production lagged far behind. Even when Japanese aircraft production peaked in June 1944 the continuing shortage of trained pilots meant no matter how many good fighters they made there was no one to fly them. From November 1943 until the war's end 3,416 Ki-84s were built.

KAWASAKI KI-100 OTSU

In March 1945, US Navy and USAAF fighter pilots reported a new and potent Japanese fighter operating over the Japanese home islands. For F6F Hellcat pilots its performance was a bit of a shock and was considered equal to and in some respects better than their own. Not found in any Allied recognition manual, the Kawasaki Ki-100 came as a complete surprise. No one expected to see such a new and advanced fighter at this stage of the war. In fact, the 'new' Ki-100 wasn't an entirely new aircraft but the work of clever engineering. At the end of 1944, 276 Ki-61 Hien 'Tony' airframes sat waiting for their liquid cooled in-line engines.

With the JAAF desperate for fighters, Kawasaki decided to fit a radial engine to the existing airframes. The powerplant chosen was the Mitsubishi Ha. 112-II large diameter radial developing 1,500hp. Adapting an existing airframe designed for one type of engine to accept another was a formidable task. In a remarkable feat of engineering and after just seven weeks of work, the first prototype took to the air on February 1, 1945. By end of May, 256 converted Ki-100s had been delivered with a further 88 being produced by July 23.

The Ki-100 excelled at low and medium altitudes and was better than anything the Allies had, except for the P-51D. Armed with two 20mm Type Ho-5 cannon and two 12.7mm Ho-103 machine guns, the Ki-100 packed a respectable punch. The Ki-100 had a top speed of 367mph at 32,800ft and was considered one of the best Japanese single seat fighters of the war.

TARGET TOKYO

"This operation has long been planned and the opportunity to accomplish it fulfills the deeply cherished desire of every officer and man in the Pacific Fleet." Fleet Admiral Chester Nimitz

On February 10, 1945 the pilots of Task Force 58 received the news. Their next target was Tokyo – the capitol of the Japanese Empire. This would be the first carrier strike against Japan since the famous Doolittle raid of April 18, 1942. Then *Enterprise* and *Hornet* and their 16-ship escort cruised to within 800 miles from Honshu and launched 16 USAAF B-25 Mitchell bombers. In the 1000 days between that first raid and February 1945 the US Navy now had 14 fast carriers and 100 escort and support ships headed to their launch point only 60 miles from the Imperial capitol.

On the evening of February 15, Task Force 58 under the command of Vice Admiral Mitscher ran northwest through heavy seas. The fleet's strike force centred in Task Groups 58.1, 58.2, 58.3, 58.4 and 58.5 was composed of nine Essex-class carriers and five light carriers. Task Group 58.5 was the dedicated night-fighter and night bomber group flying from *Enterprise* and *Saratoga*.

For the upcoming raids seven of the air groups embarked would be undertaking their first combat operation. At 0640 hours on February 16, two hours before the rest of Task Force 58 launched their strike, a solitary TBM Avenger took to the air. This was a specially modified TBM-3D configured for Radar-Counter Measures (RCM). Its job was to confuse Japanese radar and disrupt the enemy's ability to track and locate the incoming raids.

The weather for the strike was appalling with rain and low-lying scud. At 0635 hours the first Hellcats and Corsairs lifted off at 15 second intervals. For the next 11 hours Japanese airfields around Tokyo were pounded by Avengers, Helldivers and strafing Hellcats and Corsairs.

Once again, the Japanese were taken by surprise. The first Japanese victims were two roving 'Betty' bombers splashed by the CAP. Led by VF-9 the Hellcats from *Lexington, Hancock* and *San Jacinto* made land fall, but the worsening weather forced them to attack the airfield at Katori near the coast.

By then more than 100 Japanese fighters were sighted over the target and after 30 minutes of frantic dogfights the Hellcats pilots claimed 48 Japanese fighters destroyed. The pilots from VF-9 took the lion's share with 12 confirmed and four probables. VF-9 would end the day with eight more victories for three losses. Although the results were exaggerated, it was clear US Navy fighters owned the airspace.

The first US Navy aircraft to fly over the Imperial Palace belonged to the Marine Corsairs from *Essex*, but no enemy aircraft were encountered. Later that afternoon 11 Corsairs from *Essex* ran into a formation of Zeros near Tokyo. In the short fight three Zeros, and one 'Val' were shot down with a further 17 aircraft destroyed on the ground at Tenryu airfield.

Elsewhere Japanese fighter opposition was scarce, but ground targets were plentiful. Eight *Yorktown* Hellcats found Konoike airfield packed with aircraft. Attacking with rockets and machine guns, they destroyed nine aircraft and damaged 21 more.

The most successful attack over Tokyo belonged to the Hellcats of VF-80 'Vipers' from *Hancock*. During the day they found repeated opportunities over Katori and Imba areas. During their first sweep of the day the pilots of VF-80 bumped into several enemy formations and claimed 24 enemy fighters. Squadron CO LCDR L. W. Keith, already an ace, shot down five fighters to double his score.

Three pilots became 'aces in a day' by destroying five enemy aircraft each. In the final sweep of the day, three pilots would claim four more victories for a squadron total of 71 confirmed and 15 probables. It is a combat record that remains unsurpassed by any other American fighter squadron. Second to VF-80's score was the impressive score of 28 kills by the Hellcats of VF-45 from *San Jacinto*.

Along with targeting Japanese airfields, TF-58 also hit factories. That afternoon, Helldivers and Avengers from *Bunker Hill* destroyed the Nakajima aircraft factory at Ota. Japanese fighters intercepted the raid however and shot down two bombers and two fighters.

On the last strike of the day the Helldivers and Avengers from *San Jacinto* and *Lexington* were bounced by a mixed bag of JAAF fighters between the Ota engine factory and the coast. The Hellcat escort claimed nine shot down, but not before several Japanese fighters got through to the bombers. The rear gunners now got their chance, claiming three kills and several damaged.

In the late afternoon, and as the weather closed in, *Enterprise* launched two divisions of F6F-5N night-fighters from VF(N)-90. Their mission was to attack the Japanese airfield at Yokosuka and prevent any Japanese aircraft from attacking the fleet.

In what had been the biggest day of air combat since the Marianas Turkey Shoot, US fliers claimed an incredible 291 enemy planes shot down. The more realistic number was 44 Japanese aircraft shot down. The over-inflated numbers were due to several factors, including the confusion of combat and pilot inexperience: well over half of the Americans were new to combat. Differentiating between an actual kill and non-lethal damage wasn't easy.

American losses were heavy with 52 aircraft being destroyed. While the majority of aircraft lost were as a result of air-to-air combat, the hard fact remained that the US Navy had the upper hand. They could absorb the losses and continue the fight but the Japanese could not.

On the 17th the strikes resumed. This time the targets were the aircraft engine plants at Tachikawa and Musashino and any shipping that could be found. Through deteriorating weather, three air groups formed up to fly the biggest strike of the day. Twenty-two F6F-5s, seven F4U-1Ds and 13 TBM-1Cs came from Air Group 4, with Air

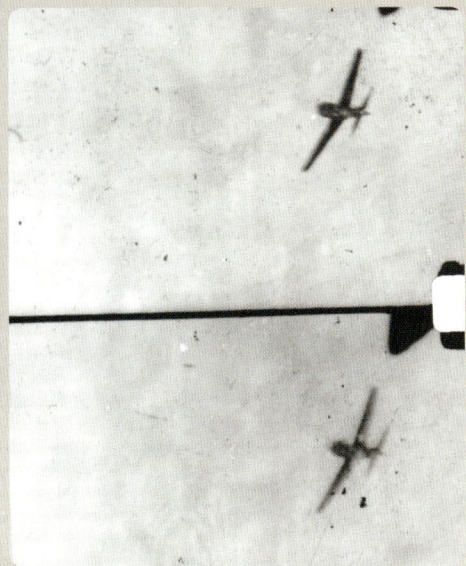

ABOVE: Gun camera image of a Ki-84 'Frank' under attack from a Corsair off *Bunker Hill* March 12, 1945, during carrier strikes on Kyushu. NARA

ABOVE: A rare gun camera image of a Kawanishi K1K1 'Rex' floatplane fighter shot down during carrier strikes on Kyushu, March 12, 1945. NARA

BELOW: Two captured Kawanishi N1K2-J Shiden Kais warm-up their engines in 1945. The largest quantity of serviceable N1K2-Js were found at the Omura Naval Base shortly after the surrender. AUTHOR'S COLLECTION

ABOVE: The Mitsubishi J2M3 Raiden 'Jack' was designed by Jiro Horikoshi, creator of the A6M Zero. Intended to replace the Zero, the J2M3 suffered from a series of teething problems related to the Kasei engine, the propeller pitch-change mechanism and the landing gear. By war's end just 625 had been built. NARA

ABOVE: One of several Ki-84s captured in the Philippines gave the Allied Technical Air Intelligence a wealth of information on the new Japanese Army Air Force Fighter. USAAF pilots found the 'Frank' only slightly less manoeuvrable than the A6M5. NARA

and 190 on the ground. On the debit side, TF-58 lost 60 aircraft to fighters and AA fire and 30 to operational causes. Actual Japanese combat losses remain uncertain. Imperial Japanese Headquarters admitted to just 78 fighters being lost in aerial combat, but the number destroyed on the ground remains unclear. While US Navy losses may have seemed high the fact remains that during two days of operations TF-58 generated 2,761 sorties. Their ability to launch strikes, establish air superiority over Tokyo itself, and remain unscathed was a testament to the US Navy's aerial dominance and professionalism.

After spending a week supporting the invasion of Iwo Jima, TF-58 returned to Japanese home waters. Launching 150 miles southeast of Tokyo, the fighter sweeps encountered sporadic combats over the airfields, resulting in US Navy claims of 46 shot down for the loss of 16.

For the Japanese there would be little respite. After ten days of rest and replenishment TF-58's air groups were back to full strength and once again Tokyo bound. On March 18 fighters and bombers from 15 flattops targeted 45 airfields around Tokyo. Fighter sweeps found few Japanese aircraft on the ground, but the Hellcats from VF-17 found a mixed bag of Zeros, 'Franks' and 'Tonys' over Kanoya. In a series of strafing runs and in the dogfights that ensued, the pilots of VF-17 claimed 25 aerial victories without a loss. By the end of the day carrier aviators had claimed 126 aerial victories, which was very close to the admitted Japanese losses of 110, including 32 kamikazes.

DIVINE THUNDER

On March 20 a thin layer of haze hung over TF-58. At dawn Japanese bombers and kamikazes rose to the attack. Taking advantage of the cloud cover and a blind zone in TF-58's radar coverage, a lone bomber emerged – hitting *Wasp* with a single bomb. Almost simultaneously a single 'Judy' hit *Franklin* with two bombs, turning the carrier into a floating inferno. In a day-long battle, damage control teams saved the ship but she was now out of the war.

The next day TF-58.1's radar plots lit up with a large bogey detected at 1400 hours 100 miles northwest of the fleet. Inbound were 18 G4M 'Betty' bombers of which 15 were specially modified G4M2Es carrying the air launched Ohka

Group 84 sending 12 F4U-1Ds, 15 SB2C-3/4s and 15 TBM-1Cs, while Air Group 45 launched eight F6F-5s and nine TBM-1Cs.

To counter the incoming raids, both the IJNAF and JAAF scrambled fighters. Seven Corsairs from VFM-124 were escorting seven Avengers to strike the Nakajima Tama Aircraft Engine Plant, near Tokyo, when they were pounced on by 24 'Tonys', 'Oscars', and 'Tojos'. Despite the numerical imbalance the American fighters still managed to keep the Japanese away from the bombers. The glide-bombing mission was a success and no Avengers were lost to enemy action.

In concert with the bombing missions, TF-58 launched several fighter sweeps – attacking airfields and coastal shipping.

Shortly after noon and in deteriorating weather Mitscher cancelled the remaining strikes and turned the fleet towards Iwo Jima. After two days of strikes in marginal weather US Navy fliers claimed 341 Japanese destroyed in the air

BELOW: The Ki-100-I Goshikisen was one of the best piston-engine fighters of the war. These examples belong to the 1st Chutai of the 59th Sentai at Ashiya Airfield in Fukuoka, Prefecture, Japan, June 1945. AUTHOR'S COLLECTION

Model 11 rocket powered suicide plane, escorted by 30 Zeros. Given the name Jinrai (Divine Thunder), it was hoped the Ohka would inflict heavy losses on the US fleet.

The Japanese knew that for the Ohka to work local air superiority was required. There were other problems as well. The modified G4M2Es proved extremely sluggish while carrying the Ohka – barely reaching 16,000ft. The Ohka's range of just 20 miles meant any chance of success was highly unlikely. Within minutes, *Hornet* and *Belleau Wood* launched 24 fighters.

As the Hellcats from VF-30 engaged the escort, the F6Fs of VF-17 and VBF-17 tore into the 'Bettys'. After 20 minutes all 18 G4M 'Bettys' had been shot down along with 12 Zeros for the loss of a single Hellcat. The introduction of the Ohka was a complete operational failure and it would have no influence in the coming kamikaze attacks.

THE LAST 60 DAYS
With the Okinawa campaign officially over in the first week of June, the carriers of Task Force 38 (ten Fleet Carriers including the night carrier *Bonhomme Richard* (CV-31) and six light carriers) and the four British Fleet carriers of Task Force 37 turned once again for Tokyo. In command of TF-38 was Vice Admiral John McCain with Admiral Rawlings in command of the British TF-37. The combined strength of these two Allied forces represented the greatest concentration of carrier air power of the entire war.

TF-38 comprised 1,190 aircraft while the BPF added another 255. On July 1, 1945 TF-38 steamed from the Philippines to launch Phase One of Operation Olympic, the invasion of Japan. This phase would involve a series of strikes lasting until mid-August. The objective of the Allied task forces was to target airfields, coastal and shore-based targets, factories and the surviving large warships of the Japanese fleet. To keep the Japanese off-balance and maintain maximum shock effect, Halsey intended to range up and down the Japanese Island, utilising the fleet's mobility to surprise the Japanese at every opportunity. For this the Allies were well equipped.

On July 10 TF-38, just 170 miles from Tokyo, launched the day's first fighter sweeps. The expected hordes of kamikazes didn't materialise, and Japanese fighters were nowhere to be seen. Rocket armed fighter-bombers made their runs unhindered, but most of the aerodromes around Tokyo were devoid of aircraft. The Japanese air forces had dispersed their strength, but the Hellcats and Corsairs managed to find their hiding spots anyway – destroying 100 aircraft on the ground.

July 14 would prove more profitable. TF-38 was ordered to sail north to commence strikes against northern Honshu and Kokkaido, targets that were just out of the reach of the B-29. During two days of strikes little resistance was met and the aircraft of TF-38 found and sank 11 warships and 20 merchant ships. Damage was caused to a further eight warships and 21 merchant ships. Twenty-five aircraft were also added to the total. Of greater importance was the destruction of seven rail car ferries in the Aomori-Hakodate area. Overnight the amount of coal delivered to Honshu's factories plummeted by more than 80%.

On July 16 TF-38 was joined by TF-37 and the following day the British Pacific Fleet launched its first strikes against the Japanese mainland. *Implacable*, *Formidable* and *Victorious* sent a mix

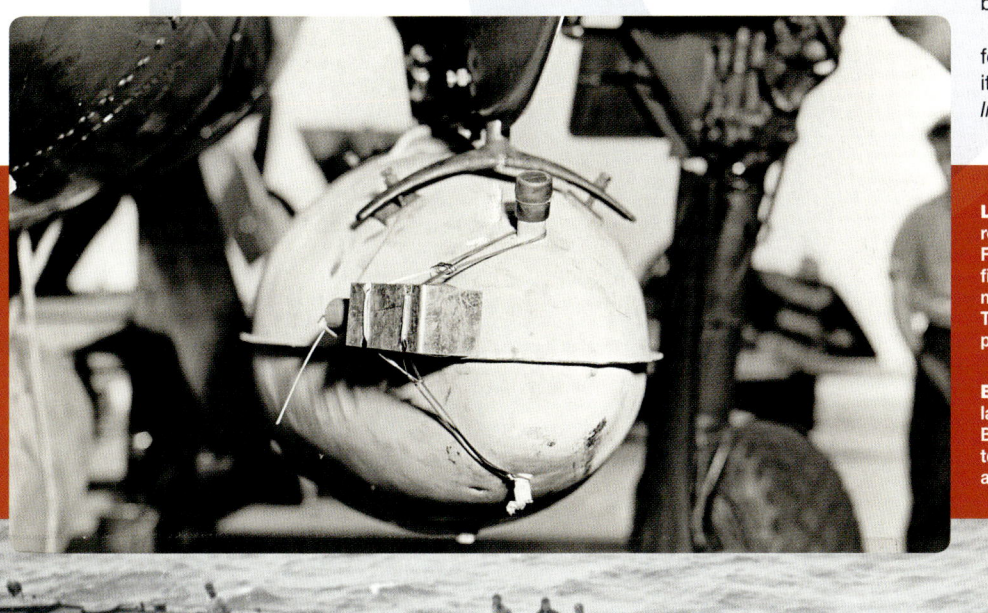

LEFT: The back end of a napalm bomb showing the rear mounted fuse assembly. Seen here fitted to an F6F-5 Hellcat, these bombs used aircraft drop tanks filled with napalm gel. As an incendiary weapon, napalm caused fires, explosions and severe burns. These bombs were introduced late in the war and proved highly effective. NARA

BELOW: An FAA Corsair of 1842 NAS off *Formidable*, lands aboard USS *Shangri-La* (CV-38), July 1945. British and American naval aircraft never operated together, with the BPF being given its own targets and assignments.

of Corsairs, Fireflies and Seafires to attack several airfields around Tokyo. Poor weather covered many of the targets but TF-37 aircraft managed to hit four out of six airfields with a mix of 88 500lb bombs and 26 rockets, destroying nine aircraft.

After TF-38 damaged the battleship *Nagato*, moored at Yokosuka Naval Base on July 18, the Allied fleet withdrew and conducted replenishment. The Americans lost 12 aircraft in the attack.

The last week of July was devoted to the destruction of the remaining Japanese battleships and carriers at the Kure Naval Base. It would be the largest and last American carrier strike against the IJN of the war. Even though TF-37 was operating as a task group of the US Third Fleet, Halsey ordered the BPF to be excluded from the attack and assigned them other targets. The US Navy had made it clear that they alone reserved the right to destroy the remaining Japanese capitol ships.

While the Japanese ships at Kure were sitting ducks, the combined shore and ship-based AA defences were formidable. The question of destroying damaged ships that had no fuel, or trained crews to operate with any degree of success was raised by TF-38 commander Admiral Cain. His objections were overridden. Admiral Ernest King in Washington ordered what was left of the Japanese fleet sunk.

In many ways, Kure offered the Japanese the greatest flak trap of the entire war.

THE KURE ATTACK

TF-38 began its two-day blitz against Kure Naval Base on July 24, 1945. Early morning fighter sweeps preceded the bombers, resulting in six N1K2-J 'Georges' being shot down for the loss of four Corsairs. The primary targets for the attack were the modified battleship/carriers *Ise* and *Hyuga* and the battleship *Haruna*. Intelligence knew the harbour was well defended by hundreds of AA guns. To neutralise them many Avengers were loaded with 260lb fragmentation bombs, while the fighters were to bomb the ships with 1,000-pounders and Helldivers with semi-armour piercing bombs.

On the first day TF-38 flew 1,747 sorties. During seven hours of repeated attacks US Navy fliers wrecked the carrier *Amagi* and sank the Combined Fleet's flagship, the cruiser *Oyodo*. The battleship *Hyuga* was targeted repeatedly and suffered ten hits. *Ise* took five direct hits with both ships settling to the bottom of the shallow harbour. *Haruna* was hit by a single bomb and damaged. Later in the day the cruiser *Tone*, stashed in Hiroshima Bay just west of Kure, was hit by three bombs. It was pushed ashore to prevent it from sinking.

While the Americans focused on Kure, TF-37 was assigned to attack airfields and shipping in and around the port of Osaka. Avengers

ABOVE: Seafire Mk IIIs from 801 and 880 NAS run up their engines on the deck of HMS *Implacable* in early August 1945. To increase their range these Seafires were equipped with ex-P-40 drop tanks giving them a respectable 200 mile combat radius. AUTHOR'S COLLECTION

THIS SPREAD: Grumman TBM-3 Avengers and Curtiss SB2C-4 Helldivers from Carrier Air Group 83 (CVG-83) aboard USS *Essex* (CV-9) dropping bombs on Hakodate, Japan, July 1945. NARA

In three days of strikes TF-38 had lost 126 aircraft (73 fighters, 53 bombers) with 102 pilots and aircrew lost. The British recorded nine aircraft lost in combat.

At the end of July, TF-37 and 38 pulled away from the coast to rest and replenish. An atomic bomb dropped by a B-29 annihilated the centre of Hiroshima on August 6, but on August 9 the harbour war resumed once again. More dead targets were attacked for little or no tactical impact. Anti-aircraft fire continued to take a terrible toll and would result in the last Victoria Cross of the war, Britain's highest honour for bravery.

TF-37 began the day by attacking airfields and Onagawa Bay on Honshu's northwest coast 170 miles north of Tokyo. In the bay were half a dozen ships of little or no military value. Leading an eight Corsair strike was Canadian Lieutenant Robert Hampton Gray off *Formidable*. Diving from 10,000ft in two plane sections, Gray led his Corsairs into the attack. Shoreline and ship-based AA guns burst into life, filling the sky with tracers and exploding shells.

Sweeping over the bay, Gray set his sights on the destroyer escort *Amakusa*. As Gray tore through the flak he was hit repeatedly. One of his 500lb bombs was shot off its rack. Pressing home his attack at just 50ft, Gray dropped his remaining bomb. The hit blew a huge hole in the starboard side, sinking the *Amakusa*. The other pilots in

bombed the escort carrier *Kaiyo*, leaving her with a broken back. It was the first time in the history of the Royal Navy that carrier borne aircraft had attacked an enemy carrier. Fifteen strikes were flown that day, resulting in the *Kaiyo* damaged, two frigates sunk, and 15 aircraft destroyed.

The July 24 attack had been proven costly however – 29 fighters and 28 bombers were lost to AA fire.

The next day, TF-38 mounted yet more strikes, sinking three tankers and a merchant ship and damaging a cruiser, plus five other vessels.

On July 28 TF-38 returned to the fight. Thirty-six aircraft from *Shangri-La* attacked the battleship *Haruna* and light cruiser *Oyodo*, both damaged on the 24th. The *Haruna* would have the dubious honour being subjected to more bombing attacks then any other Japanese battleship by both Navy and USAAF aircraft. The *Oyodo* was hit several times and capsized. *Haruna* was hit by at least eight bombs and later that afternoon 70 Okinawa-based B-24s added to the maelstrom but no hits were recorded. After taking on tons of water, *Haruna* sank next to the pier. The light carriers *Katsuragi* and *Ryuho*, which had escaped damage in the first raid, were heavily damaged. At 1930 hours the fast carriers withdrew to the south-east at 23kts.

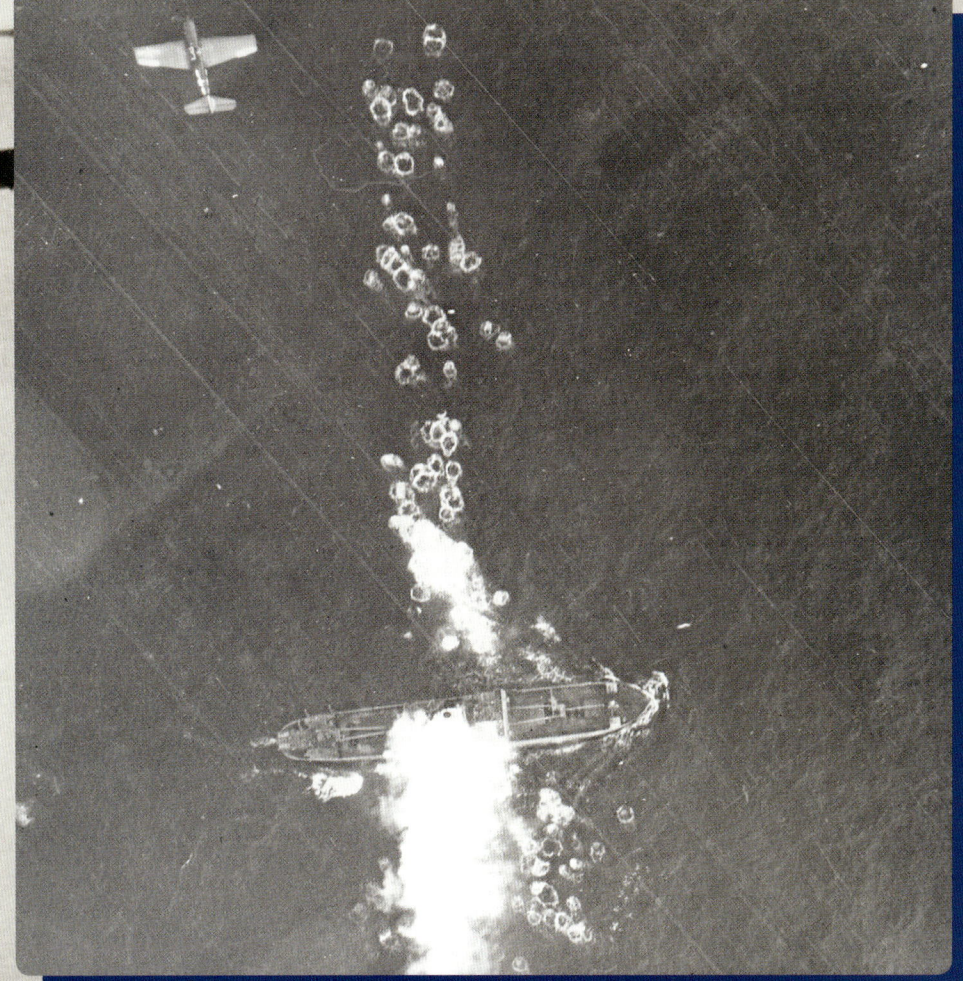

ABOVE: The Japanese inland seas proved to be target rich environments for Allied naval pilots. Here a Hellcat finishes its strafing run on a Japanese cargo ship, July 1945. NARA

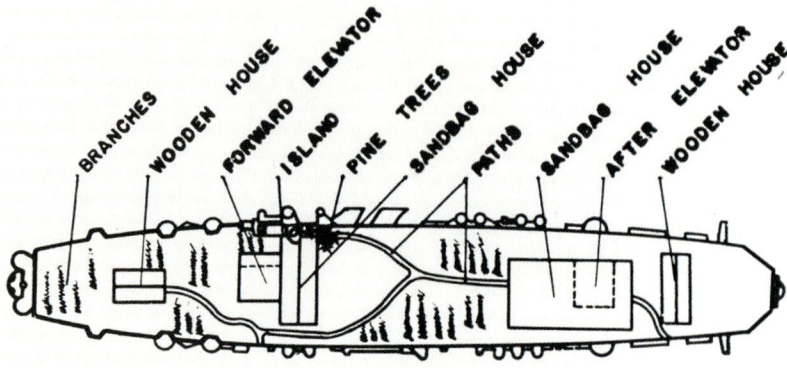

ABOVE: With their fleet stuck in harbour, the Japanese expended a great deal of effort to confuse US Navy reconnaissance aircraft with elaborate camouflage patterns. This US Intelligence illustration shows the camouflage scheme used on carrier *Katsuragi* in March 1945 while moored at Kure. US NAVAL HISTORICAL CENTER

ABOVE: Carrier Operations off Japan, August 1945. A Japanese aircraft is shot down just off the starboard bow of *Wasp* (CV-18), during operations off Honshu, Japan, August 9, 1945. US NAVAL HISTORICAL CENTER

the flight watched in horror as Gray's Corsair – streaming smoke and flame – rolled to the right and crashed into the sea.

Gray was most likely the last Canadian to die in action during the Second World War and only the second Fleet Air Arm pilot to be awarded the Victoria Cross.

That same day the aviators of TF-37 and 38 learned that a second atomic bomb had been dropped on Japan. Later that day the Soviet Union declared war on Japan. Despite the massive destruction, Admiral Halsey decided to immediately continue strike operations against targets in Japan.

LAST DOGFIGHTS OF THE WAR

High above the Japanese homeland at 0340 hours a force of 134 B-29s from the 315th Bomb Wing were making their way home. Their target had been the Nippon Oil Company Refinery at Tsuchizaki. Below them lay two cities devastated by the world's first two atomic bomb attacks. Other cities fared no better. Incendiary attacks had burned out 40% of the built-up urban areas in 66 cities, resulting in the destruction of nearly a third of all Japanese houses.

The war was effectively over, but for the Japanese high command there was no other option but to fight on. Bent upon extinction rather than surrender, the Japanese offered the Allies precious little middle ground. The cultural divide between Japan and the West was a vast chasm of disbelief and unconscionable moral logic. While the world waited and prayed, powerful US and British carrier task forces were preparing for the last air strikes of the war. The question is why? There were no military targets left of any consequence and Japanese resistance in the air was virtually nonexistent.

The night before, pilots aboard the carrier USS *Shangri-La* had heard rumours and reports all day. Corsair pilot Dick DeMott recalled, "that Japan has broadcast and has accepted our peace treaty… I wish to hell we could find out if the Japs are surrendering before we go needlessly groping over Japan again and lose more pilots".

It was the last day, the final desperate 24 hours in a long and barbaric war. It would also be the last time Allied and Japanese fighters would tangle in aerial combat. Who would lay claim to the last dogfight of the war? American history says it belongs to the US Navy Hellcats of VF-88, but as recently as June 2001 claims were made that the Seafires of Royal Navy No 24 Naval Fighter Wing may have been the ones to fire the final shots.

To assess who participated in the last dogfight of the war, we have to return to the morning of August 15, 1945. Several fighter units including US Navy squadrons VF-6, VF-31, VF-49 and VF-88 flew missions in and around Tokyo on that fateful day. The British were also involved with sorties by Fireflies, Avengers and the Seafires from 887 and 894 Naval Air Squadron. The Allies had planned two strikes for Tokyo for that day with Strike Force Able being launched first at 0415.

Sunrise over Japan came at 0435 hours on August 15. The sky was a patchwork of clouds and scattered showers. TF-38's carriers began launching combat air patrols and assembling two strike missions. Aboard the HMS *Indefatigable* at 0400 hours four-rocket armed Fireflies were launched, followed by six Avengers with an escort of eight Seafires led by Sub-Lieutenant Fred Hockley.

Their target was Kisarazu airfield near Tokyo. At 0415 hours 12 Hellcats from VF-88 roared off the deck of the USS *Yorktown*. VF-88 was battle trained but untested, its pilots eager to get into the fight. They rendezvoused with

ABOVE: Seafires and Fireflies are ready to launch for another strike against Japanese targets from *Indefatigable*. The Seafires are equipped with 90-gallon slipper tanks. The slipper tank gave the Seafire an escort and strike capability. AUTHOR'S COLLECTION

ABOVE: The Japanese cruiser *Tone* under air attack near Kure on July 24, 1945. NARA

24 Corsairs from the carriers USS *Shangri-La* and USS *Wasp* and their mission was a sweep of the airfields at Tokahasi and Atusgi, northwest of Tokyo. Hellcats from VF-6, VF-31 and VF-49, as part of Strike Force Able, were also launched.

Despite their hopeless situation, the IJNAF and JAAF were still mounting air defence sorties. One of the units involved was the 302nd Kokutai AG. There were very few veterans left in its ranks by the final weeks of the conflict, however, and most of its pilots had been transferred in from other branches such as seaplanes, flying boats and carrier bombers. By May 1945 the 302nd Kokutai was down to just ten operational aircraft, a mix of late model Zeros and J2M3 Raidens.

The 252 Kokutai, based at Mobara airfield, east of Tokyo Bay, was also assigned the task of air defence. Like the 302nd, it too was equipped with a limited number late model Zeros.

As the 14 Fleet Air Arm aircraft (six Avengers, eight Seafires) climbed through low cloud, they finally broke through to better weather at 6,000-8,000ft. The Seafire pilots were greeted by the new day's summer sun and all was quiet except for the steady throb of their trusty Merlin engines. As the tiny strike force was crossing Tokyo Bay, a pair of A6M5 Zeros was sighted well below the Avengers. This was a common decoy tactic used by the Japanese but the Seafire pilots didn't bite. Then a gaggle of a dozen A6M5s was seen coming down from the 3 o'clock-high position. The time was 0545.

R/Ts snapped with the calls of 'Bogies three o'clock'. The diving Zeros passed the top cover headed for the Avengers and the close escort Seafires below. Sufficient warning was given for the pilots to counter the bounce, but not all were able to jettison their drop tanks. R/T failure doomed Sub-Lieutenant Hockley and he was shot down in the first pass. He was the last Royal Navy casualty of the war.

As the first Zeros passed out of range, Sub-Lieutenant Vic Lowden turned his flight and met the second Japanese element in line abreast. Opening fire at the extreme range of 800 yards, Lowden hit a Zero and saw it "flaming nicely, going down". His No 3, Sub-Lieutenant Williams,

ABOVE: After being damaged by US carrier strike aircraft in March 1945 the battleship *Haruna* was finally sunk by Task Force 38 during this July 28, strike. US NAVAL HISTORICAL CENTER

CARRIER STRIKE 125

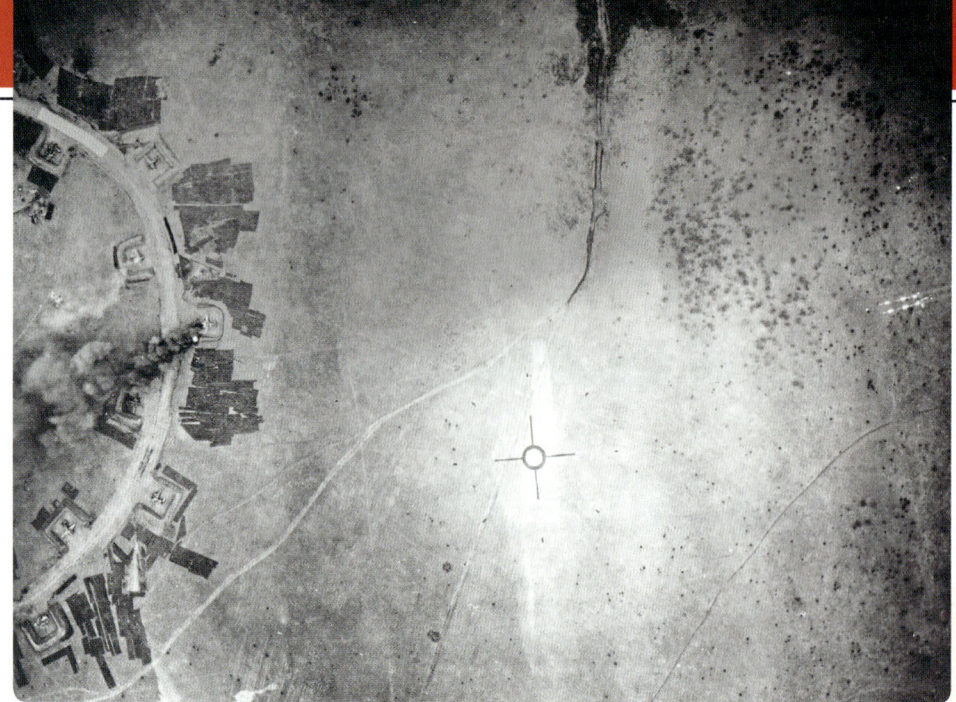

ABOVE: An F6F-5 Hellcat, on the right, unleashes its full load of 5in air-to-ground rockets towards the 'Betty' bombers in their revetments on the left, July 1945. NARA

also made a contribution hitting the same aircraft with cannon shells. Lowden soon found another Zero. Opening fire from about 200 yards he saw pieces fly off as it fell away.

He later wrote: "I then found one of the original attacking 'Zekes' climbing at 8000ft about 1000 yards from me. I closed to 100 yards at 11,000ft, kicking on the rudder to have a look at the markings, and then went back astern and fired two two-second bursts of machine gun fire – the cannon ammunition had already been exhausted. Following strikes all over the aircraft, the pilot baled out. His fighter dived past him, smoking somewhat."

Lowden would be credited with two destroyed, a third shared and two damaged.

In his memoirs, Lieutenant Saburo Abe of the 252nd AG claims to have shot down a Seafire on August 15 but his description does not match what happened to Hockley: "Immediately, it turned into a chaotic battle. Both the enemy fighters and ours were coming and going from all the directions. I did not know how to determine my target. Suddenly, an enemy plane appeared from my right and flew down to the left. At that moment, I remembered what Tetsuzo Iwamoto, a pilot officer, taught me before. Quickly, I banked to the left with full-throttle and chased the enemy fighter.

"On the ground, I was pretty good at shooting. However, it was not the same when I had to shoot while flying the fighter plane. I always missed my targets. So, I had decided that I would not pull the trigger lever until I was close enough to see an expression on the enemy's face. On that day, I did the same.

"The enemy pilot probably felt my presence, and he looked back. Our eyes met for a moment. I saw his despairing look, and I opened fire at the same time. I did not need to use a gun sight. If I remember well, the distance between us was less than 20m. I pulled the trigger lever, and the next moment, I witnessed that half of the pilot's head was blown off. The windscreen of his airplane became all red being covered with blood. His plane was tossed upward into the air as if it was bending its back. I flew under him and just managed to avoid a crash."

Lt Abe also claims to have been shot at by Seafires, causing a forced landing of his fighter: "I heard a loud noise and felt pain in my right leg as if someone hit my leg with an iron bar. I felt like I was awakened from my trance or something. Still, I was thinking 'Idiot! Who are those stupid ones that cannot tell their friends from the enemy? I'm going to punch them when they get out of their planes,' still thinking that they were Japanese fighters.

"I looked up and the two planes passed above me and to the left. 'There was no rising sun painted on the bodies,' I said to myself. They were not the American fighters. Their marking was different. 'Who is that? That's British. What are they doing here?'"

Hockley was shot down but he escaped by parachute. He was later captured and executed by his captors. The remaining Seafires turned in to the Japanese fighters. With the first Japanese element now out of range, Lowden moved his flight into a line abreast and engaged the second group of fighters.

The close escort, tied as they were to the Avengers, still managed an impressive score. The first Zero was shot down at long range by

ABOVE: Starved of fuel and trained crewmen the Japanese fleet became little more than a series of floating targets. Here the Japanese battleship *Ise* is attacked at Kure, July 24, 1945. US NAVAL HISTORICAL CENTER

ABOVE: After being hit by 22 bombs between March 19 and July 28, the Japanese Battleship *Ise* finally settled to the bottom of Kure harbour. US NAVAL HISTORICAL CENTER

BELOW: By July 1945 both the JAAF and IJNAF had all but ceded air superiority to the Allies. These smoking 'Bettys' at Honshu Airfield attest to the Allies' overpowering presence. NARA

Lowden. He continued to score, hitting another Zero at 250 yards; after three short bursts it blew up. The opening moves had proved decisive for the Seafire pilots. Lowden shot down two Zeros, with a third shared and two others damaged. Now it was Sub-Lieutenant Murphy's turn: "The enemy approached our Avengers in fairly close starboard echelon, but with flights in line astern. They peeled off smartly in fours from down sun and headed for the Avengers. One section of four appeared to be coming head-on for us, but I didn't observe their guns firing. Their original attack was well coordinated, but they seemed to lose each other after that, and could not have kept a good lookout astern.

"I opened fire with my flight leader from the enemy's port quarter. Saw strikes on fuselage of enemy, which was finished off by flight leader or No 3. Disengaged from above to attack another 'Zeke' to port and 500ft below. Closed from above and astern, obtaining hits on belly and engine, but I was closing too fast and over shot. Pulled up nose to re-attack No 2 and saw a lone 'Zeke' at same level doing a shallow turn to starboard. He evidently didn't see me, and I held fire till some 100 yards away. Observed immediate strikes on cockpit and engine, which burst into flames. Enemy rolled on back, plummeting in flames into cloud."

Sub-Lieutenant Don Duncan RNVR chose to retain his slipper tank and keeping his speed up, as recommended in Naval Air Tactic Notes, engaged three of the Zeros, coming away with two probables. The last Seafire to leave the combat area was Duncan's' section leader, Sub-Lieutenant Randy Kay. As a Zero closed on the Avengers he made a quarter attack, setting it on fire in the port wing-root area. Switching targets he then concentrated on another Zero and with a high deflection shot blew its tail off with his

ABOVE: These A6M5C Type 52cs of the 252 Kokutai warm up their engines prior to flying another home defence mission in the summer of 1945. AUTHOR'S COLLECTION

first burst. Searching for a third target he found and damaged a third A6M5.

All six of the Avengers delivered their bombs on target. Only one was badly damaged by the attack, but the pilot brought the crippled aircraft back to the Fleet and ditched alongside one of the radar picket destroyers.

En route to the coast VF-88 and the Corsairs encountered low cloud cover, forcing the squadrons to separate as they climbed through the overcast. The cloud cover extended to 18,000ft and when the group emerged, only eight of the original 12 Hellcats were together, the Corsairs nowhere to be seen. Lieutenant Howard M. Harrison of VF-88 ordered two of his Hellcats to remain near the coast and provide a communication link with the fleet in the event that a recall message was issued. Six Hellcats remained, piloted by Lieutenants Harrison, Maurice Proctor, Joseph Sahloff and Theodore Hansen, and Ensigns Wright Hobbs and Eugene Mandeberg. They pressed on towards their target at Atsugi Airfield, home base for the tough 302nd Kokutai.

On the morning of August 15, Allied carrier aircraft were reported inbound towards the Tokyo area. The 302nd commander, Captain Yasuna Kozono, ordered all serviceable fighters airborne. Led by Lieutenant Yutaka Moriaka, four J2M3 Raidens and eight A6M5c/A6M7 Zeros took to the air. The 252nd Kokutai also launched fighters. Lieutenant Commander Moriyasu Hidaka led a group of eight or nine Zeros towards a large formation of enemy aircraft.

The air space over Tokyo Bay and the surrounding area proved to be a crowded place. Along with the aircraft from HMS *Indefatigable* there were the Hellcats from VF-6, VF-31, VF-49 and VF-88 and Corsairs from VBF-8. It has been recently claimed that the Japanese fighters the British Fleet Air Arm encountered that morning "were almost certainly the 302nd AG led by Lieutenant Moriaka". But this doesn't mesh with Moriaka's claim of a single Hellcat shot down that day.

Moriaka's original orders were to head to Kisarazu airfield. There he found a hangar on fire and smoking violently. Could the earlier Firefly Ramrod launched ahead of the Avengers and Seafires have reached Kisarazu airfield before the weather closed in and attacked the airfield? According to Moriaka his flight was then ordered back to Atsugi Air Base "now under attack by Grummans". There he spotted six F6F Hellcats and shot one down. He described the base as being under attack by rocket firing F6Fs (the Hellcats of VF-88 were armed with four HVAR rockets). Moriaka recalled: "This is it. I ordered my flight to spread out into combat formation. The Grummans were at 3,000 metres, rocket-bombing Atsugi. There were six Grummans right in front of me, flying in two groups of three planes. We were in an advantageous position, like a cat getting ready to pounce on some unsuspecting mice.

"Then I suddenly saw one plane circling around. 'OK, there it comes.' I placed this plane squarely in my gunsight. There were three planes below me and they could climb up to get me. That could be dangerous. I pulled up, circled, and dived down. I could see the pilot wearing a purple muffler. I opened up with my 20mm cannon and could see red-coloured projectiles striking the Grumman's engine. The plane spun around and I saw the pilot with the purple muffler parachute out. 'I did it!' The other one or two Grummans fled the area."

Maury Proctor, one of the two Hellcat pilots who survived that day describes a different scenario: "At 0645 we were within seconds of starting into our dive on Atsugi airfield when Hardesty relayed the news that the fleet commanders had broadcast, 'all Bronco planes cease hostilities and return to base, the war is over'. Needless to say, everyone went ape over the news and flew in all directions doing aerobatics to vent the enthusiasm that we felt.

"By the time we could get organised and rendezvous the flight, several precious minutes had lapsed." Shortly after Proctor and his five remaining Hellcat pilots were attacked by "approximately 20" enemy fighters made up of Zeros, Franks and Jacks.

The six relatively inexperienced F6F Hellcat pilots claimed they were bounced by 'Franks

ABOVE: Some of the Fleet Air Arm's best. These pilots were involved in the Royal Navy's last air combat of the war. From left to right, Sub-Lieutenants Don Duncan, Randy Kay, 'Spud' Murphy, Vic Lowden, Ted Gavin and 'Taffy' Williams, all from No 24 Naval Fighter Wing from HMS *Indefatigable*. They were credited with seven Zeros shot down on August 15, 1945. AUTHOR'S COLLECTION